THE SILENT WAR

The Cold War Battle Beneath the Sea

John Piña Craven

A Touchstone Book
Published by Simon & Schuster
New York   *London*   *Toronto*   *Sydney*   *Singapore*

Touchstone
Rockefeller Center
1230 Avenue of the Americas
New York, NY 10020

First Touchstone Edition 2002

TOUCHSTONE and colophon are registered trademarks
of Simon & Schuster Inc.

For information regarding special discounts for bulk purchases,
please contact Simon & Schuster Special Sales:
1-800-456-6798 or business@simonandschuster.com

Designed by Deirdre C. Amthor

Manufactured in the United States of America

5   7   9   10   8   6   4

The Library of Congress has catalogued the Simon & Schuster edition as follows:
Craven, John P.
The silent war : the Cold War battle beneath the sea / John Piña Craven.
p.   cm.
Includes index.
1. Craven, John P.   2. United States. Navy—Civilian employees—Biography.
3. Ocean engineering—United States—History—20th century.   4. Nuclear
submarines—United States   5. Fleet ballistic missile weapons systems—
United States.   6. Deterrence (Strategy)   7. United States. Navy—Submarine
forces.   8. Military intelligence—United States—History—20th century.
9. Espionage, American—History—20th century.   10. Cold War
11. Law of the sea.   I. Title.
V63.C73 A3 2001
359.9'33—dc21
00-054755

ISBN: 978-0-7432-2326-3

Acknowledgments

I am indebted to agent Peter Matson for taking a chance on an un-proved author; to writer Robert Katz for teaching me the crisp prose of a "best-seller"; to Maja LaBelle Clark for helping me bridge the generation gap; and to editor James Wade, who extracted coherent history from a set of uncoordinated tales.

I acknowledge that I have been, at best, an anthropological in-formant for the men and women of the Navy and the nation's intel-ligence services, who collectively and heroically won the Cold War.

This book is dedicated to my granddaughter
Anna Makena McGuire,
that her generation may enjoy Life, Liberty,
and Pursuits of Happiness.

Contents

Prologue

The Polaris Marching and Chowder Society meets for breakfast on the first Wednesday of each month at the Columbia Inn, a classic Honolulu eatery. It has met without fail for more than two decades. Its members became joined at the hip for their roles in the genesis of the Polaris Fleet Ballistic Missile submarine system—the first undersea fleet dedicated to the deterrence of nuclear war. Most of them are graduates of the United States Naval Academy and all were actively involved as submariners in World War II—all but one, the author of this book.

After their retirement many of the society members continued as civilians employed in transforming the silent service into the most effective source of the intelligence that won the Cold War; the most effective suppressor of conflicts in Southeast Asia, Asia Minor, and the Middle East and the preserver of peace in the perilous days that lie ahead. What prevents this breakfast from being just another gathering of old-timers volleying memories is the regular attendance of the active duty commander of the submarine forces of the Pacific fleet (COMSUBPAC) and members of his staff. This is a family breakfast and a rare opportunity for the family elders to offer their wisdom to the young in command.

I am the adopted member of this family. My undersea career in a civilian capacity does not qualify me to wear the submariner's Dolphins. But I share with the most weathered of these veterans a lifetime of naval experience and a key role in the genesis of the Polaris system. I was a battleship sailor in World War II and share "anchors aweigh" memories of Pearl Harbor departures for missions in that seemingly endless war. On those last nights in port we would "drink to the foam" and seek, but rarely find, intimate company with that mythical Polynesian maiden who sang:

Now is the hour when we must say goodbye.
Soon you'll be sailing, far across the sea.
While you're away, O then remember me.
When you return you'll find me waiting here.

Uncertain that he will ever return, the battleship sailor casts off bow and stern lines on the mooring piers of Battleship Row. The crew, lining the rail in spotless whites, renders honors to the sunken *Arizona*, whose rusting superstructure protruding from the waters marks her grave. Slowly steaming out of the channel that separates Ford Island from Hickam Field, all eyes on the port side are fixed on a bordello-pink structure on the hill above the harbor. Wreathed in the orographic clouds that cover the mountaintop, or under the arch of morning and evening rainbows, the building, Tripler Army Hospital, looks like the anteroom to heaven. The same fantasy plays behind every sailor's gaze—that he will be wounded just enough to spend the duration of the war rehabilitating in that hillside retreat.

As the hospital fades from view, another vision in pink appears, enticing and no more attainable than a mirage. It is the Royal Hawaiian Hotel on Waikiki Beach. Surface ship sailors are jealous, even angry, for the "pink palace" is the exclusive rest and recreation domain of the submariner. There are no purple hearts for sub-

mariners, but awaiting all who return from patrol is an idyllic vacation in a sailor's paradise.

Every submariner is a volunteer who has chosen to gamble his
life at high stakes. The submariner casting off bow and stern lines at
the sub base is certain that he will come back whole or not at all.
There is no thought of Tripler. Instead, as they pass the Royal Hawaiian, all aboard fantasize that this submarine will return from its patrol for one spectacular fling at the Royal Hawaiian.

Regardless of service, submariner and surface ship sailor shared
the same fatalistic view that the Second World War was endless.
Anyone planning for the future did so expecting the war to last ten
years. Then on August 6, 1945, the power of the atom bomb was un-
leashed on Hiroshima. Lives were vaporized, steel beams twisted into
writhing ghoulish forms, and the mushroom cloud was burned into
our collective consciousness as the icon of nuclear war. From that
day on, everyone knew that World War II was over, but no one understood the full consequences of unleashing the nuclear genie.
Who could have anticipated the puniness of human flesh and habitat against the power of the atom released from a single airborne
weapon?

Sailors, submariners, and others in the armed services celebrated
their freedom. Those who had families could return to them. Thanks
to the GI Bill of Rights, most veterans of the war could enjoy four
years of education at the school of their choice. Those who at war's
beginning had not yet set foot on a career path pursued new profes-
sions with vigor. Some continued their career in the service or as
civil servants for the military. I was one.

The formation of the United Nations seemed to assure hope for
years of peace. And there was the hugely comforting thought that
our side had the monopoly on the bomb and its technology. It would
be our shield as we waged peace.

An iron curtain descended over Europe and soon the Cold War

became a hot war. Times were then, as they are now, dangerous. The Korean War was one of the bloodiest short wars in history and the warriors of World War II were participants. I was one. The conflict was stanched in 1953.

The United States had lost its nuclear monopoly to the Soviet Union in 1949. The Navy responded by establishing the Special Projects Office to develop the Polaris Fleet Ballistic Missile System. The office was manned almost exclusively by officers and civilians who had experienced combat in World War II and had learned that carnage in the abattoir of battle was the most obscene human activity. They were determined to devote their careers and their lives if necessary to preventing and deterring war. I was one.

Deterrence was not enough. The same cadre of dedicated individuals, the same group whose alumni would form the Polaris Marching and Chowder Society, embarked on a four-decade program of undersea intelligence whose missions, whose very existence was so clandestine and so classified that participants knew they would go to their graves with their success and sacrifice unacknowledged by the nation they were defending. I was one. This submarine espionage program would uncover and expose cracks in the Soviet Union so that Soviet leaders could eventually see for themselves the risk of nuclear war engineered by renegade military elements. Only then would the leadership transform itself and adopt policies of openness and restructuring, glasnost and perestroika. Then in 1998 a book entitled *Blind Man's Bluff* unveiled this espionage program, or a part of it, as a tribute to these "unsung heroes of the silent service." Only a few of the protagonists could be identified. I was one.

Thus chance and fate marked me as a spokesman for this silent service. Most of my colleagues urged me to write a book that only a participant could write—a book that tells their story, as it should be told, but without compromising national security. Others urged me to be silent, fearing that I would inadvertently put at risk ongoing ac-

the *Nautilus* slowly made her way to the Electric Boat Company dry dock. She had been tried at sea and had won every praise and laurel. Now, however, she was silently limping home. She was "down by the bow," as keen observers could see, but no one except her captain, Commander Eugene P. "Dennis" Wilkinson, had the slightest indication that the mighty *Nautilus* might be in grave danger.

Wilkinson's concern was communicated to retired Admiral Andrew McKee, chief designer for Electric Boat. By the very quaintness of its name, the Electric Boat Company proclaimed that it had been around a long time; it had in fact been building battery-powered submarines as long as submarines had been built for the United States Navy, and McKee was long in experience, too. His own name had become synonymous with World War II submarine design. In the early days of the war, the S-boats were doomed to sink if the engine room flooded. McKee added a sixteen-foot section to each hull that was no more than a buoyancy module, but it saved a fleet. As Electric Boat entered the nuclear age McKee's accomplishments kept pace. Like Wilkinson, he already knew that the *Nautilus* had been experiencing severe vibrations at high speed. The skipper had complained forcefully to the Navy's Bureau of Ships, whose structural engineers had measured these vibrations but had been unable to find their source. The problem had been assigned to the flow studies section of the David Taylor Model Basin and handed over to me.

At thirty-two years old, I was the new kid on the block—a physicist at the Washington, D.C., David Taylor Model Basin—considered by virtue of my California Institute of Technology master's degree and University of Iowa Ph.D. a theoretical whiz in hydrodynamics and structures, though few knew of my practical experience with ships at sea.

How could they? It had been more than a dozen years since I had twice disgraced my father by failing to get into Annapolis and then by joining the Navy as a mere enlisted man—breaking the long line of revered Craven family naval officers who had gone on from the Academy to distinguished Navy careers. A third and perhaps intolerable disgrace would have been my lockup on a court-martial offense in the brig, following an unjustifiable fistfight with a fellow enlistee while on duty. Instead, the apparent emergency of the gory injury to my fighting hand landed me in a hospital, where a magnanimous Navy doctor decided, after putting two and two together, that the break in my protruding bone had occurred when I ran into a door, or, rather—to remove all fault on my part—a door ran into me. When the hospital staff finally noticed that Seaman Craven, who was basking in a monthlong convalescence, was again fit for duty, I was summarily transported to still devastated Pearl Harbor. Assigned to the battleship *New Mexico*, I found her moored alongside the sunken but balefully visible battleship *Arizona*, which had been lost in the surprise attack. It was the first day of 1944 and we were headed for the Marshall Islands to fight the rest of the war, but luck had somehow attached itself to my side, where it stuck. My brief (six months) but intense encounters in battle were experienced as a helmsman of the *New Mexico*, flagship of a task force of some 100 ships of the line and the train.

Here I would meet naval officers who were destined to one day be my subordinates. Here I would participate in and hear firsthand of battles won or lost by technology or skill, or both. Here, as the lowest-ranking seaman, I would acquire the helmsman's feel of the sea in calm, wind, and storm, in head sea, quartering sea, beam sea, and following sea.

By war's end I was enrolled at Cornell University in a naval science training program, graduating two years later near the top of my class with a commission as an ensign in the Naval Reserve. It was too late to fulfill my family destiny but a career as a naval scientist might make for a happy compromise. Accepted for graduate studies at Cal Tech, one of the nation's elite science and technology institutions, I went on for the next few years as a GI Bill student with scarcely enough time to leave the laboratory or look up from my books. Thus had I been rendered the "whiz kid" who now stood on the pier with my seasoned elders, Commander Wilkinson and Admiral McKee, and the world-famous *Nautilus* in dry dock.

We inspected the submarine from stem to stern. Our first concern was the integrity of the pressure hull. This is the inner space capsule that resists the pressure of the deep ocean. At test depth it is exposed to more than one thousand pounds per square inch of seawater pressure. Ideally the hull should be a complete shell of steel with no openings to the sea. But the crew, the machinery, and the supplies must be loaded on board at the beginning of a patrol or a dive and so there must be a hatch or hatches. The standard hatches on submarines are only twenty-five inches in diameter; they are open in port but closed and battened down whenever the submarine is submerged. The inside of the pressure hull is maintained at atmospheric pressure or close thereto. But outside there is a forest of machinery and tankage that is exterior to the hull. There are anchors and winches and all sorts of marine hardware. There is a propeller, which has a shaft that penetrates the pressure hull. There are periscopes and masts that project from the command and control center up through the sail. All of these must be covered by plating called "fairwater" if it covers machinery on the deck or the "sail" if it covers the masts and the surface observation bridge. The hydrodynamic shape of a submarine is thus a composite of the bare hull, the fairwater over the machinery on the deck exterior to the hull, the sail that surrounds the periscope, the masts, and the bridge, and the exterior of the ballast tanks, which envelop the hull fore and aft. There are in addition appendages in the form of bow planes or sail planes, stern planes, and rudders.

Archimedes' principle states that a body will displace its own weight in water. Most submarine hulls are designed so that when they are empty their weight is about 0.4 times the weight of water they would displace. Thus the hull by itself would float on the surface and be unable to submerge. The depth to which the hull can go is a function of the material of which the hull is made and its configuration. Small submersibles use a spherical shell, larger ones use a cylinder with spherical end caps, but a large military submarine employs a cylinder reinforced by girders of steel called stiffeners. These girders or stiffeners are inside the pressure hull for that part of the hull where the hull plating is a part of the hydrodynamic shape of the submarine. For those portions of the hull where ballast tanks and fairwaters completely surround it, the stiffeners will be external to the hull but are not exposed to the flow. In either case the stiffeners are attached at regular intervals to the pressure hull. These "pressure hulls" are designed so that there is a balance between one failure mode, called "buckling," and another, called "elastic failure." Everyone understands buckling because any empty can of beer or soda can be squeezed or stomped on to demonstrate the phenomenon. Everyone has also witnessed elastic failure, which means that a structure, say, the beer can or a car fender, will not return to its initial shape after it has been deformed. The interaction between the cylindrical hull and the ring stiffeners is vital to the submarine's ability to resist buckling and to maintain elasticity.

When Wilkinson, McKee, and I had completed our inspection of the hull we were in a state of shock. What we saw were ring stiffeners that had been torn away from the hull as though a giant hand had repeatedly twisted them until they failed in fatigue. We could put our hands between the hull and the stiffeners. McKee was in shock because that discovery implied that he had completely underestimated the forces between hull and stiffener. Wilkinson was in shock because he now realized that he had come closer to losing the *Nautilus* than he had ever thought, and I was in shock because I had studied the theory of inelastic buckling under the renowned Professor George Hausner at Cal Tech and I knew that McKee and Wilkinson were dead right. I had never before seen or imagined a structure so completely destroyed by stress and fatigue. It was well known that aircraft could fail from aeroelastic vibrations known as flutter, but it was assumed that the massive hull structures of submarines would not be affected by hydrodynamic forces produced by the sea as the submarine plows through the water. Something was happening to separate the ring stiffeners from the hull and as a result the collapse depth—the level beneath the surface of the sea at which even the most powerful submarine hull will implode without warning as a result of the pressure of the water around it—was greatly reduced.

But there was more. A submarine is more than a pressure hull. It must include mechanisms that allow it to submerge, to surface, or to maintain a specified depth. This is accomplished by the use of ballast tanks. These are nothing more than inverted cans shaped to match the contours of the hull with openings at the bottom. There are no valves on these openings, so air can flow in and out as the submarine changes depth and air pressure inside the tank is equal to the water pressure outside. For this reason these tanks are called soft tanks. The exterior of the ballast tanks is part of the skin of the submarine that gives it its good hydrodynamic shape. There are valves at the top of the tanks, which permit the tanks to be flooded with water and cause the submarine to submerge. There are bottles of compressed air inside the tanks that, when the valves at the top are closed, cause the water to be expelled from the tanks to be replaced by buoyant air so that the submarine can rise to the surface. All of these simple mechanisms must work or the submarine will sink.

Our inspection disclosed, to our horror, that all the ballast tanks showed splits along their sides. If the ballast tanks leak, then water will flood the tanks unless replacement air is continuously added. Otherwise the submarine sinks. For the *Nautilus*, already down by the bow, the splits in the tanks limited the size of the bubble that could be contained and caused a continuous drain of the air stored in the ballast tank air bottles. It was only a matter of hours before the onboard air supply would be exhausted. The air bottles that contain the precious compressed air had broken loose from their attachments to the hull inside the ballast tanks and were dangling from the piping that carried the air from bottle to tank. In a few hours, or at most a few days, the air bottles would detach completely and then the frames would separate from the hull and the *Nautilus* and her crew of 116 hands would be doomed. Thus three modes of failure were imminent: destruction of the pressure hull, loss of ability to hold ballast air, and the loss of air with which to blow ballast and provide the buoyancy to raise the submarine.

When McKee, Wilkinson, and I wriggled out of the ballast tanks and alerted Washington, there was the kind of glowering consternation that precedes the dreaded public embarrassment of the Navy. The long shadow of a national disaster was falling and heads might have to roll. All of the top brass of the Bureau of Ships—that powerful department of the Navy that oversees all aspects of naval vessels from the drawing of plans through commissioning and right through to the end of a ship's life—descended on Connecticut.

A notable exception was Hyman Rickover, who never allowed his name to be associated with failure. He would leave the mess to Wilkinson, his personal choice as the first skipper of the *Nautilus*. At the emergency meeting in New London, Wilkinson briefed the BuShips admirals on the damage, and a consensus emerged that the *Nautilus* should be laid up for a reevaluation of the design to uncover the mechanisms of the failure. When at the end of a long day they got around to me, I pointed out that I had a plan and a package of instruments designed to investigate the problem. "Why don't we repair the damage," I said, "and try to find the cause." The breakdown had taken place over eighteen months and was not likely to recur during the short period of my investigation. As against the grim alternative of a high-profile crippled *Nautilus* in sick bay, there seemed to be no harm in this approach and they agreed.

I discussed it with a senior naval architect for the Electric Boat Company, Robert McCandliss, a man whose judgment in crisis I trusted. He had been a fighter pilot in World War II. His plane had been shot out of the sky in a dogfight, and when he bailed out, the straps of his parachute got caught in the fuselage. Instead of panicking, he instantly analyzed the nature of the entanglement and reasoned that if he were to rotate his body in a certain direction, he would be freed. He was right. Now, with respect to the equations I was using to analyze the situation, he suggested that there might be unknown factors at play and that I ought to instrument for every conceivable and far-fetched scenario. I did.

The instrumentation consisted of small pressure gauges designed to measure the fluctuations in fluid force on each submarine appendage and the pressure inside and outside the ballast tanks and in each cavity of the superstructure. I hoped that the magnitude, frequency, and location of these pressures would reveal the nature of the mysterious forces that had produced such damage.

The Electric Boat Company would not allow me to install the instrumentation on the boat and insisted on doing the job themselves. It was apparently a matter of pride and, though no one could know it at the time, it was the kind that goes before a fall. The pressure gauges were distributed throughout the outside of the pressure hull of the submarine. Each gauge was meant to measure the difference between the pressure at its own location and the average pressure associated with the depth of the submarine at any given moment while submerged. It was therefore necessary that all the gauges be exposed to this average pressure. The method devised by Electric Boat was to connect each gauge by long lines of thin tubing to a single large bladder, or balloon, filled with air that was placed in a cage aft of the submarine's external vertical structure known as the sail. As the submarine changed depth the bladder would compress or expand, placing the appropriate air pressure on the back face of each pressure gauge. With the test instruments so installed, we put to sea.

This was my first extended voyage aboard a nuclear submarine. It was unlike any ship I had been on before. Gone was the reek of the diesel oil that permeated the conventional submarines of my experience, and it was neither cramped nor confining; there were no hammocks like those on the battleship I had served on. Nor was there any of the rolling, pitching, or heaving that I had known on minesweepers. As soon as we left port we submerged into the quiet world of the undersea. I was treated as a junior officer, and my mechanic, Louis Louistro, as a member of the crew. After dinner that first night, I went to my quarters to set up and calibrate the instrumentation, very much aware that I was missing the poker game that had begun in the wardroom. It was a bit hard to bear. I realized that no one aboard knew of my skill at that great psychophysiological game, a huge advantage in setting out to take one's opponents to the cleaners. But after I had had the opportunity to discuss the quality of the poker played on *Nautilus* with the supply officer, I had reason to pause.

The CO, he told me, was the greatest poker player in the Navy. Before commissioning, when Wilkinson assumed command, the high-stakes wardroom poker game had spun out of control, with losers out a lot more than they could afford. Wilkinson's expertise was such, it seemed, that he could literally control who won and who lost. The big losers found themselves recouping, and soon he had reestablished equity, at which point he reduced the stakes to a more reasonable level. The supply officer shook his head in wonder as he recalled Wilkinson's uncanny ability to detect the best bluff from the real thing. I, too, was impressed but spurred on, resolving to one day break the captain's hold on the game. When I was still a boy, my uncle on my mother's side, Eddie Pinna (the spelling of the family name had been altered), a Brooklyn cabdriver, had taught me the poker arts: how to spot a cheat, first of all, but mostly how to read between the lines of a player's body language, the giveaways of butterflies, thrill, excitement, anger, disappointment, the sweat on a brow, and other nuanced, involuntary manifestations associated with a pat hand, a flush, or a full house aces high. For now, however, I would have to defer my aspiration to be part of the Navy's poker stories. There was a submarine in distress and I was on the spot.

Early the next day, we were on station and my gauges were all functioning. I notified the skipper of my readiness and he began to bring the boat up to speed. Suddenly, however, all the gauges failed simultaneously. Buoyancy and high-speed flow had torn the external average-pressure bladder loose from its moorings, destroying all the gauges as well. There was no point in continuing and we turned back to port, our mission further than ever from accomplished.

As I emerged from the hatch, three admirals peered down at me eager to know the results. I had to tell them that we had none and I did so unabashedly. These officers had fought a war in which all too many skippers had to return from patrol with the mission frustrated. It had taken more than a year before our torpedoes in World War II were functioning. They knew then, as they knew now, that despite all our best efforts, the sea is relentless and will find a way to thwart the mariner. Long ago I had learned that when you bring something new to the sea, the sea will bring something new to you. To the uninformed observer the discussion at the hatch would have seemed almost laconic. If the admirals were testing anything, they were testing my competence in coping with the sea. Electric Boat's insistence on installing the instruments was not my alibi. It had done its best in the installation of new and untested oceanic instrumentation. That the instrumentation had failed did not diminish its credibility and left my own intact.

It was, therefore, with a certain equanimity that I approached the next conference of admirals. The same group had again flown up from Washington and it was in fact a repeat performance, except for my negative reaction to the shipyard's proposal that we berth, rather than dry-dock, the *Nautilus* for reexamination. They did accept my suggestion to repair and reinstall the gauges and go back to sea.

I decided that each gauge should have its own bladder. When Louistro and I could find nothing suitable in the Navy's supply facility, we went to a Woolworth five-and-ten-cents store and bought thirty-six brightly colored beach balls that seemed perfect for the task. The venerable Electric Boat Company thought otherwise. If beach balls were to be installed on its high-technology submarine, I was informed, Louistro and I would have to install them ourselves. Furthermore, neither Electric Boat nor the Navy was willing to foot the bill for returning the *Nautilus* to dry dock. Instead, holes were cut in the tops of the ballast tanks to permit my mechanic and me to inch our way through and make the installation. To prevent water from flooding the ballast tanks as we did this, temporary covers were placed over the ballast tank openings at the bottom of each tank. Unfortunately these covers leaked and water was entering the ballast tanks. To compensate, pumps were installed to keep the ballast tanks relatively dry. No sooner had we started working than, inexplicably, the pumps stopped operating and water began to pour through the leaky covers, flooding the bottom of the tanks. Two very wet individuals shot out of those tanks like rockets and the Navy dipped into its pockets and ordered the ship dry-docked.

Finally, the gauges repaired and reinstalled, we were ready to give it another try. Back at sea, my equanimity began to give way to raw emotion after we completed the first run. As the submarine gained speed, all the gauges began acting in unison and soon all indicator needles were hitting a point on the dial that I'll call X. This was a value we had assigned for the pressure fluctuation that we rated as dangerously high. Our instruments allowed us to record values well in excess of X and I set the scale on the instrument panel to 2X. All the indicator needles were hitting the stops at 2X. The tension mounted. I went to 5X. The needles hit those stops; same result at 10X. The intensity of the forces due to the vibrations could not be measured until I set the scale to record values of 30X, positive and negative. All the needles were oscillating in synchrony when the limit had been reached. I knew then that only a "little brown jug" phenomenon could explain the fluctuations in pressure. The water flowing over the opening at the bottom of each tank caused it to behave like a jug when you blow over the top of its neck and produce a sound. In the little brown jug case the frequency of the sound depends upon the volume of air in the jug and, to a lesser extent, its shape, and the amplitude depends on the amount of air that passes over the top of the jug. For the submarine the frequency of the sound depended not only on the volume of water in the ballast tanks but on the elasticity of the hull and the ballast tanks. The amplitude depended on an unforeseen resonance phenomenon similar to flutter on aircraft. It is this particular resonance phenomenon that I am reluctant to disclose (for security reasons), but I knew what it was and I knew what modifications could solve it. I also believed that the *Nautilus* was again at risk of sinking—if not immediately, within the next few hours or days.

True, all the repairs had been made on the stiffening rings and the pressure hull—the rings were reattached to the hull by welding— but there could be no doubt that these forces were creating new damage and we could not be sure that the repairs were completely effective. I called for a pause in the test program long enough to develop the records and be sure that the data would not be lost. I then went to the CO.

"The good news is," I said, "I found the problem. I have the data to demonstrate it and there is a simple solution."

Wilkinson nodded. "And the bad news?"

"The bad news is that we should slow the ship down and proceed directly back to port."

Wilkinson looked at me with a pat-hand smile. He suspected that my reluctance stemmed from a first-time submariner's fright. "Sorry, Craven," he said. "I have two days of tests to carry out."

I smiled in return, for I was the one with the high cards. "But I prepared that test program and I advise you not to."

Wilkinson, knowing that all the damage had been repaired and knowing that he had operated for eighteen months before the condition was serious, said, "Well, I am going to carry it out. You never know what else you might learn, son."

Sure, I thought, maybe the last lesson of my life.

Now I had to make a decision. I could, with little effort, make my instruments mysteriously stop working, forcing termination. Or I could take the easy way and not, as they say, rock the boat. First, I assessed the wisdom, if any, of the CO's call. Quite clearly his education did not include an understanding of the relationship among stress, elastic resonance, fatigue, and failure. Whatever understanding he had of the situation was based on intuitive knowledge acquired from experience, not a solid grounding in theory. From what I had heard about his card-playing prowess, I felt safe in surmising that he was a man who soaked up this sort of knowledge in all of his life experiences. He had skippered this ship for thousands of miles at high speed, fully aware of the vibrations and their intensity. Was that enough? I wanted poker—I wanted cold calculating unemotional thought in an assessment of skill and chance. I was getting poker, in spades. High-stakes poker is not a game—he was betting his life. I decided to go on with the tests—looking forward to what I might learn. And learn I did.

The next set of tests was conducted at maximum operating depth and at flank speed. This is the most dangerous operation for any submarine even when all systems are go. The distance from maximum operating depth to collapse depth is a little more than the length of the submarine. For the officer of the deck it is like being a pilot with the Blue Angels flying in formation. One misstep by any operator on the team means disaster for all. One stern plane jam, one rupture in the seawater system, one failed repair to the hull or structure and there is no opportunity for recovery. First-timers on a submarine will experience extreme stress during this operation. As the submarine reaches the maximum operating depth the compression of the hull will induce "snap, crackle, and pop" in the light plating of compartment bulkheads, inducing beads of sweat on the brow of the neophyte. Qualified submariners will have no qualms. For the *Nautilus*, I estimated that the forces I had measured would reduce the collapse depth by not more than one hundred feet. I was wrong. Subsequent analysis would show that two thousand of the ship's fifteen thousand horsepower were absorbed by the resonance. That meant that the ship was being battered by the equivalent of twenty-one-hundred-horsepower sledgehammers at more than ten times per second. Failure could occur at any depth. Luckily the maximum speed tests at maximum depth were uneventful except for the cheerful revelation that at maximum stress the needles hit the stops no higher than 30X. My Grandmother Pinna's old saying about what life had taught her—"If I live through Monday, I live through the rest of the week"—was comfort as never before.

The next tests were conducted at shallow depth. All hands were relaxed when suddenly there was the sound of a violent explosion in one of the ballast tanks, then in another—an intermittent series of powerful blasts in one or more of the ballast tanks. The officer of the deck quickly reduced speed and the blasts stopped. I must admit I was alarmed. The crew informed me that they had experienced them before not knowing what they were. I had a sudden insight, recognizing this as a phenomenon known as "cavitation." Vapor was being generated by negative pressure in the ballast tanks that exceeded the pressure of water at depth. In shallow water, or at atmospheric pressure, this negative pressure is about one atmosphere, or some fifteen pounds per square inch. We were getting more than double that inside the tanks. Each bubble was like the first bubbles in a pot of water that is about to boil. If any of the officers or crew were alarmed it did not show, but all were eager to hear my opinion on the source and severity of the cavitation bursts. I pointed out that the explosive sounds were produced by nothing more than great pockets of collapsing vapor. The vapor itself was pressure-relieving and the collapse had merely reinitiated the pounding to which the ship was continuously exposed. It was hard to tell how much that reassured them but cavitation was a phenomenon I had studied in the laboratory and that knowledge was good enough for me.

When the tests were over, the *Nautilus* surfaced. For our trial purposes, large steel plates had been bolted over openings in the fairwater, the sail, and superstructure, and at this point the test program, which could not anticipate that the problem might have been solved, called for removing these temporary plates so that other hydrodynamic phenomena might be investigated. The CO, Louistro, and I went topside. With the *Nautilus* heading directly into a moderate sea, we climbed to the top of the sail. Because nuclear submarines are continuously submerged few nuclear submariners see what we were about to witness. Only a small number of officers and crew are in the sail while underway on the surface and thus able to see what is happening outside the sub. What we saw was, under the prevailing conditions, a manifestation of a natural phenomenon at sea. A great sheet of accelerated water covers the bow. Being thin, and moving at the same velocity as the submarine, this sheet of water appears as a lustrous transparent glaze. As it proceeds toward the stern it slows and at a certain speed suddenly produces a standing wave of foamy water known as a hydraulic jump. The ship itself generates great diverging bow waves like a giant knife cutting the water. The wedge containing the bow waves invariably makes a perfect 19 degree 28 minute angle with the path of the ship. Similarly, the bow waves diverge tangent to a line that is always 35 degrees 16 minutes with the path of the ship. Behind, the great rolling following waves have a length (lambda) that depends on the speed of the ship.

I had learned the formula by heart as a form of poetry, and now I shouted, "C squared equals g lambda over 2 pi." These beautiful and immutable patterns are the same for a rowboat as for an aircraft carrier. Some may think that such knowledge detracts from the beauty of the scene but when one knows the details of the wave pattern one knows precisely what further beauty to look for—the undulating reflections of the moon by night or the glittering shimmer of many suns by day. One appreciates with new insight the luxurious rolling, trailing waves—as did we on the *Nautilus*, with those towering waves breaking over the bow, hurling their refreshing foam and spray into our faces. In a cathartic release of tension—we were going to live to tell the tale—our whole beings were filled with exultation as the skipper, Louistro, and I crawled along the deck, secured by safety lines, unbolting the steel plates and hurling them into the sea with fiendish glee. Our lungs bursting with the exhilarating breath of the sea, these words rang out in my memory:

> *Roll on, thou deep and dark blue ocean, roll!*
> *Ten thousand fleets sweep over thee in vain;*
> *Man marks the earth with ruin, —his control*
>   *Stops with the shore.*

Lord Byron notwithstanding, for eighteen months the *Nautilus* had taken on the ocean, fury and all, and the *Nautilus* had prevailed. The mission done, a simple, straightforward, and still classified modification of the ballast tank openings in hand, there remained only the debrief on our return and maybe my chance to extract wages from the CO at his own game. But that was not to be. Back in port, Wilkinson was besieged in the wardroom by reporters eager to hear of the latest exploits of the *Nautilus*, but oblivious to the real-life drama that had just unfolded. In the background, a radio was blaring the only sour note—Yankee Don Larsen was pitching a World Series perfect game against my beloved Brooklyn Dodgers. The secure telephone was ringing incessantly with calls from the BuShips admirals. The true story of our voyage, even though it was top secret, would spread swiftly though the fleet and soon enough I would be summoned to the science and technology helm to steer another ship away from rocks and shoals.

2

Design for Deterrence

When on a late autumn day in 1955, Admiral William F. "Red" Raborn took up his post as director of the Navy's brand-new and as yet unstaffed Strategic Deterrence Systems, he had been handed sweeping powers by Navy men cut from the same cloth as he. A highly decorated World War II Navy fighter pilot and subsequently commander of an aircraft carrier, Raborn would handpick forty naval officers and a like number of civilians without regard to status or seniority, each of the eighty possessing a special competence. Almost all of the officers would be men who had experienced both victory and defeat in battle; almost all of the civilians selected had been involved in the technologies that had turned the tide in World War II. Due to their wartime experiences, these individuals had enough imaginative foresight to know that nuclear war could not and must not be an option.

The organization called the Special Projects Office started small. It was housed in the Old Munitions Building on the Capitol Mall and had been created only weeks before Raborn took charge. It had been given the Defense Department's assignment of developing the sea-launched version of the Jupiter missile. But the Navy had vested Raborn with responsibility for an as yet undefined larger, fleetwide role. Thus, while complying with orders regarding the Jupiter IRBM (intermediate range ballistic missile), he set out to develop alternatives to the Jupiter system. That alternative to the Jupiter missile would be called Polaris. Toward that end, he called on the man who would soon become his technical director, Captain (later Admiral) Levering Smith, and a civilian strategist, William F. Whitmore, to be his Chief Scientist. Raborn as vice admiral and Whitmore as GS18 (the highest civilian rank) were at the top of the organizational pyramid. Levering Smith, as the technical, organizational, and management genius, would be the de facto project director. Raborn, as leader, would select and galvanize the team into action.

Whitmore, an operations analyst from the Navy's Office of Strategic Planning, fit the description of Chief Scientist. Bespectacled, shaggily mustached, and dressed in baggy tweeds, he was the archetype of the intellectual academic. His knowledge of the technical literature was prodigious and he was intimately familiar with the host of strategic concepts espoused by each of the military services, the politicians, and academia. His finest and most valuable contribution was in establishing from the very start of the program that Polaris, as the missile of the Fleet Ballistic Missile System, was not a war-fighting system but a deterrent to nuclear war.

His day-to-day occupation was the coordination of the Navy Laboratories in support of a Special Projects Office program that would not mature for nine years. It was a long-range program leading to an unspecified deterrent system.

Smith, a gunnery officer, who, rescued from sea, had learned the technical lessons of the disastrous battle of Savo Island at Guadalcanal and who had shepherded the Hiroshima and Nagasaki bombs on the ill-starred USS *Indianapolis*, could immediately see that the liquid-fueled Jupiter missile launched from a vulnerable surface ship heaving on the high seas was a formula for failure as well as an easy target. A more sensible approach would be to launch missiles from submarines, undetectable in the still waters of the deep, thus less vulnerable to attack. And although they would have to be larger, the missiles would be solid- rather than liquid-fueled, eliminating the need for last-minute loading of the fuel.

But Smith kept his theories to himself for the time being, knowing that direct confrontation with authority—in a politically charged atmosphere as the country prepared to fight a nuclear war—courted instant failure. His opportunity to promote the use of the submarine service for nuclear deterrence came in 1956 when the National Academy of Sciences conducted a summer study to determine the ideal system that the Soviets might develop for any near-future strategic confrontation. Smith volunteered to staff that study and Whitmore participated in the selection of the strategic analysis participants. As a result, a Russian submarine with solid-fueled ballistic missiles was designed. The constraints associated with the necessarily lightweight missile and inadequate yield of contemporary warheads were resolved by the nuclear scientist Edward Teller, father of the hydrogen bomb (and no friend of mere deterrence), who confidently and, as it soon turned out, correctly predicted a weight-to-yield ratio that no one else dared conceive.

Any study bearing the seal of approval of the National Academy of Sciences is guaranteed to receive top-level attention and serious consideration. When Smith's submarine study was completed, Raborn presented it to the Chief of Naval Operations with the statement, "If the Soviets can build this system, then the United States can do it also."

Smith's submarine study received scrutiny over Labor Day weekend. While the rest of the country was flipping burgers, an emergency meeting was called by Clark Millikan, a famous physicist from the California Institute of Technology, who was in charge of a committee overseeing the nation's strategic systems. In attendance were the Secretary of Defense, the director of defense research and engineering, the Secretary of the Navy, the undersecretary of the navy for research and development, the Chief of Naval Operations, and the admiral in charge of strategic systems planning. Smith, Levering, and Whitmore were given the floor.

Smith led the technical discussion while Raborn outlined the Navy's organizational capability for the conduct of the mission. Whitmore presented not only the submarine study's strategic philosophy, but also an "Air Force Eyes Only" report authored by the RAND Corporation that cited the cost effectiveness of the National Academy of Science's "Russian System." By Monday the decision had been made to abandon the Jupiter project and institute a new "fleet ballistic missile" weapon system with a solid-fueled missile. Raborn named it Polaris, after the North Star, which has guided navigators through the centuries. It would be housed in a nuclear submarine.

Until the *Nautilus* had slid down the ways in a spray of champagne in January 1955, diesel-powered submarines spent most of their life on the surface, submerging on time-limited battery power only in close proximity to the target to attack and escape, and then resurface and recharge. Polaris, which would become the backbone of a new strategy of deterrence, would have been a pipe dream were it not for the nuclear-powered *Nautilus*, the world's first true submarine, a revolutionary innovation more far-reaching than the transition from sail to steam. Steam had liberated ships from the caprice of the winds but only in exchange for the tethers of constant refueling; nuclear power had set them free.

But the darkest hour for *Nautilus*, as she limped back to port in October 1956, was, fortunately, not exposed to the media and was quickly overcome through urgent and effective action. And fortunately, much of what took place over the next forty years in developing our undersea warfare capability remains secret to this day. As this book demonstrates, our programs, like our submarines, ran silent and ran deep. What would have happened if we had lost *Nautilus* in October of 1956 and with her the momentum that carried us to decisive supremacy in our defensive, deterrent, and intelligence capabilities in the depths of the oceans? It is almost unthinkable.

Another October later, Sputnik changed everything. There was nothing secret about this accomplishment of Soviet science, and Russia's projection of military capability into space. There it was, a twinkling man-made satellite passing over our country several times each day, emitting a faint but taunting radio beep-beep that was a wake-up call of major proportions. It was a terrific shock to the United States; it suggested the nation faced a possible nuclear Pearl Harbor because Sputnik vividly demonstrated that we were far more vulnerable to an attack by the Soviet Union than we had realized. The "balance of terror" was suddenly and perilously out of balance. Stunned beyond measure, the United States nevertheless reacted swiftly. The creation of a triad of deterrence began (one system for each service, with bombs or missles launched from land, sea, and air).

The United States had lost its nuclear monopoly to the Soviet Union in 1949, and whatever advantage it recovered in 1952 by exploding the world's first hydrogen bomb was lost again the following year when the Soviets exploded theirs—ushering in the age of the balance of terror. Moreover, intelligence reports were revealing that the devilish balance was tipping the other way. Moscow was making rapid strides in the race to develop long-range nuclear missiles—the ultimate weapon of the day—while America's ICBM program was facing knotty problems in propulsion, guidance, and reentry. The ICBM had been assigned to the Air Force, with the Army given the task of developing an intermediate range ballistic missile. The Navy, reaching a historic nadir in its mission, had no ballistic missile role.

The Air Force's Strategic Air Command now supplanted the Navy as America's strategic arm. But naval officers steeped in a tradition of deterrence through the persuasive display of irresistible power could see that a sea-launched missile capability, which would carry the threat of certain annihilation close to enemy shores, could restore the Navy's preeminent role. They sought participation in the Air Force missile program, but were promptly turned away by the new guardians of strategic warfare. They finally gained a foot in the door only when the Department of Defense assigned the Navy to develop a ship-launching system for the Army's liquid-fueled Jupiter IRBM. We were still a long way from putting the nuclear deterrence triad into place. Such was the picture—until late 1957.

On December 9 of that pivotal year, with Sputnik 2 overhead, the Polaris program was shortened from the original nine-year completion date to four years and assigned BrickBat01 priority, the highest in the land. The Special Projects Office expanded its management team, new management concepts were promulgated, and one of the most remarkable and technologically complex development programs in the history of mankind was set in motion.

When I returned from New London in October of 1956 as head of flow studies at the David Taylor Model Basin in Washington my plate was already full. I was in charge of a team of oceanic detectives who were evaluating the technical performance of ships and submarines that would play a leading role in America's defense throughout the Cold War (and the century to follow). These scientists and technicians were at sea on all sorts of experimental craft that were part of a fascinating story largely untold to this day. But it was not clear that the nation or the Department of Defense shared our enthusiasm. In these early days of developing the full potential of the submarine we were dismayed to be told that one of the most urgent priorities, based on a congressional request, was the evaluation of visibility through the ports of the Disneyland submarines. Apart from "grave" national concerns like this, there was no international crisis on the immediate horizon that would require deployment of submarines that existed only on drawing boards. True, the Polaris program had just been established, but it was not expected to mature for almost a decade.

My life at the David Taylor Model Basin was idyllic. This whimsically named naval research facility is located in suburban Maryland on the shore of the Potomac. It features two parallel basins of water each more than a half mile in length and, as I remember it, about ten to fifteen feet in depth and from twenty to thirty feet wide. Each basin has a bridging structure, called a carriage, which is mounted on wheels that run on tracks along the sides. The carriages are driven by electric motors whose electricity is supplied from a generator room at the end of the basin. Wooden or wax models of ships and submarines and their appendages are instrumented and towed in the basin to evaluate design, design flaws, and hydrodynamic theory.

Our work day closed at 4:15; it took only fifteen minutes to drive to a beautiful new home in wooded suburban Maryland. I would soon complete a leisurely bit of intellectual self-indulgence, spending seven years at night school acquiring a law degree. My wife was embarked on her own career as a professor of speech pathology and audiology at the University of Maryland. Neil H. McElroy, onetime head of Procter & Gamble, was Secretary of Defense and he was instituting a major reduction in the budget for Defense Department-sponsored research and development.

But this relaxed existence came to an abrupt end in December of 1957 when the Special Projects Office mission was accelerated. I was summoned to the office of Admiral Alvey Wright, the newly designated commanding officer of the DTMB, to be given a new assignment.

He congratulated me for my work on *Nautilus* and told me that the Special Projects Office was now ready to move full steam ahead in the development and deployment of the Fleet Ballistic Missile submarine and its Polaris missile. Unlike other services where system development is managed by contractors, the Special Projects Office had management responsibility for every aspect of the Fleet Ballistic Missile System. This included design and development of every component of the submarine, the missile, and the support facilities. This included supply ships, submarine tenders, the support bases in Charleston, South Cardina, Guam, and Holy Loch in Scotland. It also included training facilities for every component of the system; management of the missile development, warhead guidance, propulsion, launch, the development of precise navigation equipment, including satellite navigation systems and shore-based low-frequency communication systems. The entire project included the most wonderful collection of "shoes and ships and sealing wax and cabbages and things." No single item involved in the development operation and deployment of the strategic deterrent was beyond the management purview of Raborn's office. Thus, Wright had been alerted to receive high-priority tasks from the Special Projects team across the spectrum of system responsibilities on short notice. He asked me to conduct or coordinate the tasks as they arose, utilizing the personnel and facilities at DTMB. I had to chuckle, for this was akin to the assignment given to Wright when he was a young commander during World War II. I knew it was important, but I did not then realize that this assignment would ring in the new year of 1958 and make it the pivotal year of my life.

Before I could savor the heady potential of this responsibility, a Captain Dennett K. "Deke" Ela contacted me. He was the head of the Polaris missile launching and handling branch, one of the project office's many subsystems. It was his job to design, develop, and test the equipment that would place the missiles in the submarines and launch them into the atmosphere with a velocity and attitude that would permit the guidance system to ignite the propellant and start the missile on its journey to the target.

It was originally thought that the easiest method of launch would be from a submarine on the surface. A Special Projects ship, the *Observation Island*, had been hastily converted from a merchant ship in 1957 and more hastily outfitted with a launch tube. Another launch tube in a complex and expensive ship motion simulator was also constructed for use on land. No missile was ever launched from either facility. Calculations of submarine motions indicated that except for the calmest of seas, it would not be possible to launch a missile with attitudes of pitch and yaw that would be within the acceptable parameters for the operation of the guidance system. There was no alternative but underwater launch. A submarine at depth could insure stability in any sea state. But no one had ever accomplished the feat of launching a missile from undersea before.

As soon as it was announced that the Special Projects Office was contemplating underwater launch, aerospace contractors and universities throughout the nation began conducting tests in model basins and test tanks with small models. All predicted catastrophe. None of the missiles in these models ever got out of the water. The problem was that no one had ever built a facility that could simulate the sea-to-air interface that would be experienced by the full-sized missile. If the model were, say, one tenth the size of the Polaris missile, then the entire launching facility must have an atmospheric pressure that was one tenth of the normal atmospheric pressure of 14.7 pounds per square inch. Such a pressure (1.47 pounds per square inch) is close to a vacuum and a facility that could maintain such a model atmosphere would be costly and time-consuming to build.

The big question in 1958 was: Could the David Taylor Model Basin build such a model test facility and conduct tests in time to freeze the design?

"Of course," I said. "When do you need the results?"

"In two months!" barked Ela.

"Surely, you must be joking, Captain."

"I am not joking, Craven. The nation needs these results as soon as we can get them. This program has the highest priority in the nation. We are already building a full-scale launching facility off the shores of San Clemente Island in Southern California, but it will only be able to conduct one test a week and we may need many tests if we run into any problems."

I had an idea. DTMB might be able to help in two months with a one-atmosphere facility if we violated modeling rules and used a very heavy missile model. The missile would be launched by a bubble of air. We would make the missile heavy enough so that the bubble of air would expand to the same size it would be in a low-atmosphere facility with a properly weighted model missile. Purists would complain, but we ought to get the right answers. But two months? We'll try to do it, I told Ela, but it would be risky to assume that the results were valid unless we could compare them with at least one full-scale test at the San Clemente test site.

"Okay, Craven, proceed with your crazy idea," said Ela. "It might work, but do it as fast as you can and let's hope that the full-scale tests at San Clemente show that we have no problems."

Construction had barely commenced on our launching facility when Ela came up with another challenge. "Craven," he told me, "the San Clemente facility is nearly operational but it is not much good unless we can prove that the missile will not be affected by waves. Can you produce a wave maker that will make full-size waves at the facility at San Clemente?" With tongue in cheek I asked when he would need it. With his eyebrows raised and that intense, fixed stare associated with wartime command, he said, "Two months, Craven, two months."

I was about to comment on the shortcomings of the launching branch's sense of humor, when I suddenly recalled my work during the Korean War on techniques for sweeping pressure mines. These sophisticated devices are activated by the disturbance in the water made by a boat passing above or nearby. One such technique involved steering a large ship directly toward the minefield and turning it away just before reaching the danger zone. The following wave train generated by its approach would then continue along the original track, pass over the mines, and detonate them.

My calculations and tests showed that such an effect was possible in this instance by using one of the Navy's largest aircraft carriers. With the test missile launcher nested in the L of the L-shaped coastline of San Clemente, the carrier could steam directly toward the shore and turn seaward just before making contact with the test platform. This would allow waves of ocean magnitude to sweep over the test launcher at the moment the test missile was launched.

The Chief of Naval Operations greeted this proposal with horror. There was no program of sufficient priority and importance to risk the destruction of the pride of the United States Navy on rocks and shoals.

When asked for an alternative I suggested that a heavy cruiser might do. The CNO responded that he would authorize the mission if there was any cruiser skipper who would volunteer for it. I was subsequently told that there was such a skipper. He and his ship would be ready on a moment's notice. The test was scheduled for early September 1958, on my wife's birthday. She was soon to give birth to our first child. David would arrive on September 25. Could I take the chance that he would be born while I was at San Clemente?

I recalled an incident that had occurred only a month previously. The navigation branch of SP, another of its many subsystems, had asked me to design a sonar dome for the Special Projects navigation test ship *Compass Island* (another converted merchant ship). They had just discovered that conventional sonar domes would allow bubbles from the ship's bow wave to pass over the dome and thereby destroy its ability to operate. They needed a new and novel sonar dome design. When did they want the design? "Tomorrow, Craven, tomorrow." There was to be an emergency design meeting at the New York (i.e., Brooklyn) Naval Shipyard the next day. Indeed, with my back-of-the-envelope design in hand, I met with the design superintendent and his staff. But where was the construction foreman? He was at the hospital where his wife was giving birth. The "Sup" slammed his fist on the table. "Doesn't he know that this is the nation's most important program? Doesn't he know what this program is all about?" A reproving voice from the end of the table said, "Tell us, what is it all about?" Yes indeed, we were in a desperate race to prevent nuclear war in order to preserve a world in which the life, liberty, and pursuit of happiness of the nuclear family could be every person's highest priority.

On my wife's birthday I gave her a bouquet of flowers. The next day, she drove me to the airport. As we parted, for the first time in our marriage of seven years she burst into tears and asked how I could leave her at a time like this. I managed to say in a confident tone, "Not to worry. I will be back in plenty of time."

As fate would have it, the tests were not delayed and the birth was not premature. But I had learned a lesson on placing my priorities and where I should expect my colleagues and my staff to place their priorities. If I was to expect them to devote their highest professional priority to making the world safe for the next generation, I should expect this mission always to be subordinate to the preservation of their family and their faith.

When we performed the test I stood on a barge at San Clemente. A ten-thousand-ton warship was bearing down on me at a speed of almost forty knots. Its approach was accompanied by butterflies—mine. It is hard to describe the psychological effect. The helmsman in me thought of this cruiser's helmsman, poised to execute the order "left full rudder" at precisely the right moment or risk running the ship aground. Even before a single wave could be discerned, I found myself shouting, "Turn, damn you, turn!" And when at last it did, suddenly, great following waves began to roll over the facility. Their amplitude was being recorded on instrumentation installed and monitored by Louistro and me, and at the appropriate moment we gave the signal to fire—or should I say "pop up," since it was a dummy missile. Pop up it did at the very height of the wave, exiting the water without deviation from its designated path. Polaris was immune from the effects of the sea when it launched, and the Special Projects Office could breathe a sigh of relief. With great relief I could now watch the cruiser's stern as she headed out to sea. (I later learned that a second helmsman was positioned right behind the first, ready to seize the helm should the first err or freeze.)

The success of this operation was such that other cruiser skippers in the squadron insisted on getting their own chance to make those waves. We got more data (and waves) than we needed. The excess did not add much to the analysis, since the first test proved the wisdom of the decision to adopt an underwater launch. In the future there would be unanticipated and embarrassing problems associated with this technique, but Special Projects was now secure in the understanding that these problems could be resolved. We had no choice but to resolve them—success or failure meant the presence or absence of nuclear war.

3

A Calculus of Terror

Nineteen fifty-eight was a year when engineering development assignments arrived at the David Taylor Model Basin from one subsystem branch or another almost daily. But the Special Projects Office was tasking DTMB and other Navy laboratories with missions that transcended science and engineering. Admiral Raborn had in one way or another organized a management structure that ensured that the entire Navy acted as a coordinated team in the development of this new and complex deterrent to nuclear war even as his subsystem managers were free to develop their own specialty. But his foresight extended beyond the immediate Polaris mission. Academy-trained naval officers had learned from tradition and experience that the enemy initiates the countermeasure to any military system at the moment of that system's birth. The only way to avoid cycles of victory and defeat was to launch the counter-countermeasure system at the same moment that the original system is first deployed. Raborn had deemed that while his organization would spend its full time developing the deterrent system, another team would focus on the future, counter-countermeasure system, whatever it might be.

The decision to organize this effort was a part of the management reorganization associated with the program acceleration decreed in December 1957. Chief Scientist Whitmore was given the assignment to organize the team and it was he who decided that the Chief Scientist of the Office of Naval Research be the chair of a group consisting of the civilian technical director of every Navy and oceanographic laboratory involved with the science and technology of strategic deterrence. By management decree no member of the Special Projects Office except for the Chief Scientist and his staff was authorized to participate in this long-range program. The team thus identified was called together for an organizational and modus operandi meeting early in 1958.

That team was called PAHGLORAD. Only a group of long-haired, wild-eyed scientists would adopt such an acronym, formed from its full name: Polaris Ad Hoc Group for Long-Range Deterrence. The development program this group would foster would be a line item in the Department of Defense budget called "Advanced Sea-Based Deterrence," and the system they would eventually recommend, in the summer of 1964, would be called the Advanced Sea-Based Deterrent. The management problem to be resolved was that the civilian directors of all the major naval laboratories involved with the Polaris program were technologists without any training in operations analysis or the strategy and science of deterrence. Therefore Admiral Wright elected to nominate me as the model basin representative for PAHGLORAD. He did this because he knew that I had recently acquired a law degree with a specialty in the law of the sea. He was aware of my experience in operational analysis as it applied to minesweeping and he knew that a group charged with the development of a future deterrent would need guidance from an individual knowledgeable in law and operational analysis as well as naval technology. Whitmore, Chief Scientist and therefore Chief Scientist of Polaris, who had assembled the team, was delighted with Wright's decision.

The group thus had a mission that transcended the competence, experience, and political acumen of any one of its members. Nobody really knew the nature of the conflict that was to be prevented. There was no script, but everyone was hoping for the leading role. The number of people who understood atomic energy on a complex level was extremely limited. The majority of these individuals were civilian scientists with no combat time among them. They had never been to hell and back, so how could they possibly conceptualize the full extent of nuclear destruction?

By 1958 the scientists and the military was split into two camps: those who regarded nuclear bombs as just another weapon in the nation's arsenal and those who saw the deterrence of nuclear war as a sacred mission to which they were prepared to dedicate and, if need be, give their lives. Our group was determined to arrive at an understanding of how deterrence could actually work to ensure that nuclear and thermonuclear weapons would never be used by any country.

The chairman of PAHGLORAD was Joachim Weyl, the Chief Scientist of the Office of Naval Research. He was the son of the anti-Nazi German émigré Hermann Weyl, one of the twentieth century's most famous mathematician-philosophers. Joachim shared his father's fierce determination that the forces of evil had to be deterred and he knew that they can never be destroyed. In addition, he had followed in his father's footsteps as an expert on the mathematics of information theory and information entropy—the word "entropy," in this meaning, being a measure of uncertainty, useful in providing guidance on the bets that one makes about the future.

Special Projects through PAHGLORAD was betting on the future of deterrence, of course, and put its money where its mouth was. It allocated unrestricted funds of approximately $1 million per year to each of a baker's dozen of laboratories to be spent on technologies that would further deterrence. Every laboratory program would be reviewed annually and its funding would either be increased or decreased by as much as 20 percent depending on PAHGLORAD's assessment of its relevance to deterrence. The group's work would continue for five years with a start date of 1959, culminating in a study that would be the basis for recommendations to the Navy and the Defense Department for the future application of deterrence as America's national strategy for the prevention of nuclear war. But many of the results of that program were ripped untimely from the schedule to cope with the crisis that resulted from the loss of the submarine Thresher—which, in turn, would put us on a path to undersea intelligence and research projects undreamed of in the 1950s and in PAHGLORAD's early years. I will describe all of this later in the book.

To establish a baseline as a point of departure, it was necessary that PAHGLORAD be fully briefed on all aspects of the developing Polaris system. Thus the committee's first meeting consisted of several days of briefings by individuals who were actively engaged in the development of the Polaris subsystems. Captain Levering Smith, the Special Projects Office's technical director, was protective of the time that Polaris experts would spend in briefings. He had determined that, except for the top people in the Pentagon, no other outside group would be given as full a perspective of the Polaris Fleet Ballistic Missile program as those inducted into PAHGLORAD.

The briefings took place in Special Projects' top secret management center. In its auditorium a podium and a large backlighted screen dominated the scene. In a room behind it "Wizards of Oz" projected every known type of audiovisual media in integrated displays as required for each management review. As I remember it Whitmore and Weyl gave the introductory overview. I did not know it then, but I would be giving similar overview briefings many times in the future.

The essence of the briefings was the same for more than a decade. I can only reveal a brief unclassified version and my memory limits

me to versions that I presented from 1960 through 1965 (when I had
replaced Whitmore as SP's Chief Scientist), but these briefings generally ran along the following lines, beginning with a discussion of
deterrence:

> *Ladies and Gentlemen:* I am the Chief Scientist of the
> Special Projects Office. This office has management
> responsibility for the design, development, construction,
> operational test and evaluation and maintenance of the
> Polaris Fleet Ballistic Missile System. This is the most
> technically advanced military system that has ever been
> deployed, and the initial deployment of the submarine *George
> Washington* was accomplished in the record time of three years
> after authorization. The annual budget for the office has been
> in excess of $2 billion per year [1960 dollars] and at any one
> time more than 200,000 people have been involved in this
> national effort. But I must tell you that all the technology I
> will now describe will be irrelevant unless it is dedicated to a
> nationally agreed upon strategic mission. SP's mission is the
> deterrence of nuclear war waged by the Soviets, by the
> Chinese, should they acquire long-range missiles, by terrorist
> nations, or by terrorists.
>
>   At the outset I must emphasize that a deterrent must be
> effective. If it is ever used, then its mission has failed and a
> worldwide apocalypse is inevitable. Thus a nation choosing a
> strategy of nuclear deterrence cannot also choose a strategy
> that would commit the nation to a tactical nuclear war. It
> should be fairly obvious that a rational Soviet leadership
> would be deterred if it were certain that our system, capable of
> launching an unacceptable number of missiles on the Soviet
> homeland, could not be defused. If, on the other hand, the
> Soviets feared that the United States might strike first, or that

the United States might even contemplate striking first, deterrence might fail. Therefore, if the United States elects to design and deploy a credible deterrent using nuclear weapons, then it must allow, nay, encourage, the Soviets to design and deploy their own deterrent having characteristics identical to our own.

There is no way the United States would contemplate striking first if it knew that a Soviet response would inflict equal or greater harm. The term for this strategy is "mutual deterrence." Ladies and Gentlemen, what would it actually take—what is the "unacceptable number" of nuclear missiles needed—to deter the Soviets? And what is the "unacceptable number" of Soviet weapons that would prevent the citizens of the United States from ever contemplating nuclear war?

I must tell you that there are strategists such as Herman Kahn who publicly advocate preparation for nuclear war and, in describing the consequences of a full exchange, find it an acceptable scenario. Although Kahn has had no personal experience or personal exposure to the effects of nuclear war, he recommends the development of an arsenal of tactical nuclear weapons. If a design group such as Special Projects discovers that politically powerful individuals in the United States and/or the Soviet Union have bought Herman Kahn's thesis, then it may find itself in a classic arms race dilemma where the number of nuclear weapons must proliferate without limit and their invulnerability must be continually updated.

The deployment of a deterrent is dramatically different from deployment for battle or deployment for the collection of intelligence. An essential element of deterrence is the conditioning of the body politic of the nation to be deterred and the conditioning of the body politic of the deterring nation to be reassured that deterrence will not fail. When

Edward Teller, an advocate of tactical nuclear warfare, foretold in 1955 the coming of lighter and more powerful nuclear bombs, this was understood by everyone to mean that the technology was almost at hand to produce a small one-megaton warhead. One megaton is the magic number. One megaton is a unit of power that people can easily conceptualize. The term 800 kilotons or nine tenths of a megaton is confusing. The atom bombs that destroyed Hiroshima and Nagasaki were about ten kilotons [equivalent to ten thousand tons of TNT]. The thermonuclear warhead of the [first] version of the Polaris missile is one megaton, or about one hundred times more powerful than that of the atom bomb [or, equivalent to one million tons of TNT].

Still, you may wonder, as the Special Projects Office does, why a single Polaris warhead has to be so powerful. Wouldn't half a megaton be enough for any rational nation to conceptualize and be deterred by? The tormenting question of design for deterrence versus design for battle is the dilemma, and the mission motivation of the designers is at the root of the dilemma. The problem for the United States is complicated by the fact that Edward Teller was the father of the hydrogen bomb and his motivation for development is the belief that nuclear war with the Soviets is inevitable. The result is the balance of terror paradox. The only rationalization for building and deploying his bombs for deterrence is the realization that powerful forces in the Soviet Union also believe that nuclear war is inevitable and are developing their own weapons for tactical nuclear war. The deterrence of such individuals may require weapons superiority even if such superiority is meaningless. Indeed the magnitude of the deterrent is at best a credible metaphor that the body politic of the deterred nation can understand. In the words of Admiral

Rickover, the only purpose of the deterrent is "to strike fear and terror in the heart of the enemy."

Having established a subjective philosophy of deterrence, it must be translated into hard, objective design. The bean counters will say that the system must be cost effective. One submarine, perhaps two, each with a capability of incinerating the entire Soviet Union—that would be ideal, they would say. The Special Projects planners, however, believe that such a system would not be credible. What do we mean not credible? The designer must adopt the lawyer's "reasonable man" concept. If a reasonable person thinks it over, even though credibility is not a quantifiable variable, he or she will come to the conclusion that total incineration is not credible. SP, therefore, has concluded that the Polaris system should threaten a significant part of the population, not with genocide, but with enough mortality to create a century of national mourning, if not eternal enmity. SP has concluded that Polaris should threaten a significant part of the Soviets' command and control, but not enough to wipe out the ability to negotiate a surrender. SP concluded that Polaris should also threaten a significant part of the industrial complex, but not enough to preclude its recovery.

Let us turn now to the submarines. Some already exist and more can be built to order. There should be no difficulty in putting in a missile compartment. But how many missiles will be needed to do the job? How about two? One on the port side and one on the starboard. Why not four? Eight? Well, something must limit the number of missiles. So the Polaris team has asked the bean-counting people for a cost effective number and, based on operational analysis, they have said sixty-four. Sixty-four missiles operated and maintained by a single hundred-man crew? That's less than two men per

missile. Each missile could destroy a city and if in the future
they are equipped with multiple independently targeted
reentry vehicles, MIRVs, could destroy many cities, perhaps as
many as five cities per man. Who would like to carry that
burden on his immortal soul?

SP must decide quickly, because the toy companies
Renwall and Revell have to develop toy models in time for the
Christmas market. The American public will learn from the
toys they buy what the strength of the American deterrent is.
SP informed the toy makers that the number of missiles would
be either eight or sixteen. Revell chose eight, and Renwall
sixteen. Before Christmas 1958, but too late for Revell, the
Special Projects Office decided on sixteen. Renwall makes a
killing and Revell is outraged. No matter, the die is cast.
Millions of plastic models tell the Americans, the Soviets, and
the rest of the world something about the envelope of our sea-
based deterrent. People can now decide if it is a weapon of war
and then they can protest; or they can decide it is a guarantor
of peace and promulgate the slogan "If it is ever used it will
have failed."

Ladies and gentlemen, if you now appreciate the strategy
of strategic deterrence, you should appreciate SP's conclusions
on the nature of the deterrent it must design and build and
update in the shortest possible time to be an effective
deterrent to the Soviet Union and nuclear war.

To satisfy the previously described threat criteria there
must be forty-one invulnerable nuclear submarines with
sixteen missiles each. Thirty-five or more submarines are to be
on station at all times. With the magnitude of the overall
system defined, the subsystems are easily identified:

• There must be a missile weighing less than a weight
heretofore unachieved with a range that will encompass the

target area from available deployment areas; it must have a reentry body that will penetrate the atmosphere and survive the burn-up effect known as ablation in a manner that has not been accomplished before.

- The missile must have a warhead that will be completely secure against accidental or unauthorized firing with a yield-to-weight ratio heretofore unachieved.

- There must be a propellant of adequate impulse that can be safely used inside a submerged submarine in a manner heretofore unachieved.

- There must be the capability for launching from underwater in all imaginable sea states with a technology heretofore unachieved.

- There must be a missile and warhead guidance system of light weight and accuracy heretofore unachieved.

- There must be targeting software with the flexibility of immediate retargeting, requiring computer technology heretofore unachieved.

- There must be a navigation system for pinpointing the submarine's precise position in the oceans with an accuracy heretofore unachieved.

- There must be a description of the shape of the earth and its gravity field with an accuracy heretofore unachieved.

- There must be officers and crew trained to operate the most sophisticated weapons system ever deployed in a disciplined manner heretofore unachieved.

- There must be a system of psychological and physiological life support to sustain the crew for two or more months without access to external supplies, in a system heretofore unachieved.

- There must be tenders, supply bases, training facilities, housing, and support for families in a manner heretofore unachieved.

• There must be a secure method of communication that can transmit a message to fire the missiles that has a false alarm rate of less than one in one thousand years, one in ten thousand years, or one in one hundred thousand years [the actual figure is classified], a rate heretofore unachieved and, moreover, a communications method that is responsive only to the nation's legally authorized executive, i.e., the President of the United States.

Ladies and gentlemen, this concludes our introductory briefing. For the next two days each subsystem manager or his representative or a public information officer will make a detailed presentation.

Such was the program communicated to PAHGLORAD at its initial briefing. But SP's task was not PAHGLORAD's task. PAHGLO-RAD's task was to develop the new technologies that would once again change the stance of national deterrence from vulnerable land-based systems to include invulnerable submarine systems. Following the path of technological imperative, however, would not be enough. PAHGLORAD had to conceive of ways in which new technology, beyond enhancing deterrence, could ensure that the nation would maintain a deterrent posture in the face of unforeseen international catastrophes (presidential assassination, Soviet power struggles, terrorist attacks, and so on), which, because they were unforeseen, would probably occur, and of course, did.

After the first day of briefings, there was a restless night for all the members of the group. The magnitude of the task that faced the Special Projects Office was awesome. How could any unit of forty officers and forty civilians conceive of, much less manage, such a complex and incredible system as the Polaris Fleet Ballistic Missile System? How could a nation that had won a war through the force of arms expect to control the future of arms through the threat of mass destruction? How could any organization in a world that had not developed the digital computer or the network of contemporary communications organize and coordinate the efforts of the more than 200,000 people who would be involved on a full-time basis in the development of this system? How could any one organization manage the research and development task of achieving all the technical miracles that needed to be achieved in the short space of nine years (much less the later space of four)? Unless the Special Projects Office was able to make Polaris a reality, there was a very real chance that we would end up fighting a nuclear war rather than preventing one.

The next day our team of senior laboratory managers returned convinced that the system being described and its proposed implementation strategy could not be achieved. But we were equally convinced that if such a system were implemented it would have to be maintained and eventually replaced, since eternal vigilance was now required if the world were to be forever free from the horrors of nuclear war. Because of the four years of World War II terror we had all endured, we were all willing to dedicate ourselves to be a partner with SP in the long-term achievement of the new and necessary balance of terror. We were now members of the expanding team. We had identified our leaders and had been identified by them and we were prepared to follow and to lead.

To my surprise and sooner than I could have expected I became a member of the Special Projects Office team. Whenever I participated in the presentation of similar briefings to new cabinet secretaries and undersecretaries, new presidents and vice presidents, and other newly elected or appointed officials, I would watch for the same psychophysiological encounter with terror at a point in the briefing that I called "the overwhelming moment." Poker players will have observed such a moment in the glaze that forms on the eyes of the neophyte when he realizes that he is out of his depth and that

he has already staked more than he can afford or its emotional equivalent on the outcome of the game. In these briefings, the overwhelming moment would invariably be followed by either a blind
surrender to the exigencies of the program or by a bracing of the
shoulders as the members of PAHGLORAD had braced their shoulders in realization of the authority, responsibility, and accountability
that participation entailed. Only one official, Defense Secretary
Robert McNamara, would not respond this way. Initially, I believed
this to be the result of a superhuman level of understanding and self-
confidence. Sadly, I would discover that this only reflected his unshakable belief in a dogma of management practice that substituted
bean-counting formulas for knowledge and understanding.

When the PAHGLORAD briefing was over there was no time to
wax poetic over our new understanding or to savor having made the
team, much less to generate an accurate record for history. Special
Projects and PAHGLORAD were moving. The Soviets were, too.
And they were moving faster.

4

An Oracle in Washington

The name of the game was now changed. It was deterrence at all costs as soon as it could be established. The Special Projects nine-year program was canceled in its entirety, the entire Special Projects Office was reorganized. A new management system was invented on the spot that included the now famous PERT program (progress evaluation and reporting technique). Its origin came from a directive from Admiral Raborn that a new management program was to be established to give the contractors the illusion that they were being managed and that the name of the program was to be PERT in honor of his new bride, whose nickname was Pert. After Sputnik, a decision was made that there was no time to be spent in salvaging any of the research and development associated with the nine-year Fleet Ballistic Missile program and that efficiency and effectiveness required that the Special Projects Office start the new four-year program from scratch. There was immediate unhappiness on the part of those laboratories and companies that were involved in the research and development associated with the nine-year program, so opportunities had to be made for them to reconnect with some other long-range strategic program. This was a major factor in establishing the Advanced Sea-Based Deterrent program under the Office of the Chief

Scientist but managed by the PAHGLORAD group, none of whose members were employed by Special Projects or were, except for a single briefing, privy to the work or activities of the Special Projects Office.

As a member of PAHGLORAD I was a part of the research and development team that was excluded from any participation with the Special Projects Office. But as the model basin coordinator for projects assigned to the laboratory by any of the many Special Projects subsystem managers, I had an intimate look at a small part of the program and could feel the pressure, pulse, and intensity of this unique project office.

This divorce between ongoing programs and long-range planning freed PAHGLORAD to make its own choices about the research and development to be conducted independently of the Special Projects Office and, more significantly, independently of the Office of Naval Research and the material bureaus. Each laboratory chose its own long-range mission. The Woods Hole Oceanographic Institution began a program for rapid precision mapping of the seafloor. This program would be carried out by the *NR-1*, a small nuclear-powered submarine about which I will say more later. The David Taylor Model Basin began a program of testing deep submergence materials—reinforced concrete, aluminum, titanium, fiberglass, ceramics, and even glass. Other laboratories, such as the Naval Ordnance Laboratory at White Oak, Maryland, the Naval Research Laboratory at the confluence of the Anacostia and Potomac rivers, and the Naval Ordnance Test Station at San Diego, California, also participated in the development of glass for submarine hulls. The Applied Physics Laboratory of Johns Hopkins University studied air-breathing rockets as precursors to the cruise missile. The Naval Ordnance Test Station at Inyokern, California, through Project Michelson, coordinated the political scientists of the nation in a study of the strategy of deterrence. All these projects came together in a summer study of the Advanced Sea-Based Deterrent project at the Naval Postgraduate School in Monterey, California, in 1964. But before that study could take place the PAHGLORAD research was ripped untimely from each laboratory to cope with a major and wholly unanticipated crisis that posed a grave threat to the future of our submarine fleet: the loss of the Navy's most advanced new submarine, the *Thresher*.

Meanwhile, in the summer of 1959 in the Special Projects Office a new role was to be added to the Office of the Chief Scientist. The primary and in fact sole focus of the rest of Special Projects was the development and acquisition of a strategic deterrent system consisting of four Polaris submarines in four years and the ultimate acquisition of a total of forty-one such subs. Four new shipyards were pressed into meeting a production schedule that ended with the Boat of the Month Club, one new submarine to be launched every month for a period of eighteen months.

To carry out this daunting task, Levering Smith, now fully in charge as Special Projects technical director, established a Steering Task Group to advise him on a continuing basis of the project's progress and problems. The group consisted of a team of industrialists, scientists, and technologists who were actively involved in the day-to-day development of the Polaris FBM System. This included the president or senior vice president of such companies and institutions as Lockheed, Westinghouse, North American Aviation, Aerojet, Sperry, General Electric, MIT, Livermore Laboratory, and others that had a major production responsibility. Smith would normally heed the Steering Task Group's advice but his was a position of absolute authority, the commanding officer of the technology fleet.

The task group's most powerful committee was to be the Systems Appraisal Committee (SAC). This committee was chaired by the Chief Scientist, who reported independently and directly to Admiral Raborn. Although the membership of the committee was fluid depending on the system function it was reviewing, at Levering Smith's insistence, no member or ad hoc member of the Systems Appraisal Committee could be a member of Smith's staff or have a line responsibility for any of the programs that had milestones and drop-dead performance dates. The Chief Scientist, in his role as chairman of SAC, was required to make his own appraisals of the system or components of the system and the development process. The Chief Scientist could, in general, call upon the appropriate naval laboratory to provide him with staff for each system study and he could undertake specific studies at the request of Admiral Smith, but the advice of the Chief Scientist on any system or subsystem had to be completely independent. The Systems Appraisal Committee would make a report at each meeting of the Steering Task Group focusing on the major changes of the program as a whole or on specific components, but the reports and recommendations were wholly advisory. In the language of anthropologists, the Chief Scientist was the system's chief priest; in the language of mythology, he was the oracle at Delphi; or in the parlance of poker players, he was the chief kibitzer.

Once the Special Projects system design and management philosophy was defined, the task of the Chief Scientist became much more technical, and Whitmore wished to move on. The qualifications for the new man (and, since we were still living in prefeminist, caveman culture times, man it would be) required the talents of a naval scientist with a feel for all of the technologies involved in the system. This was a tall order. The Polaris FBM system had already been divided into subsystem branches working day and night on their discrete specialties. The duties of the Chief Scientist also included identifying technical problems that had not been anticipated, evaluating proposed solutions to such problems, and acting as the program's wise man. The only pool of potential candidates appeared to be the members of PAHGLORAD. They had unique and intimate knowledge of the Polaris system, years of experience as directors of laboratories involved in the development of naval hardware, and membership in the club of laboratory directors. There was only one junior member in the group, and that was me. At this point I was a lowly GS-12 technologist, and I did not know anyone in the Special Projects Office except Whitmore and a few members of the launching and handling branch—though I had forged some strong bonds with those operating our subs.

Every member of PAHGLORAD more senior than I was offered the job of Chief Scientist for Special Projects, and every one of them turned it down. All of them were in their late fifties or early sixties. They knew that the position of Chief Scientist would be a high-pressure, physically and intellectually demanding position. It would also be interdisciplinary, and all of them had achieved their senior civil service position by focusing on the technologies of their laboratory. There was only one PAHGLORAD member left at the bottom of the list, so Whitmore phoned me and asked if I would be interested. I could not suppress a wry smile. This was obviously a good-natured joke, an expression of frustration with the turndowns from the others. If it were serious it would be a once-in-a-lifetime opportunity for me, but I was certain that Whitmore had made a mistake. I was six notches below his rank in the civil service and the way the system worked, you went up, if you went up at all, one notch at a time.

"Bill," I said, "you're a GS-18 and I'm a GS-12."

Whitmore gulped. "Gosh, Craven," he said. "I thought you were much older and much more senior." He hung up.

I flung the telephone against the wall but when our little exchange sank in, my mind began to race.

Good God! I thought. What does it mean to be the Chief Scientist of the Special Projects Office? What is its mission? To deter nuclear war, Craven. To prevent the destruction of civilization in the face of all conceivable scenarios. What must an organization know to carry out this mission? Doesn't need to know a thing, Craven, just to take direction from its superiors. Who, the President? The Secretary of Defense? The Chief of Naval Operations? Good God, I know them all and they are completely unqualified to make technical decisions to produce a workable deterrent. Certainly they are less qualified than Red Raborn and his team. Then we're back where we started from, right, Craven? So, if one could be a member of such a team and make some small positive contribution, that would be an opportunity that few individuals would ever come by. But Chief Scientist—what does it really mean? These Special Projects guys are only going to come to the Chief Scientist when they're in trouble. Good God, they're going to be in trouble every day. If they're not smart enough to solve the problems in the field of their competence, how can anyone else help them? Ergo, no one is qualified to be Chief Scientist. Which makes me as unqualified as anyone else. I can be as good a Chief Scientist as the next guy. But the Chief Scientist must have unassailable integrity, must be internally secure, unflappable, must be completely aware of the global significance of decisions that he will influence. And he must know that if things start to go wrong, he is allowed to have regrets but not paralyzing guilt. He must keep on. Did I, I wondered, have the right stuff?

In the midst of my agonizing, the phone rang again.

"This is Admiral Raborn. Why won't you be my Chief Scientist?"

I began to explain that a GS-12 cannot become a GS-18 overnight.

The admiral interrupted. "Are you trying to tell me what I can do and what I can't do?"

"No, sir."

"Well, then, are you going to be my Chief Scientist?"

"Yes, sir."

"Very well. Report in the morning."

I did. On a date that I cannot recall in 1959, I walked into my new office, which contained a mahogany desk and a flagpole. I met my new secretary but didn't have time to meet the rest of my new staff because I was suddenly besieged by senior officers and technologists of the SPO's navigation branch and given a lesson in what it meant to be Chief Scientist.

They needed my advice on the purchase of a maser amplifier for the radiometric sextant.

A what for a which? I don't know how much they detected of my ignorance, but one of them jumped in with an explanation.

"You know, the maser magnetic amplification through stimulated electromagnetic radiation and the radiometric sextant that tracks stars by day from their radiometric signal."

"Of course. And when do you need this advice."

"Tomorrow at 1300."

They left and I reached for the phone. I called the resident guru at the Office of Naval Research. The maser, I learned fast enough, had recently been invented but all my informant knew was that a young professor named Charles Townes was the expert on this device (he would later win a Nobel Prize for the invention of the laser). Townes, reached at his laboratory, was more than kind, walking me like a schoolboy through the basics of how electrons can be amplified, until we got to something more complicated involving signal-to-noise ratio. The next day, receiving the navigators at 1300, I pontificated: "I have been thinking all night about this problem." I then rattled off the signal-to-noise ratio and concluded, "Yes, this is something that will work. We should get it right away."

I was now, at the age of thirty-four, a Chief Scientist and a member of the tribe—one comprised of men like Raborn and Levering Smith as well as other intrepid mariners of their school such as Lawson "Red" Ramage and Eugene "Lucky" Fluckey, both Congressional Medal of Honor submariners. Both had earned their awards in heroic encounters with Japanese warships. But what I and other submariners to this day treasure most about Lucky Fluckey is our inscribed copies of the *Submariner's Song Book*, which he compiled and published and which became the submariner's cherished morale booster of World War II. There was Hank McKinney, damage control officer on the carrier *Ben Franklin*, which survived damage from a sustained Japanese attack so severe that she should not have been able to remain afloat. Another early member of our tribe was Gus Eble, whose repair of a battle-damaged radar permitted them to rescue the crew of the USS *Harder* when it had run aground. One man whom I already knew was Robert Herrol, my division officer on the *New Mexico*. After I was detached from that ship, my relief was on the bridge when it was hit by a kamikaze, killing the captain and incapacitating everyone else on the bridge. Through Lieutenant Commander Herrol's brave and immediate action, the *New Mexico* lost not a moment as a fighting ship. Among the civilians was Charles Stark "Doc" Draper, who was to play a decisive role in my life. He had developed the "shoe box" gun sight that turned the antiaircraft war around in the bleak early days in the Pacific. These men had the fighting spirit, tempered by the effect of their wartime experiences. All were dedicated to deterring nuclear war.

The Navy heroes of World War II were my heroes and now, as one among them, I would count myself the most fortunate of all. Their motivations and aspirations were the same as mine. I was confident that our goals would be achieved and peace preserved. But I could not know that all my colleagues, all my prior experience, and all that I knew had not prepared me for the life I was yet to lead. I had been conditioned to believe that there is nothing more dangerous than the arrogance of ignorance; now I would learn that it does not compare with arrogance of knowledge, knowledge that often is confused with wisdom.

But at this period of my life I looked forward to orientation and . clarification of my role in this fast-moving program, only to discover quickly that finding my way would be left exclusively to me.

As soon as I was named Chief Scientist I was simultaneously

chairman of the Systems Appraisal Committee. I was required to make a report at every meeting of the Steering Task Group. The task group, composed of the most senior, technically qualified executives of every major corporation and institution having a significant role in the Polaris FBM program, would serve as a jury. When it met, each naval officer in charge of one of the Polaris subsystems would brief the task group on the progress and problems of his particular responsibility. The group would then cross-examine the officer in a process called the "murder board"—if the officer didn't pass muster, he was soon out of a job. For Steering Task Group chairman Levering Smith, the group's deliberations served as his best guide to whether or not the total project was on course.

The task group met at least once a month or whenever a critical decision was on the immediate horizon. I realized that I would have to make a systems appraisal to them, which, if deficient, could lead to my untimely demise before the murder board. I contacted subsystem managers, who invited me to participate in one of their on-site program reviews. As a result, in my second week on the job I was scheduled, in my role as chairman of the Systems Appraisal Committee, to be in a different city every day: in Sunnyvale, California, visiting Lockheed on missile problems; in Baltimore at the Applied Physics Laboratory, discussing navigation problems; in Los Angeles at North American Aviation on gyro problems; and finally back to Washington, D.C., for the mandatory Saturday morning SPO staff meeting. This appeared manifestly impossible and I went to Admiral Raborn to find out which meetings had the highest priority.

Raborn smiled his biggest smile. "You're going to find out what I tell the whole staff: 'I want to see you going and I want to see you coming and I don't want to see you staying.' Decisions on millions of dollars of taxpayer money are going to be made during each of those visits."

Fine, I thought, but which should I go to? He must have read my mind.

"All of them, Craven, all of them."

So in my second week on the job I was crisscrossing America by air and, on the ground, wrestling with problems associated with Polaris thrusters and whether to go with high-strength steel or fiberglass for missile motor cases. The task group would hold its monthly session the next week.

Preparing for that meeting, I noted that clearly the most significant item on the agenda was a report by a commander assigned to the Office of the Director of Defense Research and Engineering (DDR&E). That office had prepared a two-hundred-page document that had implications for the future of the Polaris system. The document itself was distributed just a few hours before the meeting. I dove in. It was for a moment such as this that I had had a lifetime of training. I scanned the two hundred pages, committing to memory the gist of the key statements and their location in the document.

When the group convened, the DDR&E commander gave his report, making the fatal error of orally presenting only the parts that he apparently believed Chairman Levering Smith would like to hear and omitting the bad news that Smith ought to hear. When the commander completed his presentation, I raised my hand, addressing Smith, whom I had just met for the first time. "Captain," I said, "I believe the commander has missed a few points in the document and in particular a paragraph on page fifty-seven."

Smith turned to the page and silently read. After a few agonizing minutes, he began to read aloud, his finger tracing every word. The hapless commander turned scarlet as the skewed information of his report was exposed word for word in a murder board executioner's song. When Smith finished, he looked up at us all. "Gentlemen," he said, "I think we have a Chief Scientist."

5
Out of the Deep
to Target, Perfect

Whatever I lost in popularity with the commander was a net gain among my peers, who now knew that I would not shrink from pointing out where things were going wrong. It is in crisis moments that the men get separated from the boys, and every leader had better have a good idea which is which and who is who in the heat of battle. For now, my ego knew no bounds—until my first fall, which was not long in coming.

During that first month in 1959 after my appointment, Raborn asked me to make a speech about Polaris out in Minnesota.

Shortly after I gave the speech and returned, I was skewered in a *Washington Post* editorial for claiming, according to the writer of the editorial, that Polaris was close to being ready when in fact it was still years away. According to the paper, for me to say otherwise was the height of irresponsibility.

I slunk into work expecting it to be my last day and of course the admiral wanted to see me immediately. Still slinking, I entered his office and he greeted me with one of his widest grins and a hand ready for a firm shake. "Welcome to the club," he said.

He then explained that the editorial was almost certainly written even before the speech was given. It was part of a campaign in support of the Air Force's program to develop the B-1 bomber. The theme was to impress Congress that America's missiles would not be ready for some time and that there was thus a "bomber gap." Raborn showed me the articles that had already been written to that end by the *Post*, all timed for ongoing congressional hearings.

The Special Projects Office's existence depended upon public perception as well as Soviet perception that our system was solely a deterrent and it would have failed if any missile were ever launched in anger. We had vigorous resistance from those in our own society who wanted nuclear war. They regarded deterrence as costly and irrelevant and too complex to ever work.

But as I occupied my new post in the summer of 1959 our number one crisis concerned the full-scale Polaris test program. The first seven missile trials were launched from surface test pads at Cape Canaveral. All had failed and had been witnessed by the press. Each report coming into the SPO's communication center was received with downcast eyes except for those of Levering Smith. He even seemed cheery, and I asked him why he was not discouraged.

"Why do you think we are conducting a test program?" he said. "It is to find the problems now before they appear in the field." That was objectively true but the naysayers of the sea-based deterrent seized on each failure as a demonstration that the program was in trouble and success was far away. One columnist, the widely read Drew Pearson, was particularly scathing.

The day finally came when an underwater test was scheduled from the submarine *George Washington*. I cannot, even today, view the film of that first launch in the summer of 1960 without skipping a heartbeat. The missile emerges from the water at an atrocious angle in pitch and roll. It appears doomed for failure, but miraculously rights itself and streaks off to its target downrange. Then with the courage born of experience in battle, Levering Smith orders a second missile fired. It inspires Admiral Raborn's message to the Chief of Naval Operations: "Out of the deep to target, perfect."

But once again, the media machine was unimpressed. The next day's Drew Pearson column began with the statement that the Navy was finally able to launch a missile from a submarine. The rest of his column, which by Pearson's own subsequent admission had been written prior to the test, recited the failures and recorded his expectation of more to come. He was not completely wrong in this regard.

The Joint Chiefs of Staff were less pessimistic, however. Along with their staff, they were on board the submarine for the next test. Four missiles were fired. None left the water. All fell back and bounced off the hull with a resounding smack. It was most difficult for these military men, particularly those of the land and air services, to maintain their normal sangfroid in the claustrophobic atmosphere of a submarine being hit by missiles loaded with high-energy fuel. To describe it in the indelicate but graphic language of the service, only the laundryman would know the extent of their fear.

The only discomfort felt by the SPO's technology experts on board was embarrassment. Otherwise, they were quite comfortable knowing that the unignited solid propellant bouncing off the hull was as harmless as a rubber ball. Indeed, SPO senior personnel had office ashtrays made from the missile propellant—a lot safer than the cigarettes that were snuffed out in them.

When the press witnessed another four failures the previous two successes were witnessed and the crisis moved to the front burner. The "crazy" test facility that I had built at the model basin now proved its worth. It showed that a diaphragm at the top of the launch tube, which served to keep the missile dry prior to launch, would not always rupture symmetrically. As the missile would rise a bubble of compressed air was formed in the space above the missile in its tube. The diaphragm was designed to rupture when pierced by the nose of the missile. An asymmetrical rupture, however, would cause the compressed air bubble to push the missile to one side of the tube or the other. As a result, the missile would tilt unacceptably, thus aborting the flight.

The diaphragms were then fitted with an X-shaped explosive ribbon and the explosive ribbon was activated on launch to rupture the diaphragm symmetrically. The problem finally solved, it was decided to test the solution out of the media's sight. As fate would have it, those unpublicized tests batted 1,000, going six for six in perfect launches.

Alas, fearful of another public relations disaster, we had failed to do range tracking of the firings, so we lacked vital data on trajectory time and impact. Fortunately the sounds of launch and splashdown had been recorded. A ship capable of very precise positioning was therefore deployed in the vicinity of the launch sound. Acoustic charges were dropped and the location of the original launch was determined by the differences in arrival time of the sound at the listening stations. The same was done for the splashdowns. Working out a way to make up for missing tracking data by using sound to make a very accurate estimation of missile flight time and impact point accuracy, we had developed a technique that I would later employ successfully in the searches for the positions of lost submarines—both Soviet and American.

In spite of the development problems and the skeptics, the system was officially operational on November 15, 1960, when the USS George Washington departed on the first FBM operational patrol, with sixteen Polaris A-1 missiles aboard. The George Washington and her sister ship, the USS Patrick Henry, had been ordered back in 1957 when the Polaris program had been cut from nine to four years. But here we were, mission accomplished only three years and two months later. It was not a moment too soon.

This triumph was followed by events that fully established Polaris FBM as the world's most credible deterrent system. Because of the deleterious environmental effects of radioactive fallout from nuclear testing, the nuclear powers agreed to a treaty banning tests in the atmosphere. The treaty would be signed in the summer of 1963, but a year earlier, in the last atmospheric tests to be conducted by any of the world's nuclear powers, the only missile ever launched with a live nuclear warhead was fired from the USS *Ethan Allen*, submerged in the Pacific Ocean and under the command of Captain (later Admiral) Paul Lacy.

The May 6, 1962, test was monitored from the surface ship *Compass Island*, on which the Polaris system's navigational equipment had been developed. Admiral Levering Smith was in command of the operation. He had the difficult task of determining whether the missile was off course and should be destroyed in flight. On the day of the test, all preparations had been going smoothly and the missile rose out of the sea and took flight successfully, but soon appeared to veer off track. The range safety officer called for termination, but the admiral stayed his hand. The missile then seemed to veer off again, then back on course and then to veer in the opposite direction. Smith let out an unrestrained "Aha!"

The irregular motion of the missile was in phase with the roll of the ship. It was the failure to adequately compensate for this roll that had created the appearance that the missile was wandering. It was not. From out of the deep to target, perfect. The bomb exploded over the South Pacific, more than a thousand miles downrange, "right in the pickle barrel" in the phrase of the day. The last and perhaps most portentous mushroom cloud showed the world, not a moment too soon, that Polaris was not a poker player's bluff.

Some months later, in October of 1962, the strategy of deterrence was tested unambiguously. Soviet ships loaded with nuclear-tipped missiles were proceeding to deployment in Cuba. President John F. Kennedy, having declared a quarantine on the delivery of these weapons, raised the threat of retaliation through the airborne alert of the Strategic Air Command and the full deployment of all operational Polaris FBM missile submarines. There were more than eight submarines each with sixteen missiles at the ready—one hundred twenty-eight in all—aimed at the Soviet Union. The world stood still in a week of excruciating tension as America prepared for nuclear war. Finally, Soviet Premier Nikita Khrushchev, faced with the ultimate dilemma, retreated. In the wake of the crisis, Khrushchev went before the Supreme Soviet and said, "Whose side has triumphed? Who has won? It can be said that reason has won."

Deterrence had won, too, won big, but not all cold warriors rejoiced.

6

War and Peace: Some Like It Hot

In the fall of 1960, when the *George Washington* had been successfully deployed, Admiral Raborn requested and received permission to distribute the largest package of civilian and military awards ever conferred on a Navy program. The task of writing each award's rationale was given to many members of the team, and I was assigned what I thought were the two hardest jobs of the lot. One was justifying a Distinguished Committee Performance Award to an obscure and unfriendly Polaris advisory committee and the other a Distinguished Civilian Service Award to Edward Teller.

I did not recall the committee in question, but I soon learned from my colleagues that its members had been vigorous opponents of the Polaris project who had been surprised when Raborn invited them to serve. They had all attended the first meeting, a full briefing about the system. They subsequently issued a single, innocuous report and never met again.

It was the nature of Raborn's leadership style to recognize that these members would, from their perspective, have had legitimate objections to the program, and this award showed his appreciation for their forbearance in opposition. It took some creative writing on my part, but the award was granted. Since then I have had occasion to visit the offices of a number of the recipients and have noted the award proudly displayed.

The literary effort for the Teller award was even more difficult. His only actual relationship to the Polaris warhead was his dramatic challenge at a National Academy of Science meeting. "Why put a 1955 warhead on a 1960 missile," he asked. Beyond that he had no involvement, but his stature as a scientist provided credibility to the Special Projects Office's commitment to design a warhead with a theretofore unachieved yield-to-weight ratio. Teller did not participate in that design effort. Those who knew him well, and there were many in Special Projects who did, knew that he had had no detailed involvement in the design of nuclear weapons since the development of the hydrogen bomb. The key to success for the Polaris warhead was the incorporation of a still classified innovation, and if it was the work of any single individual, that person was Commander Robert Wertheim, who also received a Navy commendation at the time of these awards.

Even after receiving his award, Teller was not a supporter of Polaris. He was a nonbeliever in deterrence. I had had firsthand experience with his fixation on the inevitability of nuclear war with the Soviets ("within five years," he would always say) as the driving force behind his call for bigger and "better" weapons. His conviction permeated the Lawrence Livermore National Laboratory, which he headed. Teller was one of the few who then believed that we needed still more weapons of war. He told me on many occasions that nuclear war was inevitable.

So it was that Livermore, spurred on by its leader, conceived of a weapon called the Low Altitude Nuclear Cruise Missile. This was to be a completely unshielded nuclear reactor, in a missile framework, that would be launched into the atmosphere. The reactor would generate heat to act as a ramjet to keep the missile aloft for days or even weeks. Compressed air at the intake would be heated by the reactor and expelled at the rear, providing the thrust for the weapon to fly at a speed of Mach 3.2.

The missile would have a bomb bay capable of carrying ten or more independently ejectable hydrogen bombs. The concept was that of an ultimatum weapon that would be launched in times of crisis as a Sword of Damocles threat to deliver one or more devastating nuclear blows to a recalcitrant enemy until whatever compliance desired was obtained.

There were, in the eyes of the designers, a couple of problems requiring further consideration. The first was that the missile in flight would leave a trail of from 200 to 300 rads of radiation over a swath of a mile or more. Proceeding at Mach 3.2, or about 1,800 miles per hour, that meant it would contaminate 1,800 square miles of land per hour with a dose of radiation lethal to all living things. Second, at the end of its mission it could not be recalled to a land base but would have to be jettisoned over the ocean, there to spew its rads for fifty thousand years or more.

It is hard to imagine that sane men would propose a weapon having such a horrendous mission profile. But humanity has yet to learn that otherwise rational individuals dedicated to revenge or victory at any cost can be completely blinded by emotion.

In the summer of 1962, under the umbrella of the Atomic Energy Commission, which was permitted to authorize the development of nuclear weapons in advance of approval by the Department of Defense, Livermore had carried out complex, expensive development to the point where it was ready for prototype testing. At this stage, the Pentagon was asked to support its weaponization. No one in the Department of Defense wanted anything to do with this project. Since it would have to be tested over the ocean and the spent missile would have to be dropped into the sea, its evaluation was thrust upon the Navy. The decision was passed on to the Special Projects Office, where it was handed to me.

There was no possibility of dismissing the project as absurd, let alone insane. There were five powerful proponents behind it, Teller's Livermore Laboratory, the Atomic Energy Commission, the Joint House-Senate Committee for AEC Affairs, and two contractors, one for the airframe and one for guidance. Any decision concerning the project's future would be accompanied every step of the way by coordinated phone calls from these five proponents urging positive action.

Nevertheless, I was not overly concerned that this nuclear-powered monster would get built. There was to be a full-scale test of one of these unshielded reactors at Jackass Flats near Las Vegas. The Los Alamos National Laboratory had a competitive program—the Rover spacecraft, which was to operate as a ramjet in its first stage—and it was known to be plagued with technical problems. I was betting that the Livermore missile would experience significant failures during its test. Experience had taught me that first tries of any complex system almost always ended disappointingly. I would then be able to halt this harebrained project on the basis of technical feasibility and development costs.

The test relied on a nuclear reactor fixed to the ground. Miles of piping supplied compressed air to be heated by the reactor to simulate the ram air at altitude. The amount of piping and air was as much as the budget would allow and, as I recall, permitted about four minutes of operation. A huge, lead coffinlike container on railroad tracks was provided to entomb the reactor after it was constructed. There this prototype would remain as a monument from this generation for all those to come for the next 50,000 years.

Since I had been charged by the Department of Defense with the evaluation of the suitability of this missile as a Navy weapon I was invited to witness the test. We watched from a shielded blockhouse. It was a classic moment of excitement in the aerospace community, everyone rooting for a win in the grand old American way. Instruments to measure temperature, stress, thrust, and a host of other pa-

Our competitor for accuracy was Minuteman, which was clearly a first-strike system. Polaris had an accuracy advantage, since its shorter range should permit greater accuracy, all other things being equal. But everyone presumed that ship motions would make the location of the direction of up (i.e., the local vertical) more imprecise on Polaris. I discovered that the limiting factor in accuracy was not ship motions but seismic tremors of the earth. Missiles launched from the land cannot avoid errors due to these small tremors because the earth is constantly shaking. Missiles launched from the sea do not encounter these errors because the ocean is not shaking. Admiral Smith was convinced of the accuracy of the Polaris determined on this basis and he established it as a system goal.

I had the privilege of making the accuracy presentation to the undersecretary of defense for research and development in 1968 and it was clear that Polaris A-3 had the best, most accurate hard target strike capability with its multiple independently targeted reentry vehicles. The Air Force was anguished because its Minuteman could not match the Polaris for accuracy. Those of us who understood the calculus of deterrence knew that if the Russians multiplied the number of warheads times the number of missiles times the number of missile-carrying subs, they would see the system as giving the United States a first strike capability that could take out their command and control facilities as well as their missile sites. The cruise missile could achieve house address accuracy but if not nuclear-armed, would not cause the kind of massive collateral damage that a nuclear warhead would.

The high probability that a sufficient number of cruise missiles would always get through to the target meant that deterrence would be diminished. It might even be defeated should a cruise missile be developed with a nuclear warhead. Alas, in the waning days of the Carter administration our well-intentioned but naive President signed an abrogation of the U.S. no first strike use of nuclear weapons policy in the NATO theater. This was accompanied by a decision to develop two versions of the cruise missile. In making this decision a meeting of the National Academy of Sciences Defense Science Board was convened in San Diego to debate the future of the manned bomber and the future of the cruise missile. The meeting was chaired by Undersecretary of Defense for Research and Development William "Bill" Perry, later Secretary of Defense for President Bill Clinton. Although I was not a member of the Defense Science Board I was invited to participate as an individual knowledgeable in submarine systems. There was little debate about continuing development of the B-1 bomber. It was regarded as moribund with the advent of small fighter-bomber–delivered precise nuclear weapons in 1968. (It would rise subsequently from the dead, transfigured by President Ronald Reagan as the B-1B bomber.)

At the San Diego meeting the debate over developing and deploying a cruise missile with a nuclear warhead was MAD (Mutually Assured Destruction) vs. NUTS (nuclear utilization of tactical systems) all over again. Charles Zraket of MIT and I led the fight against the nuclear cruise missile. We did not want "every policeman in Europe to be armed with a flyaway nuclear weapon," but we lost. When Reagan became President he purged all the identifiable opponents of tactical nuclear systems. Reagan, like Teller, was traveling the road to Armageddon.

I was, by chance, witness to the last chapter of the Reagan-Teller partnership in behalf of SDI (Strategic Defense Initiative, or as it is more popularly known, Star Wars). President Reagan was preparing for his second meeting with Soviet president Mikhail Gorbachev on October 11, 1986, at Reykjavik, Iceland. The sticking point in the arms limitation negotiations was the future of Star Wars. Reagan was determined to develop this space-based laser system for full deployment in ten years. Gorbachev would only agree to per-mitting laboratory development of the system, with a ten-year moratorium on testing in space. Just before Reagan's departure for the summit I was seated in the lobby of the Cosmos Club in Washington, D.C. Members waiting for guests or reading the *New York Times* and the *Washington Post* were frequent visitors to this private reception hall with its Victorian decor and its rule of silence.

There was a telephone in the lobby that was available for club members primarily to receive messages of late or early arrival of their guests. The discussion of business or politics was strictly forbidden by the rules of the club. All of a sudden on this day the tranquility of the lobby was interrupted by the loud and unmistakable voice of Edward Teller talking on the lobby telephone. We all knew in an instant that he was talking to the President. The President must not yield on the deployment of Star Wars within ten years, he insisted. In fact, he must use all his negotiating skill to restrain and contain the Soviets until that time. Teller correctly predicted that a right-wing coup was in the offing that could not be contained by the Kremlin.

In making these rather apocalyptic predictions his voice reached the level of a shout and it was obvious to all in the lobby that by speaking so loudly he was indirectly telling his fellow scientists there that they were wrong in their negative assessment of the Star Wars system. A psychoanalyst might say that he may also have been trying to reassure himself of the rightness and righteousness of his own belief. In any event Reagan did not yield on the Star Wars issue and an agreement on arms limitation was not reached.

Reagan, Teller, and Gorbachev have left the stage and for better or for worse "We thank what Gods that be that no man lives forever, that dead men rise up never, and that even the weariest river runs somewhere out to sea."

7

Fail-Safe

Admiral Raborn, if I were you, I couldn't sleep at night knowing . . .
Admiral Smith, if I were you, I couldn't sleep at night knowing . . .
Dr. Craven, if I were you, I couldn't sleep at night knowing . . .
Captain W., if I were you, I couldn't sleep at night knowing . . .

The paradox of using nuclear weaponry as a deterrent is that no system failure of any kind can be tolerated because unintended nuclear war may result; yet, if deterrence fails, the United States must have the means to retaliate. This capability must be an absolutely reliable and unstoppable means of measured nuclear retaliation as well as a deterrent to further attack. Those who were responsible for developing and deploying such a system had to make it fail-safe. Who was responsible? The Special Projects Office? The Chief of Naval Operations? The Secretary of the Navy? The Joint Chiefs of Staff? The Secretary of Defense? All were responsible, but ultimately the reliability of the system depended on the one man who had his finger on the button—the commander-in-chief of the armed forces, the President of the United States.

On November 22, 1963, President Kennedy was assassinated in Dallas. The Steering Task Group of the Polaris program was meeting in Washington, D.C. At about three o'clock in the afternoon I was beginning to present my Systems Appraisal Committee report when a messenger interrupted the meeting and passed a note to Admiral Levering Smith. Smith informed us that the President had been shot in Dallas and was not expected to live. I suggested to Admiral Smith that we have a recess to recover from the shock. His response was brief and curt.

"No, you should continue your report."

Fresh in our minds was Kennedy's viewing of a Polaris firing six days earlier on November 16. On November 19 he wrote in a letter to Admiral Galantin, then director of Special Projects:

> The Polaris firing I witnessed from the USS *Observation Island* on 16 November was a most satisfying and fascinating experience. It is still incredible to me that a missile can be successfully and accurately fired from beneath the sea. Once one has seen a Polaris firing the efficacy of this weapon system as a deterrent is not debatable.

On November 22, the President was scheduled to deliver a speech at the Trade Mart in Dallas. In the remarks we had prepared for him he was to have said:

> In less than three years we have increased by 50 percent the number of Polaris submarines scheduled to be in force by the next fiscal year, increased by more than 70 percent our total Polaris purchase program . . .

All this was racing through my mind as I attempted to continue with my report. At about 3:30 P.M. the messenger returned and Admiral Smith announced that the President had died. Once again I suggested a recess. The admiral was even firmer in his response.

"It is much more important now that you continue with your report and that we prepare the program to meet all of the exigencies that will flow from this tragic event."

I should have said, "We must brief Lyndon Johnson immediately," but my mind was numb. The only appropriate thing, it seemed to me, was to ad-lib a reminiscence.

John F. Kennedy was one of us, a World War II veteran who performed under fire and had experienced the horrors and tragedy of war. His older brother, a fighter pilot, was killed in combat. He was a PT boat skipper. He was already a legend as an intrepid PT boat commander who closed with the enemy in spite of certain destruction. The training base at Newport, Rhode Island, was also the training base for PT boats and they could be observed every day whipping up the water with high-powered, high-speed maneuvers. We would observe them most every day. Inspired by the observation and legend, I, as a seaman in 1943, attending the Navy's school for quartermasters [navigators] and signalmen, had volunteered for PT boat service. I was virtually assured of the assignment until my misconduct put me in the hospital from where I was summarily sent to sea.

After the war I met my hero in the club car of the night train from Washington to Boston via New London. He was then Senator Kennedy and he agreed to be a fourth at bridge. It took a few hands before all four players knew that they were dealing with tournament champions or most probably card sharks. There was one hand that I will never forget. I was dealt six spades queen jack high with lots of honor count in the other suits. I opened with one spade. My partner's response led us to a small slam. When my partner laid down his hand he had four spades to the ace but not the king. There were three spades out against us. Kennedy, on my left, led with a small spade. Could

This particular problem was eliminated by mandating the use of nonflammable silicone oils in pressurized machinery. But how can project managers at the top of the management pyramid avoid design defects? Subordinates and nature itself are perverse, and disaster eludes even the most careful preparations.

When Special Projects was first established it was mandated to produce a version of the liquid-fueled Jupiter missile. But missile experts like Levering Smith refused to carry out the assignment because they knew it was a recipe for catastrophe. Instead they proposed a more stable solid propellant. But even that was not enough.

As the new Chief Scientist of Polaris I had absolutely no knowledge of missile and ordnance chemistry. So I was referred to Dr. Dwight Gunder, the oldest and most experienced rocket scientist on the Special Projects team.

He said: "Craven, there are old ordnance scientists and there are bold ordnance scientists, but there are no . . ."

I interrupted him, "Yes, I know, I know."

"Craven, you always think you know what someone is going to say. You don't know because I was going to tell you that you will never meet a young bold scientist—for in this business your first mistake is your last."

"Wow, as young bold Chief Scientist, that means I can't make one misstep when it comes to rocket fuels or ordnance."

"That's right, Sonny Boy," he said and then he told me his secret for avoidance of mistakes.

"It's all very simple," he said. "There are chemical elements that are called oxidizers. These include oxygen, fluorine, and chlorine. When they come into physical contact with a fuel like hydrogen and carbon or with metals like lithium, aluminum, sodium, they burn. The only thing that stops them is that they are kept apart by an element called nitrogen, which is hard to burn. If you look at chemical formulas you will see lots of molecules that have lots of nitrogen in structures that look like chicken wire. The more "chicken wire" there is, the less likely the probability that they will release their oxidizer or fuel. There are solid propellants called double-based propellants in which the oxidizer and the fuel are part of the same molecule. There are a lot of salesmen who will tell you that their double-based propellant will not accidentally detonate. But when for any reason their propellant deteriorates, it ends up as nitroglycerin ($C_3H_5N_3O_9$). Any schoolboy will tell you that nitro will detonate if it is shaken. Just look at that molecule, seventeen atoms of oxidizer and fuel held apart by just three atoms of nitrogen."

"Surely," I said, "no one on the Special Projects team is proposing double base for our submarines."

"Check it out, Sonny Boy, there are a number of projects going on in your Navy and industry laboratories at this very moment which are trying to do just that."

I asked Gunder if Special Projects was sponsoring any of what he called hot propellants. He said yes. Fortunately they all burned up in the laboratory. (The lithium hydride fire was spectacular and thankfully no lives were lost.) A few weeks after my Dwight Gunder tutorial a salesman came to see me proposing chlorine trifluoride (CLF_3) as an oxidizer. "Where is your nitric chicken wire?" I asked. There was none, and he didn't understand as I ushered him out the door.

But knowledge and vigilance were never good enough. Sneak hazards would inevitably appear. A near fatal explosion took place on a Polaris submarine when the housing on a specialized instrument, the radiometric sextant, manufactured by a corporation with no submarine experience, dieselized as a result of the hydrocarbon oil used for lubrication.

NASA experienced far more tragic results with oxygen-rich mixtures when three astronauts died in a fire in Apollo 1. Three divers were lost in an oxygen-rich decompression chamber at the U.S. Navy experimental diving unit in Washington, D.C. Normally, air at atmospheric pressure is safe. But oxygen-rich mixtures at atmospheric pressure or air that is compressed and therefore oxygen-rich can be hazardous.

There was a joint workshop between NASA and the SeaLab people to examine this potential for disaster. George Bond, who attended the workshop, was concerned over the oxygen-rich mixtures in the command module of the Apollo spacecraft while it was sitting atop the booster on the launch pad. In the case of the rest of the Apollo components, the interior pressure in them would be low throughout the flight. Thus, to provide enough oxygen for life support, the air in the command module would have to be oxygen-rich. To simplify the mechanical system, it was decided that it would be no health hazard if the astronauts were exposed to this oxygen-rich mix at atmospheric pressure for the short period of time associated with launch. This was the fatal mistake and they were consumed by fire during a test on the launch pad. Subsequent launches adjusted the oxygen levels in accordance with cabin pressure.

The tragedy at the diving school occurred for a very different reason. Decompression dives on air face the danger associated with oxygen-rich mixtures under pressure. Thus scrupulous attention was given to create a spark-free atmosphere and a fuel-free vapor environment. Alas, the air filters that were provided to ensure this pure atmosphere had been drawn from standard Navy stock. Unbeknownst to the divers, these filters were also used in jet aircraft. In a maintenance procedure, every so often a filter would be removed from the stock and tested with aviation fuel. If functional, it would then be put back into the inventory. One of the filters chosen to eliminate explosive vapors was, in fact, filled with aviation gasoline. The resulting mixture exploded due to a form of dieselization.

After that, spare parts for the Special Projects Office were no longer obtained from the Navy supply system, but from a system designed to serve only the needs of the Fleet Ballistic Missile system.

These lessons we had learned and were still learning were those of a team that was first taught in the unforgiving environment of total war. Other major national system projects were ably manned but not so blessed with hard and painful experience. On January 28, 1986, NASA's *Challenger* spacecraft was on the pad preparing for launch. This was to be a zenith event in America's conquest of space. Seven astronauts were aboard, including Christa McAuliffe, who was to be the first schoolteacher in space. The launching had been delayed for several days for various reasons. The only conceivable factor for further delay on this day would be the air temperature, which was below the temperature that had been established as the required minimum. Few, if any, were aware of the implications of attempting launch at less than this apparently moderate temperature. The pressure from the White House and the media to proceed was intense. Schoolchildren all over the United States were riveted to their television sets to witness the event that would loft Ms. McAuliffe into space as a surrogate for their own beloved classroom teacher.

What difference could a few degrees Fahrenheit make in the safety of the launch? Certainly the President could not know. The range manager could not know why this temperature was chosen for this particular rocket. Our post–World War II society has been conditioned to believe that top executives need not have technical expertise. As the world now knows, the launch was followed by the most watched, horrifying, traumatic failure in history with the loss of all of the *Challenger's* astronauts. Somewhere far away from the launchpad, far away from command and control, a few engineers had the sickening feeling in the pit of their stomachs that told them what had happened. It was the nightmare of NDT.

NDT—nil ductility temperature—is the temperature below which a material, when under stress, becomes brittle and behaves like ice or glass. The O-rings in the *Challenger* rocket nozzles had an NDT of about 40°F. Just one or more degrees below this value, they became brittle and failed to seal the joints between two of the lower segments of a solid rocket motor.

The Polaris program had experienced a similar problem with the liner of its solid propellant motors. These liners became brittle and pulled away from the missile case when exposed to low temperatures. The initial separation of the liners seemed small and unlikely to increase, but Levering Smith acted immediately on a new design to be implemented in the event that the problem became serious. It did, and the new design was ready.

The Navy had learned the bitter lesson of NDT as far back as World War II. The attrition in our merchant fleet by German submarine attacks at the outset of the war required the rapid construction of hundreds of Liberty ships for the transport of cargo. Sadly, much of the steel employed for the hull and structure of these ships had an NDT that made the decks brittle when exposed to the extreme winter conditions in the North Atlantic and Arctic Ocean. The temperature of the water never went below 32 degrees Fahrenheit but the air temperature could be as low as minus 50. The disasters were horrible. The ships, without warning, would break in two like a matchstick. The bow and sterns sections would sink too quickly for the launching of lifeboats or alerting of the crew. Worse yet, there was little time for the radio operator to communicate the tragedy to other ships at sea. Some of these Liberty ships just disappeared and were never found. Thus the principle of NDT was well known to mariners.

Probably the worst NDT experience I ever had concerned our Polaris subs. A special steel was developed for the hulls of the Polaris submarines, called HY80 for its eighty-thousand-pounds-per-square-inch yield strength. It was so tough that a pressurized tank made of such material would not rupture if hit by a bullet and would not fail explosively in a brittle manner. The alternative steel, known as HTS (high tensile strength steel), was a good substitute except in a pressure vessel subject to bullet or shell damage. The first Polaris submarines had sixteen banana-shaped flasks, nested against the interior of the pressure hull, which held high-pressure air used to launch the missiles. Technical director Smith had specified HY80 for the flasks.

One day, the launching subsystem manager reported a delay in delivery of some flasks because of an explosion at the manufacturing plant. Smith asked about the details of the explosion. The manager did not know and was advised to find out immediately. A few hours later, we were shocked to learn that what had exploded was one of our flasks sitting on a test stand at three quarters of the operating pressure. An inclusion (a mixture of slag) in the flask had caused the failure. But this did not explain why an HY80-strength flask would have exploded, well under maximum pressure. Red-faced, the project manager acknowledged that the flask was made of HTS instead. The steel manufacturer, he said, had claimed that HTS would be cheaper and equally as effective. He had cited twenty years of anecdotal experience to the effect that there had never been a failure. So, at the subsystem level, orders had been violated for the sake of economy. The outcome was infinitely more serious than a mere in-plant accident. Now there were sixteen potential time bombs on every Polaris submarine deployed at sea.

It was one day before the nuclear submarine *Robert E. Lee*'s commissioning. The boat, which would serve in the Polaris fleet, was being spit-shined and dressed with cordage, bunting, and signal flags. The words of Longfellow resonated in my ears: "Nothing useless is, or low;/ Each thing in its place is best / and what seems but idle show/ Strengthens and supports the rest."

We rejected a recommendation that sixteen cuts be made in each pressure hull, the flasks removed and replaced, and new ribs for the hull welded into place. This solution would have required a permanent reduction in the operating depth of the subs. Instead, we were able to insert ultrasonic probes through piping into each flask and conduct an examination of its walls. If the flasks had the slightest indication of flaw or inclusion they were depressurized and the missile associated with that flask was taken off the line. The flasks on each submarine were replaced at the boat's first major overhaul. It would be four years before all the defective flasks could be substituted, the last on the *Robert E. Lee*. During those four years, there were flasks deployed at sea that if ruptured by a bullet or high-velocity shrapnel, could sink a Polaris submarine. This being our watch, we could not qualify for a "Certificate of No Responsibility," but we did all that we could do to ensure the national deterrent, so we could sleep. We did more. We retained our sense of humor.

NDT had to be flushed out of every nook and cranny. In the process of planning the Deep Submergence Recovery Vehicle (which will be described later in this tale), the subsystem manager reported that the Sears, Roebuck catalog had a "camper toilet" that was very similar to the portable toilet to be used on the rescue vehicle and was being sold at a fraction of the price. He suggested that we switch to the Sears toilet. "Good idea," I said, "but find out from Lockheed how much it will cost to qualify it to meet military specifications." The answer was $35,000 just to carry out the military certification tests. Military specifications required that the toilet be operational in the polar regions. Unfortunately, the Sears toilet seat had an NDT much higher than the specified temperatures. I could imagine a sailor being rescued in the Arctic who, having had the living daylights but not all else scared out of him, is seeking a measure of relief on the Sears toilet. As he settles his cold posterior on the seat, NDT breaks the seat in two and he plunges into an icy oblivion. The Lockheed toilet, on the other hand, would save this poor sailor from the devastating embarrassment of a moment of ignominy in an otherwise heroic rescue.

8

Triumph to Tragedy

On April 10, 1963, the Commander Submarine Forces Atlantic, Elton "Joe" Grenfell, of World War II fame, convened a meeting of his top commanders with the top submarine brass of the Pentagon, the top engineering duty officers of the Bureau of Ships, and the top management of the Special Projects Office. SPO's Admiral Raborn, due to address the group, described it as a "revival meeting." Its purpose was to review the operation of the successful Polaris FBM system. The program's future course and speed was to be established in an atmosphere of fair winds and following sea. It was probably no accident that this was the day for the deep submergence trials of the USS *Thresher*. The successful development of this submarine was part of the day's celebration. *Thresher's* hull design was the prototype for both the new missile boats that would come after *George Washington* and *Patrick Henry* and the next generation of attack subs.

As Chief Scientist, I was one of the few civilians in attendance at this meeting Admiral Rickover, as usual, was not there, although he may have had a representative. I was seated next to engineering duty officer Harry Jackson. He had just completed his tour of duty as EDO for the *Thresher*. Until now, Jackson had been aboard the boat for every test, inspected every installation of new equipment on the boat, and every repair, and he had declared the submarine fit for sea. With bulldog tenacity, he had monitored the construction of the hull and the installation of its machinery and witnessed its performance at sea. He was one of the most admired and respected of the EDOs on active duty.

The meeting had barely proceeded past the introductory remarks when Admiral Grenfell was called from the speaker's platform. He returned ashen-faced to announce that *Thresher* was down and was almost certainly lost with all hands. The traumatic impact of that announcement cannot be adequately described. One hundred and twenty-nine members of your most immediate Navy family lost in a single moment. Among them were four men from the Naval Ordnance Laboratory scheduled to carry out tests for me. The night before, I had received a telephone call telling me that only four out of my team of seven had been allowed to go and would I intercede on behalf of the entire team. I had, and had been turned down. Three lives saved and four lost. But at that moment my heart reached out to Captain Jackson seated next to me. He kept repeating, "I should be . there, I should be there."

"What could you do, Captain? What could anyone do?"

I no longer recollect the immediate end of the meeting, but I was certain that every man in that room knew what his duty was now, and would carry it out to make sure that such a tragedy would not occur again.

Until we knew the probable cause of the *Thresher*'s loss the Special Projects Office had to assume that the entire Polaris fleet was vulnerable to a repeat of the *Thresher* scenario. The press and the public would want to know the cause and fix the blame. But there was no time for recrimination. That would be left to a board of inquiry.

As chairman of the Steering Task Group's Systems Appraisal Committee I had to prepare a report on the implications of this tragedy to the total Polaris FBM system. My evaluations were made independently of the board of inquiry and were perforce made on the basis of privileged conversations with naval officers and civilian scientists who were involved in the events leading to the loss.

As Chief Scientist I had participated in the planning for the development of the Thresher-class submarine and its somewhat novel function as prototype for both FBM and attack subs. This dual mission gave rise to a bitter controversy. The origins of the controversy really go back to the earliest days of the nuclear-powered submarine. The Atomic Energy Commission–sponsored reactor that went into the Nautilus was developed by Westinghouse. The attack boat skippers wanted a boat that would be designed to fit their perceived needs so they persuaded the Ships Characteristics Board to authorize the parallel development of a reactor by General Electric that would power a new attack sub named Seawolf. This reactor would use liquid sodium for heat transfer from reactor to power plant rather than the pressurized water used in Nautilus. But the liquid sodium leaked, which delayed Seawolf's development, deployment, and evaluation. In the same period of time the Navy undertook construction of a conventionally powered sub with a unique hull and control surface configuration. This was the Albacore, prototype for hull, stability, and control features for future nuclear subs. My unit at the David Taylor Model Basin worked on evaluating the hydrodynamic performance and structural interactions for all three submarines. Albacore proved a resounding success, and her hull design and control features were employed in the first set of attack submarines.

The differing submarine designs came directly from an analysis of their missions. The designers of attack boats presumed, quite correctly, that these hunter-killer submarines would in the course of their lifetime go in harm's way. The probability of nuclear weapons being used against them was low, since the attacker itself would be in the same vicinity. They would be subjected to depth charges, so the sub had to be resistant to shock. Machinery had to be shock-mounted and rugged; piping had to be flexible. These attack subs had to be able to recover from a wide variety of damage scenarios. The attack boat had to be highly maneuverable and fast for short periods of time. It had to be quiet at low speed, as it lay in wait for its prey. It would betray its position during attack by virtue of the incessant pinging of its active sonar and would be noisy during its escape. Recognizing that its vulnerability increased with the overpressure of the sea above, it would go deep only to get below a thermal layer in order to mask its acoustic signal from detection by surface ships. These thermal layers are rarely deeper than one thousand feet.

As a result of these requirements, a practice had developed of subjecting the hulls to shock testing. These tests consisted of exposure to depth charges detonated at a safe distance from the hull. This would insure that minor flaws, which could be identified and repaired after the shock tests, would not sink the ship during actual combat.

The Special Projects Office, however, had an operational doctrine diametrically opposed to shock testing. Deterrent missile submarines had to be kept as far removed from harm's way as possible. The Polaris submarine had to drift in shallow water only when it was positioned for launch. Otherwise it had to run deep. Any effective assault on Polaris when she was running deep would most likely originate from a nuclear weapon launched from afar with a large radius of kill rather than from depth charges. A depth charge has to detonate close by to kill and exerts a *localized* pressure on *part* of the hull—a localized pressure that can break the back of a sub if the depth charge is close enough when it detonates. (A missile sub is, of course, also vulnerable to attack from a hunter-killer sub, but that is another sort of threat, one countered by making the missile sub as silent as possible—and keeping its position as secret as possible.) The pressure wave from a nuclear antisub weapon is large compared with the dimensions of the sub. The stronger the hull the less likely it is to fail when exposed to the *uniform* pressure of the sort that a nuclear detonation would produce. There is a trade-off here—a stronger hull means more weight, which in turn limits what you can put into the sub—reactor weight, ordnance, and so forth. If your reactor is limited, your speed is limited. Attack sub skippers don't want anything to cut their speed. They don't need the capability to operate as deep as the missile sub, which needs more hull strength. The missile sub can live with that trade-off, since speed matters less to a missile sub than it does to an attack sub. (If, however, you use scarce, costly titanium for a hardened, deep-diving hull—and we were concerned that the Russians would do just that—you get a much better weight-depth-speed trade-off.)

A submarine with a collapse depth of two thousand feet will be, in nuclear parlance, 1,000 pounds per square inch hard, a figure several times higher than the hardest missile silo and thus the least vulnerable of the nation's deterrence weapons. A Polaris sub skipper is not worried about a localized pressure from a depth charge (except during the brief periods at shallow depth). He's not worried about speed. But an attack sub skipper worries about depth charges, so he wants a stronger hull to withstand that localized pressure exerted when a depth charge detonates close in. It is unlikely that his adversary—another hunter-killer sub or an antisub surface ship—is going to use a nuclear device on him.

One of our most dreaded scenarios envisaged the loss of a ballistic missile submarine while on patrol as a result of an undetected flaw induced by shock testing done early in the sub's life. Any missing submarine, until found and the cause of sinking determined, would confront the President of the United States with the possibility that the loss was due to deliberate enemy action. In the case of a nuclear-armed ballistic missile submarine, the magnitude of the President's quandary, in terms of international security implications, would be enormous. It could precipitate a world crisis. It could escalate into nuclear war.

Thus when it was proposed that the *Thresher* and *Thresher*-class submarines be shock-tested the Special Projects Office vehemently objected. A second disagreement related to test depth. Under the urging of Special Projects, the operational depth of the *Thresher* was to be increased as much as possible. The Soviets were moving toward titanium hulls for their ballistic missile submarines, giving them a depth capability of five thousand feet or more. Their hulls would be lighter and their power plants heavier, giving an advantage in speed. They would soon be ahead of us and we would have to catch up.

Zeal for shock testing and conservatism in design, which limited a sub's capability for deep submergence, carried the day. I was present at, and retain a vivid recollection of, a bitter conference between Special Projects and BuShips at the end of which the chief of the bureau, Admiral Ralph K. James, leaned over the table, went eye to eye with Raborn's successor, Admiral Ignatius "Pete" Galantin, and said, "Admiral, if I were you, I could not sleep at night knowing that my submarines had not been shock-tested." Galantin replied with the same intensity, "Admiral, if I were you, I could not sleep at night knowing that they had."

Thresher was shock-tested. Rumor has it that the charge was mistakenly set off too close and *Thresher* became the most shock-tested ship in the United States Navy. Design for deep submergence was given short shrift. The stage was set for tragedy.

Was the shock testing the proximate cause for the tragedy? It certainly initiated the chain of events. Did it create the damage that caused the failure that flooded the hull? Probably so. That was the reason for the shock test. Was the failure that of a four-inch seawater pipe? One would have to assume so, for that was the largest penetration of the hull. Would such a failure cause the ship to sink? It should not. The ballast blow systems for pre-*Thresher* submarines were designed to compensate for the failure of a four-inch pipe while operating at test depth. In fact the captain had a protocol that required him to scan the surface with sonar—thus adding a certain delay in execution—to be sure there were no ships or obstructions above him before calling for an emergency ballast blow. If, while operating at a deeper depth, the captain had employed that protocol during *Thresher's* sea trial, would, should the sub have recovered? Alas, simple calculations indicate that it would not. Was the protocol given to the captain the one that would not work in such a major emergency flooding situation (because by the time he had scanned the surface it would have been too late to execute the emergency blow successfully) or was he given another designed for emergencies at the greater depth? We did not know. We did not have to know. It was now obvious that, in any event, the ballast blow system was inadequate and required immediate major redesign and installation. My Systems Appraisal Committee report made the single recommendation that the operating depth of the existing fleet be reduced to the safe operating depth until these changes were made.

When I submitted my report, SP's technical director, Captain (soon to be Admiral) Smith, was already ahead of me in those observations. The Bureau of Ships was also already ahead of me. Their civilian designers and engineering duty officers were working overtime on a new design based on the gas generators employed for the launching of Polaris missiles. The installation of this new design, one that gave a sub the capability to execute an emergency blow far more effectively, would be known as the Sub Safe program. The submarine desk of the Pentagon was way ahead and, taking a broader and longer-range view, had appointed the oceanographer of the Navy, "sea dog" Admiral Ed Stephan, to chair a committee that would lay out a program to dramatically transform the submarine Navy into a Deep Submergence Systems Navy.

Stephan's first action was to assemble a staff of experts. He first sought the assistance of the Bureau of Ships, but they were fully involved with the Sub Safe program. He then tapped the resources of the Navy Laboratory participants in the PAHGLORAD program. They were ready, willing, and able, and they were already at the cutting edge of research and development in the deep ocean. They did indeed possess the information required to design a Navy capable of a wide range of operations in the deep ocean but there was almost no thought given to new missions that might be possible because of such new capabilities. The recommendations of the Stephan committee would have everything to do with deep ocean technology and almost nothing to do with deep ocean intelligence and combat missions.

Before long—but held up by the necessity to wait until the congressional funding came through at the beginning of the fiscal year 1964—the Stephan committee made its report. It recommended the development of a Deep Submergence Rescue Vehicle, a Deep Submergence Search Vehicle, and a Large Object Salvage System. To everyone's surprise, it did not recommend that the Ship System Command (the new name for the Bureau of Ships) manage the program. For the first time in the history of the United States Navy the responsibility for the design and development of ships and submarines was to be given to a separate organization. The Special Projects Office, now officially under the direction of Admiral Smith, who had moved up from technical director to director, was chosen. But Special Projects was already deeply involved in developing a new missile, the Poseidon, and new submarines to carry the Trident missile. They would be the next-generation system after Polaris. SP was also involved with the British in the development of their version of the Polaris system. Smith elected, therefore, to establish a subproject called the Deep Submergence Systems Project and assigned it to the Special Projects Office.

Shortly after that, in the fall of 1964, Smith elected to spin off this DSSP from the rest of SP and assign it, as a separate project, to the Chief Scientist. It became, after Polaris, only the second independent project in the history of the United States Navy. Most people believe that Admiral Rickover ran such an independent program when he worked on developing the nuclear submarine. But Rickover's only design responsibility was the nuclear reactor. Everything else was the responsibility of the Bureau of Ships and the other material bureaus, such as BuOrd, the Bureau of Ordnance. (All of the bureaus would be renamed "commands" in the mid-1960s, so, for example, BuShips became Ship System Command.) The public thought otherwise because Rickover caused them to think so. This is the bone that sticks in the craw of every designer and operator involved with nuclear submarines. Rickover had no responsibility or authority that was not related to the nuclear reactor unless he usurped such authority, which he certainly did when possible. Rickover made his share of contributions to the modern submarine Navy, but he was only one among many who made it possible, as this book demonstrates.

So in 1964, we were moving toward three different submarine missions—deterrence, attack, and intelligence. The Deep Submergence Systems Project was the embryo of the intelligence Navy.

.   There was great consternation within the Navy when this program was set up as an independent entity. Tradition had been broken, not only by keeping this program outside the domain of the Bureau of Ships but also by appointing a civilian to a post normally occupied by a naval officer. The Ship System Command protested to the Secretary of the Navy and questioned the competence, experience, and command capabilities of the Chief Scientist and his staff. Special Projects stoutly defended his and its qualifications to do the job, arguing that this was the kind of assignment for which SP's staff of innovators had already proved their competence.· In the heat of the argument there were avid SP proponents who even proposed that Seaman Craven be called back to active duty with the rank of commodore. In a compromise, I remained a civilian but was given the full legal status of a commanding officer of the United States Navy.

Thus had another John Craven, by the grace of a technicality, finally passed through the portals of the Craven family naval pantheon. My father, shrugging it off as inevitable, saw it as the work of God fulfilling destiny. I saw it as a calculated expedient of line officers of the Academy who had reluctantly decided to start a new arm of the Navy, divorced from the conservatism of attack boat mission analysis and dedicated to the full occupation of the sea. No one had expected the small cadre of the Special Projects Office to be even marginally successful, much less revolutionary, in the management and development of the most complex weapons system yet known to man. No one expected the Deep Submergence Systems Project to come anywhere near the Polaris program in its contribution to national security. The Ship System Command was understandably wounded and engineering duty officers were loath to take on a role that smacked of disloyalty to the bureau. There were many who believed that DSSP would fail, so they adopted a wait-and-see attitude.

During my transition to this new responsibility and while the debate raged, in the waning months of 1963, I visited an offshore oil platform as part of my duties as chairman of the Interagency Committee on Oceanography. Sipping coffee in the Galveston ready room I was telling the helicopter pilot that I would much prefer to go out to the platform on one of the new hydrofoil boats. They were nearly as fast as the helicopter, had a very smooth ride even in heavy seas, and were much safer. The pilot delivered the classic cliché reply, "There are old helicopter pilots and there are bold helicopter pilots, but there are no old bold helicopter pilots, and I am an old pilot."

"Not to worry," the pilot went on to reassure me. "This helo is highly reliable, is well maintained and continuously inspected, and I have been trained in emergency procedures. But I would hate to be in a hydrofoil whose propulsion failed in a heavy sea."

Coffee finished and professional needling concluded, pilot and committee members strapped themselves in the helicopter's seats. Safety checks complete, rotors engaged, the helicopter rose vertically to about one hundred feet and then was tilted over to initiate forward velocity when we heard a loud crack. A shudder ran through the airframe. The tail rotor shaft had failed, the rotor had lost power and stability, and the craft began an uncontrollable rotation.

I can still recall every moment of it. My mind begins to race; we are in the "crescent of death," the term for failure of forward velocity and loss of control of the helicopter. I must estimate the nature of the certain crash if I am to optimize the possibility of survival. I expect that the helicopter will begin to rotate, and then because of gyroscopic action will begin to nutate and swing like a pendulum. If the helicopter is nearly vertical there is some hope that it will stay where it lands when it crashes, but if the main rotor strikes the tarmac, the helicopter will be cartwheeled across the field. The rotors will break and broken pieces of blade could pierce the cockpit with catastrophic results. I instinctively check the hard hat that had been provided and the fastenings of my seat belt. But the potential for fire is such that I must be ready to release the belt right after impact. I must be aware of all of the possible locations of egress and, oh yes, I must be mindful of my responsibilities for the safety of my committee members. All these thoughts are racing through my mind. Good Lord, this is no time to indulge in panic or contemplation of mortality. The crash is imminent.

The old experienced pilot is equally occupied working the problems of emergency control. He has dropped the helicopter as rapidly as possible. Thank God, it crashes nearly vertically. The main rotor slashes into some tires lying on the tarmac, but does not impact the ground. Now we must wait until the rotor stops before crawling out on the ground. We look around and smell the air in the cabin for possible indications of fire or flame. There are none. The door of the cockpit has broken open due to the crash. When the pilot says "Go," we scramble out the door, crawling on our bellies to safety. The pilot and I are the last to leave. As we clear the main rotor we are side by side on the ground. With a supercilious smile, I say, "I told you, helicopters are dangerous."

The pilot is furious; he has used every ounce of professional skill to save the lives of all on board. He has not had time to feel, much less absorb, the psychological and physical shock of this traumatic experience. And now he has to crawl to safety alongside a smart-ass.

Shaken, we all return to the ready room, where there is a profound silence while the pilot informs the authorities and the company of the accident. The corporate executives in Houston are greatly concerned about public image and make an initial offer to send another helicopter so that the mission can be completed. Unanimously rejected. They then propose that the committee rent a car and drive to corporate headquarters where they will arrive in time for cocktails and dinner at their executive club, which has a glorious helicopter-like view atop a Houston tower. As chairman, I agree, with the proviso that I be the driver of the car. I point out that the highway journey is much more dangerous than the helicopter journey. It is most important that the driver be cool, calm, and collected.

The drive complete, committee and corporate executives assemble in the luxurious club atop the tower. They pretend to admire the view below. I, the "cool, calm, and collected" driver, have two double scotches on the rocks, go to my room, and pass out.

The next morning I awake before sunup, and discovering that I am still alive and feel no pain, I perform my Royal Canadian Air Force exercises (fifty push-ups), shower, shave, and take a taxi straight to the airport. I catch the first plane back to Washington. They have nearly killed me in Texas and I don't want to give them a second chance.

Back in Washington, I assumed my new role as Director of the now-independent Deep Submergence Systems Project. The project mission appeared to be limited to engineering development with tasks to be carried out by a cadre of engineering duty officers, civil servants, and aerospace contractors. I borrowed the chief civilian technologists from the launching and handling branch, the navigation branch, the FBM System branch, and the integrated controls and computer branch of the Special Projects Office and other administrative staff as the in-house management team. We had to plan for the development of a Deep Submergence Rescue Vehicle and its associated support, a Deep Submergence Search Vehicle and its associated support, and a Large Object Salvage System, presumably from a newly designed salvage ship.

This program did not enjoy the priority status of Polaris, and it was clear that there was a long haul ahead as we passed through Secretary McNamara's gauntlet of contract definition, cost effectiveness studies, budgets and program plans, congressional appropriations, contractor selection, hardware design and development, operational test and evaluation, and—finally—acceptance by the fleet. As old hands we sat around the office consuming large quantities of coffee sketching out rough designs and schedules associated with these designs. We decided to begin with the Deep Submergence Rescue Vehicle, which regardless of design and complexity could not be deployed earlier than 1970. We phased the design and development of the Deep Submergence Search Vehicle in a way that would bring it on line about two years after the DSRV. We deferred consideration of the Large Object Salvage System until the first two programs were underway. In the end, DSRV was mother to quite a brood—and some of her chicks were hatched before she was fully operational. This is a classic example of the secret intelligence paradigm; the cover (DSRV) is real and it produces covert progeny.

We could not have anticipated the difficulties and triumphs that lay ahead in the development of the Deep Submergence Rescue Vehicle, the NR-1 nuclear-powered oceanographic submarine, the Man-in-the-Sea Program, a deep submergence search and rescue capability, the recovery of a lost hydrogen bomb, the salvage of SeaLab III, the search for the lost submarine Scorpion, and, most of all, the top secret, special intelligence "Hunts for the Red Whatever" (Chapter 15).

Whatever our future fate would be, the die was cast. A Deep Submergence Systems program had been established under the direction of an ex-Navy mustang (an enlisted man and definitely not an Academy graduate)—or a long-haired mad civilian scientist, depending on one's political perspective. In either case, I was on the spot, a very hot spot.

9

The Deep Submergence Rescue Vehicle

The Moving Finger writes; and having writ,
Moves on: nor all your Piety nor Wit
Shall lure it back to cancel half a Line,
Nor all your Tears wash out a Word of it.

—Edward FitzGerald,
The Rubáiyát of Omar Khayyám

The *Thresher* was lost. Moving fingers had written furiously in various committees and up the chain of the military command, in Congress, at the CIA, and in the media. The KGB, the Kremlin, and every nation that possessed or desired to possess nuclear submarines for deterrence or attack also analyzed the loss of *Thresher*. But even as the reports were being written, we were responding to the tragedy.

The Sub Safe program produced an immediate modification of the ballast tank systems in all submarines. For the time being, the depth of operations was drastically reduced. The Sub Safe program priced out at about $300 million, and the Navy believed that it would have to go to Congress for an emergency appropriation. But Special Projects' Admiral Smith had surreptitiously sequestered a contingency fund (for the Polaris A-3 missile) that he did not now need. He offered the $300 million. Many people wondered where this windfall had come from. In my new role as project manager of the Deep Submergence Systems Project, I knew exactly how it had originated, because Admiral Smith had taught me a lesson in thrift. Although the McNamara Pentagon did not allow budgeting reserves for contingencies, Smith had always found ways to put aside a million here and a million there.

The Sub Safe program thus financed, a new budget was available for the Deep Submergence Systems Project. Funds, mission, and organization in hand, I set out to define the objectives of the DSSP, tackling the Deep Submergence Rescue Vehicle first. The mission of the DSRV was to rescue personnel from a downed submarine of any nation wherever that emergency might occur.

A realistic assessment revealed that this was for all practical purposes a nonmission. When a nuclear submarine leaves port, usually for a sixty-day patrol, it heads directly for deep water. On the West Coast of the United States or from an island, it takes about twenty minutes for the sub to reach deep water. From the East Coast continental shelf it takes about two to three hours. Thus the probability that any sunken nuclear submarine would be in waters where rescue would be possible was very small. Even so, should a casualty occur in shallow littoral waters, the existing rescue capabilities would be nearly adequate. Low-cost modifications would make them more than adequate.

All submariners are required to pass an escape test in a diving tower one hundred feet in height. They employ a hood that permits them to inhale and exhale during the ascent. In addition, ASRs (Auxiliary Submarine Rescue Ships) are available with McCann rescue chambers that attach to the submarine hatch. With the addition of teams of SEALs who can dive to depths of six hundred feet or more in order to clear the hull, effective rescue capability already existed. Our first order of business was to provide additional elements to enhance these rescue capabilities. We could now sleep at night knowing that should rescue be required, we could respond.

Why then would we insist on investing large sums of money for the development of a rescue vehicle that in all likelihood would never be used? Only an anthropologist can explain the human desire to rescue people from the sea wherever and whenever they are in danger and then, should that effort fail, to return their bodies for burial on the land. If such be the human motivation, what then could a DSRV offer a society seeking reassurance that men could be delivered from the implacable grip of the deep ocean? Practically speaking, we had to dream up every conceivable scenario in which individuals lost at sea might still be alive in a submerged or floating structure and theoretically capable of rescue. This included individuals in submarines, in sunken surface ships, and free swimmers or divers separated from their decompression chamber, their support ship, their life raft, or their life preserver. The DSRV would have to be designed to accommodate every scenario as well as it could, given the limits of technology and budget, and regardless of cost effectiveness.

There was also another answer, one that never appeared in a directive but was tacitly understood. There were many highly classified missions associated with national security that could not be accomplished without a DSRV system. The specific operational needs for these missions could not be anticipated but they were certain to occur. Thus a DSRV designed, constructed, and deployed for every conceivable rescue mission would also be available for the intelligence "mission impossibles" that were sure to occur.

This "mission impossible" DSRV now defined in our minds, we suggested the framework for its design. The craft had to be transportable by the largest cargo plane—say, a C-141—that could fly from the DSRV's home base fast enough to permit recovery of imperiled seamen anywhere in the world. This set the limits on the DSRV's weight, diameter, and length.

The airfields around the world that could receive the C-141 were identified along with the location of the port or ports nearest to the airfield. A road transporter that could be carried on a companion aircraft had to be provided and roads identified that would allow the DSRV to be carried from the airport to the port. The port itself would have to be configured with a berth for the submarine of opportunity (that is, the nearest available submarine) that would be used to bring the DSRV to the rescue site. Obviously, the coverage would be less than the Navy desired but the program would still be unique in the world because of its geographic scope.

The dimensions of the craft established the configuration of the pressure hull. Now the interior had to be designed. For structural efficiency, the DSRV would be either a ring-stiffened cylinder with spherical end caps, or two spheres connected by a tunnel, or three spheres connected together. My staff and I chose the three-sphere configuration.

Our decision was largely dictated by the nature of the mission. When a submarine is submerged, the occupants breathe fresh air usually obtained from compressed gas bottles. And, of course, they exhale carbon dioxide. Consequently, the atmospheric pressure in the boat increases from accumulated, unvented exhalations of CO_2. Above a pressure of five atmospheres, the ability to survive is almost nil, but it is possible that the pressure in a downed submarine could reach that level with rescuees still alive. In order to be rescued they would have to be decompressed in the DSRV. Thus the decompression sphere would have to be maintained at a different pressure from the sphere in which personnel are entering and leaving the downed submarine. In the third sphere, the pilot and copilot would remain at an atmosphere close to normal.

The crew, apart from the pilot and copilot, would consist of one or two persons to assist the rescuees. The rescuees would number up to twenty-four. Their physiological and psychological capacities might be impaired, and some might be irrational and wish to take control of the DSRV or interfere with its operation. It was thus vital that the pilot and copilot be protected from such irrational behavior by rescuees and work in a separate forward compartment that could be completely isolated from the transfer and transport compartments. It was desirable that each rescuee, once on board, be separated from the crew members handling the rescue (medical corpsman and salvage personnel). This dictated the three spheres, one for pilot and copilot, one for other crew, and one for rescuees. The dimensions of all three spheres were limited by the size of the transport aircraft. From previous designs it was known that the weight of the hull must be about 0.4 of the displacement. The hull must go as deep as possible—at least to the collapse depth of existing and future hulls, and at least to the depth of the continental shelves—which meant it had to operate at a depth of at least three thousand feet. The actual depth is still classified.

So far, so good. But the DSRV was going to be carrying a lot of equipment, such as life-support air bottles, navigation sonars, communications equipment, propulsion motors, and thrusters for vertical and horizontal control. It had to be equipped with a mating flange and a double-hatch entrance and egress system to provide access to the sunken vessel. If the DSRV were to have three spheres, there would be space outside the hull in which to nest a lot of equipment. The space was a limited bonus based on geometry. On the other hand I was forced by the same geometric constraints to use electrically powered thrusters and propulsors outside the hull that would be powered by batteries or, rather, fuel cells that would be especially developed for the DSRV.

In early 1964 I started establishing the in-house design of this and other submersibles. My preliminary design for the DSRV was almost complete but would have had failure built in had it not been for my experience with the Polaris submarines, which must hover during launch. The DSRV also must hover. Its ability to remain in a location in the vertical would depend on the adjustment of its ballast. Is it neutrally buoyant or is its buoyancy slightly negative or slightly positive? If there was a current, then there might be a lift on the DSRV in either direction. But there would always be a current because the DSRV would always set the fluid of the ocean into motion. The pilot could not be relied on to sense these factors, because we had discovered that such sensing is outside the parameters of human capability. The pilot, it had been shown, always got it wrong, adjusting trim instead of ballast and vice versa.

There had to be a brand-new, smart-vehicle control system in the DSRV that required internal motion sensors and external flow sensors on the hull. The equations of motion would have to be programmed into a computer. The sensors would feed their data into the computer, which would tell the ballast system and the propulsors what to do. There had to be an integrated control and display system in the DSRV with all mission profiles programmed, and the DSRV had to be capable of carrying out these programs. I had already made up my mind that the only organization capable of designing this system was the MIT Draper Laboratory under Stark Draper, the legendary gun sight designer. His laboratory would later produce the computer and displays for the Apollo landing system that would guide America's astronauts to their first landing on the moon. As it turned out, a more complex computer system would be needed for the DSRV, since it was much more difficult to control a hovering craft in a fluid medium than in outer space. MIT was equal to the task although it required two of the Apollo computers. Today a laptop would be overkill.

Parallel to this effort was a similar project associated with the Deep Submergence Search Vehicle, the Large Object Salvage System, and various interim search and rescue systems. As noted earlier, the magnitude of these programs made it difficult to manage them within the structure of the Special Projects Office so a decision had been made by the Navy that the DSSP should be set up as an independent project under the Chief Scientist's supervision. I now had to effect the transfer of some of the Special Projects Office officers and civilians to the DSSP. With a certain trepidation, I met with Admiral Smith. I was headhunting, as it were, for his most creative personnel.

There were times when the slow pace of the admiral's thought processes were simply maddening. Instead of fussing with a pipe or cigar as a delay mechanism, he would take out his comb and groom his hair, slowly and deliberately, and then light one of his chain of cigarettes. While his eyes searched whatever document you had prepared for him, he would leisurely puff or comb, or both. Finally, snuffing out the cigarette in a forest of butts, he would raise his eyebrows and say something you least expected. True to form, including surprises, he fulfilled my every request. He pointed out that Special Projects was past the need for innovation and that innovators can't help but innovate. They now stood in his way unless some unforeseen problem would arise in the Fleet Ballistic Missile System. He suggested and I agreed that I retain my title as Chief Scientist in the Special Projects Office and that the personnel transferred to DSSP be recallable on demand to the Special Projects Office if needed. He also arranged for a meeting with the director of civil service to ensure that none of the transferees would be reduced in grade. As a result, the DSSP team consisted of the same highly motivated and innovative individuals who had created Polaris, and I structured the organization accordingly.

With the team assembled and the preliminary system package prepared, DSSP was ready to brief the contractors. Excitement was running high in the aerospace community because it was the first time those contractors had had the opportunity to design and develop undersea craft. It was incorrectly assumed that the Navy would soon be buying many small submersibles with a budget that matched its purchase of aircraft. Lockheed, Westinghouse, North American

Aviation, and, of course, the Electric Boat Company all expected to be major players. They all made mock-ups of the rescue compartments and demonstrations of how many human beings could be packed into one small sphere. Lockheed had built *Deep Quest*, a small submersible, to demonstrate its abilities. Westinghouse had *Deep Star 4000*, capable of descending to the deepest part of the continental shelf. North American belatedly entered the submarine-building business with DOWB, the Deep Ocean Work Boat. Electric Boat Company had already developed *Star I*, its own small, moderately deep-dive-capable submarine, and soon launched *Star II* and *Star III* as advanced versions. Not to be outdone, the Ship System Command began work on *Turtle* and *Sea Cliff*—small, two-man deep submersibles. By the end of 1965 there was a fleet of small experimental submersibles built by companies vying for the DSRV prize. The award was finally made to Lockheed in 1966, but subcontracts for the integrated controls and displays were given to the MIT Instrumentation Laboratory (as it was known before it became the Draper Lab) and contracts for the manipulators were given to Westinghouse. *Jane's Fighting Ships* in a 1970 photograph shows the submarine *Hawkbill* at sea clearly modified for support of the DSRV with the DSRV mounted on its deck.

This new technology was evolving during the period from 1964 to 1970. The DSRV and its support structure also served as cover for all the other projects, and more than half of the equipment designed and built for the DSRV was actually designed and constructed to serve as "spare parts" for almost all the advanced deep submergence vehicles produced by DSSP—*Trieste II*, *NR-1*, and the intelligence submarines. Thus the DSSP had a cost overrun of 2,000 percent on the DSRV.

As soon as they learned that DSSP/DSRV was underway the Soviets got into the act. Their Shirshov Institute of Oceanology was part of the Soviet National Academy of Science. Military science was, of course, a part of their academic repertoire. Thus any oceano-graphic ship of the Shirshov had to be presumed to be, and in fact was, an oceanographic ship for the conduct of military missions. When the Shirshov tried to purchase Star 1 (this first small sub-mersible built by Electric Boat Company was in fact designed and constructed by one of its employees in a "backyard" facility) for use on its oceanographic ship *Vityaz*, there was great surprise on our shores. The State Department referred this request to the CIA and the Special Projects Office for approval.

Admiral Smith and I concluded that the Soviets would bend all efforts to obtain a small submersible from someone or else develop one themselves. Star I, we knew, was the most obsolete of our small submersibles. We believed that the best way to slow the Soviets was to permit them to develop a dependence on that craft. The CIA con-curred and the sale was about to be authorized when it came to the attention of Admiral Rickover. He promptly called the Director of the CIA. Over the speakerphone in the Director's office Rickover could be heard calling him an "unpatriotic son of a bitch." He threatened to bring the workers of Electric Boat out on strike if the sale were consummated. His threat worked. In response the Soviets immediately acquired Pisces II, a much more advanced vehicle, from the Canadians. They then established a development program under the direction of their most dynamic and innovative underwater technologist, Anatoly Sagalevitch. He would become my counter-part in the Soviet navy and our lives were thus destined to be inter-twined. It was he who commissioned the Finns to develop the famous Mir submersibles. The world knows these submersibles through their featured use in the film *Titanic*. They are said to be the most advanced deep submergence vehicles in existence.

While the contractors were preparing their response, I decided that the project engineers of DSSP should acquire a personal famil-iarity with small submersibles and their operational capabilities. At that time in 1964, Jacques Cousteau was in La Jolla, California, with his small submersible *Soucoupe*. When approached, he welcomed the idea that we hire him to give familiarization dives to members of the project. Although I had already been on dives aboard the small submersibles *Alvin*, *Star*, and *Aluminaut*, I exercised my prerogative as director to go first, timing it with a cross-country automobile vacation trip with my family. I presumed that my five-year-old son, David, would be impressed with his father diving on a Cousteau submarine. He did not appear to be.

On the morning of the dive, I was briefed by Cousteau and his pilot, Albert Falco, on the characteristics of the submarine and the nature of the dive. Cousteau pointed out that although French was Falco's native language, he was perfectly able to communicate with me in English should the need arise. Falco and I boarded the submarine and closed the hatch. The craft, sitting on the deck of a ship, was lifted by a crane and, held by three slings, lowered into the sea. Almost immediately, a torrent of water came gushing into the submarine. My first thought was that this was a seal that would close with depth, but I had never seen so much water flooding a boat. I looked at Falco, who had gone white, losing his "perfectly able" English. "*La première fois,*" he said repeatedly, while I summoned up enough French to translate that this was the first time such a thing had happened, to which I replied acerbically, "Well, let's not make it *la dernière fois.*" The submarine support divers were busy unhooking the slings. Falco was dropping the emergency ballast weight and shouting a stream of commands in French into the underwater acoustic microphone. Most of these I did not understand, although I could have sworn at one point that I heard "*sacrebleu!*"

Fortunately, the last sling had not yet been detached. The others were reattached and the *Soucoupe* was hoisted out of the water. Back on the deck, it was discovered that an O-ring was out of its groove and in effect the hatch had been locked in the open position. Falco, dripping water from head to foot, was given a hand for his courageous actions in the emergency. As I emerged, I realized that I must have lost my cool, for I was only wet from the pants down. It may have been my imagination, but I was sure I heard hands stop clapping in midair. I would never be sure how much my Cousteau adventure would have impressed my five-year-old, but I was thankful he wasn't there that morning, and I kept the details to myself. Nevertheless, by the afternoon, the submarine (and my pants) had dried and my cool had returned, so we descended again, without mishap.

Later that week I took my son to Disneyland. As my wife and I stood in line to ride the Disneyland submarine David disappeared. He was going down the line telling everyone, "My father designed these submarines." I remonstrated, "No, David, I did not." He stamped his feet and clenched his fist. "Yes, Daddy, you did, you told me so." The vehemence of his conviction reminded me that I had indeed tested the Disneyland submarine windows for visibility. I suspected that most people, like David, would agree about the relative importance of the Disneyland sub vis-à-vis the United States Navy subs.

The in-water experiences of my staff and me convinced us that although real progress was being made in the design and development of small submersibles, the aerospace industry was not yet ready to manage the development of the DSSP. For the time being, all of the significant technical decisions would be made in-house as they were with the Special Projects Office. Industry now joined the Ship System Command in its disappointment at being denied a leadership role in the conquest of "inner space." The Lockheed modification of the DSSP design was the winner, but not without complaint from others. Then when the costs and complexity of the DSRV were in the public domain, Senator William Proxmire awarded the project his famous Golden Fleece Award for its world-record overrun (which, as I've explained, was largely due to its cover for related intelligence projects). Anxious officers and staff, fearful of the nega-tive impact on the public support for the program, wanted to brief the senator on the existence of the classified program. Wiser heads prevailed. They calculated that the Soviets would also be lulled into the false belief that the DSSP program was an expensive failure.

It was at this juncture that a bitter ex-submariner wrote a novel entitled *Event 1000*.

It begins with an American nuclear submarine down in twelve hundred feet of water. The on-scene "commander for search and rescue" criticizes the Navy's "benign neglect" for the lagging development of the Deep Submergence Rescue Vehicle. The project director of DSSP, a thinly disguised caricature of myself, is not spared having to down a heaping plate of crow. The denouement has the Soviets coming to the rescue. This book appeared in 1971 when the full panoply of deep submergence systems, although highly classified, had already been deployed. When it was published, U.S. officials at every level of security were furious and wanted a public repudiation of the book by the Navy. But again, wiser heads prevailed. Instead we hoped that the novel would be translated into Russian and widely read throughout the KGB.

In the early 1970s a public demonstration of the DSRV system was carried out. Although the DSRV command knew that a test would take place within the fiscal year they were suddenly ordered—at a time that they least expected—to mate immediately with a British submarine sitting on the bottom of the North Sea. Although it was announced as a drill, all hands performed as though it were real, and the submarine was "rescued" in a short time. With the success of the system well publicized, the author of *Event 1000* rewrote his book as a screenplay and made the DSRV the hero of a movie entitled *Gray Lady Down*. Then the DSRV was featured in *The Hunt for Red October*. With the success of that novel and the movie made from it, the public became aware of the splendid capability and performance of the first real inner-space vehicle. The DSRV's technical sophistication and complexity surpassed the space vehicles of that day and perhaps of today. This was a vehicle ahead of its time, with versatilities still unpublicized, and the potential to conduct missions not yet publicly articulated. In 1990 the integrated controls and displays were redesigned by Draper Laboratory to incorporate the newest in information technology and to refurbish these vehicles for another twenty years of service to the nation.

The DSRV was the first and the last element of the DSSP to be carried out with mature and deliberate speed. The new missions that were created as a result of the DSRV's success would engulf the DSSP office. These new missions could only be accomplished by cannibalizing design, development, spare parts, and personnel of this first DSSP project, which itself was the child of the Polaris Fleet Ballistic Missile System.

10

Spooked

"Wouldst thou"—so the helmsman answered—
"Learn the secret of the sea?
Only those who brave its dangers
Comprehend its mystery."

—Henry Wadsworth Longfellow

In early 1965 I received a call from the Pentagon from a man who said he was a naval intelligence officer. He asked me to meet with him at the Pentagon and not to tell anyone on my staff, including my secretary, that I was going to this meeting. This was my initiation into the world of Special Intelligence.

When I arrived, a man whom I knew well as a submarine officer involved with the Polaris program greeted me. I was soon to discover that his involvement with Polaris was a cover for a program that was itself a cover for a more secret program whose name I am bound to this day not to reveal. But the name of this program, Sand Dollar, is already in the public domain and there is no national security reason for keeping it secret.

I was immediately taken to and locked in a room that was, in fact, a vault, secured internally and externally by combination locks. I was then informed that the organization that had requested my presence was the Defense Intelligence Agency. This agency is charged with the gathering of military intelligence by covert or clandestine means. I was then subjected to a briefing on the security requirements of Special Intelligence before the reason for my presence was revealed.

I learned that the DIA, operating in support of national security policy, developed and carried out specific missions. The DIA is completely independent of the CIA. Any important intelligence it gathers is first transmitted to the National Security Agency, which decides, on the guidance of the National Security Council, whether the information should be released to the CIA. The head of the DIA is an admiral or general of one of the armed services. Each service has a chief of intelligence and an intelligence corps. The DIA has a civilian board called the DIA Scientific Advisory Committee.

The activities of the DIA are highly compartmentalized. Most activities are categorized as Special Intelligence projects. Even the code name of each project is highly classified. A list of individuals with a need to know is designated for each project. The list is as short as possible. Information acquired under the program is kept in tightly guarded security spaces and nothing may be removed except when transferred to another secure facility. In that event, material is transported in a locked briefcase shackled to guards who have no knowledge of what they are carrying. Participants can tell no one, not even their families or closest professional colleagues, of their involvement in a Special Intelligence project. In addition, every participant must have a true personal cover story to account for his whereabouts twenty-four hours a day.

Every project must have a cover project that must be true. Thus is formed a hierarchy of projects, with one or more Special Intelligence projects at the top of the pyramid. Most participants in a cover project do not know that it is a cover project. One or more individuals who are cleared for both projects make the link between Special Intelligence projects and their covers. The chain proceeds all the way down to unclassified projects. Thus, I was told, the DSSP could serve as the host for projects at every level with a structure that deflected penetration anywhere. If someone stumbled on information to which he was not privy, he was briefed at the lowest level of security for which he was cleared and warned against further release of that material.

Those who understood the system appreciated the fact that the project they were working on was real and significant but at the same time might be a cover for a project whose mission was more sensitive. You would never know whether you had penetrated the "seventh veil" except by the length of the clearance list. If it was ten or less, you could be fairly certain that the information gleaned would be transmitted only to the admiral or general who was the director of the DIA, who, in turn, would provide the information to the President's National Security Adviser and finally to the President.

These and other techniques for preserving security were discussed in our hour-long meeting in the vault, after which I was duly cautioned on the damage to national security and the threat to the lives of those involved should any breach occur. I was then placed under written oaths and briefed on the mission that required the development of a Special Intelligence project or projects in which I would play a major role in initiation and management.

The Sand Dollar mission was the identification and retrieval of military hardware located on the seabed, possession of which by a foreign power or unauthorized individuals would be inimical to national security. The location and recovery of sunken nuclear weapons in particular was the highest priority. I was shown an inventory itemizing the items known to be on the seabed and a map of their distribution throughout the world. Could I organize and manage a program to carry out this mission using the assets of DSSP? Furthermore, could I carry it out in such a manner that my family and friends and closest professional colleagues would have no idea that I was involved in such a project?

My instructions were coming from the director of the DIA and his immediate staff, who were guided by the Defense Intelligence Agency Scientific Advisory Board. The civilian chairman of that board, Gene Fubini, was the resident genius who dreamed up ideas at the national level. It was he who had seen in DSSP a mechanism for implementing an undersea intelligence system of great national value. I know nothing about his background. Special Intelligence is a world in which one does not ask and, if asked, does not tell how he got involved. Now that Fubini is deceased and can no longer be targeted, I can venture a guess that he was an anti-Fascist Italian who served as a technical intelligence agent for the United States during World War II. He would become my mentor, and later, when I was no longer a civil servant, I would serve as a member of the DIA advisory board.

A captain whose name I can no longer recall and his relief, Captain Jim Bradley, a nonnuclear submariner, whose career was similarly shrouded, were the DIA staff members who would be my co-conspirators. Now retired, Captain Bradley has suffered two serious strokes, is unable to communicate, and is therefore invulnerable with respect to the disclosure of Special Intelligence information. Mutually cleared for this unnameable project, we would study the map and determine how to carry out the mission. Then we roughed out the system.

The salvageable items of interest were spread around the globe. I was soon disabused of my vague belief that there was some grain of truth in the contention that an area in the Atlantic, the so-called Bermuda Triangle, was the location of an extraordinary number of aircraft and ships that had mysteriously vanished. There were plenty of interesting objects on ocean floors worldwide, not just in the

Bermuda Triangle, and there was an equal distribution of these objects between those that were lying on the continental shelf and those in the deep ocean. There was a skew in favor of the continental shelf because of shallow water, rocks, and shoals, but much of that hardware had either been salvaged or scattered by storms.

It was clear that three capabilities had to be developed. The most immediate was a means of conducting a clandestine search in the deep ocean. We had a particular interest in finding and recovering Soviet missile reentry bodies and guidance systems. The possibility existed that the Soviets had not hardened these items with respect to electromagnetic impulse, which was probably our only hope for an effective antiballistic missile defense. The second immediate requirement was to develop a capability for manned inspection and recovery of small and intermediate-sized objects from the deep sea floor. The third was the capability to clandestinely place divers on the seafloor for the recovery of objects that required some form of handling.

My first task of substance was to present these mission requirements that I had identified to the DIA Scientific Advisory Board. I was to discover that on this board sat the high priesthood of the Department of Defense. Anthropologists would say that admittance to this priesthood required only a complete set of security clearances. The entry-level requirement to this inner sanctum was clearance for Top Secret. The next level was Top Secret, Q clearance. The Q clearance category was for nuclear matters. I had reached that level as soon as I became Chief Scientist and underwent a one-week individualized crash course at the Sandia nuclear weapons facility near Albuquerque, New Mexico. Those with this clearance are eligible for the most intimate knowledge of nuclear weapons whenever they have a need to know. Parallel to this level was Top Secret, Special Intelligence. Those with this clearance are eligible for the most intimate knowledge of intelligence operations whenever a need to know arose. Captain Bradley and his predecessor were in this category. The pinnacle of clearance was Top Secret, Special Intelligence, Top Secret Q. Every member of the DIA board possessed these security clearances. They were cleared for access to material at these top levels of classification if they had a need to know and as a consequence they were part of a pool of high priests at the Pentagon who wielded exceptional power.

I soon learned that collecting information about Soviet military hardware was not the DIA's highest priority. The DIA intelligence people understood that the Cold War ought to end, not through a clash of arms, but when the Soviet leadership made fundamental changes in policy (such as agreements to arms control), driven by their appreciation that their command and control system had broken down so badly that some kind of upheaval or coup was inevitable. This, of course, is ultimately what happened when in the 1980s Mikhail Gorbachev adopted his policies of glasnost and perestroika, openness and restructuring. It was therefore the mission of the DIA to observe from satellites the smallest details of Soviet activity on land, to intercept their most private communications on land or sea or in the atmosphere, to detect the cracks in their system before they were recognized by Moscow itself and to allow the Soviet government to discover through its own intelligence system that we knew, before they knew, that they were losing control and that it could not be regained. But much remained to be done in 1965 to develop the intelligence capabilities that would give us early warning that this was actually happening.

Some who are in a position to speak with authority, like Senator Daniel Patrick Moynihan, find the CIA a tad remiss in not waking up to the fact, even quite late in the day, that the Soviet Union had, in John Le Carré's felicitous phrase, turned into a skeleton inside its armor. Others maintain that the agency has a tendency to work on the basis of what William James called "the will to believe"—in its own beliefs and estimates, which encourages it to tell its masters what agency employees think their masters want to hear. The Bay of Pigs is one example and as history emerges via declassification many more examples are coming to light. The DIA tends, like Sergeant Joe Friday of *Dragnet* fame, to adopt a "just the facts, ma'am" approach, although the Department of Defense always has its share of woollier thinkers.

Absent such indications that the Soviet monolith was cracking up, the deterrence of nuclear war was a major element of our strategy, and the DIA, unencumbered by service rivalries, was fully appreciative of how the Special Projects Office could help establish a credible and unassailable deterrent to surprise nuclear attack. Until the establishment of the Deep Submergence Systems Project the DIA lacked the means to exploit fully the potential of the technology of the sea in furtherance of its Cold War mission. DIA therefore gave quick approval to the development of the three capabilities I had identified, but limited immediate development to the Sand Dollar mission.

In March and April of 1965 plans were submitted to DIA by DSSP and approved, and the appropriate budgets were allocated from congressionally mandated authorizations and appropriations in a very complex way in which those involved were allowed only to see "through a glass, darkly"—and only at the level of their need to know. As a result, authority, responsibility, and accountability were vested in the hands of a very few individuals. We had no choice but to trust that the actions of we few, we secret few, would be carried out properly on missions of vital importance to national and international peace and security. Most of us, veterans of a world conflict, understood the nature of that trust.

Bradley and I were now authorized to proceed with the development of search and recovery vehicles that could pick up from the ocean floor such things as nuclear warheads. Since security required that the number of cleared participants be kept to an absolute minimum, individuals involved in various programs had to make design decisions and equipment choices on the basis of experience and in the absence of any formal design or operational studies. This was virtually identical to conditions in wartime, where technical and operational decisions were made by veterans on the spot, on "the back of an envelope," a classified envelope. I immediately concluded that our mission required the use of nuclear submarines. The Office of Undersea Warfare, that part of the Pentagon that oversaw submarine intelligence (Bradley was head of it), determined that we could choose from a number of possibilities, among them the submarines *Seawolf*, *Whale*, and *Halibut*, to carry out missions of recovery of items on Sand Dollar's wish list of material on the seabed of interest to naval intelligence. The choice was obvious, at least for the immediate deep ocean search capability.

Halibut had been designed to carry a Regulus cruise missile inside her pressure hull. As a result *Halibut*'s twenty-foot-diameter hatch, which opened into the pressure hull, was unique. No other submarine in the world had the capability for underwater launch of small, unmanned vehicles, either towed, tethered, or independently operated. Our plan was to secretly refit *Halibut* with deep ocean search and intelligence capabilities without alteration of its external appearance and without reassignment to missions other than publicly announced unclassified training and research missions completely unrelated to DSSP. As part of this plan, *Halibut* was reclassified as an attack sub in July 1965. My involvement and DSSP contractor and personnel involvement was to be completely secret outside the intelligence establishment and not to be disclosed even to members of my family, my closest friends, or members of DSSP who did not have a need to know.

It did not appear that the second capability, manned, deep ocean recovery of small objects, could be realized without use of a *Trieste*-type submersible. *Trieste* was an extremely deep diving craft developed by Jacques Piccard, the Swiss submarine designer, in the late

1950s in Italy. This unusual deep submergence device consisted of a heavy pressure-resistant gondola capable of going to the bottom of the ocean without collapse. The gondola was attached to a large float of high-octane aviation gasoline that provided the buoyancy to bring the gondola back to the surface. At this time there was only one such "bathyscaphe," and it had been purchased by the Office of Naval Research from Piccard in 1957. Piccard and Lieutenant Donald Walsh took this vehicle to the deepest part of the ocean in the Challenger Deep in 1960, setting a record for deep submergence that cannot be broken. But the *Trieste* had very little operational capability, and modification of that boat would have been more expensive than new construction, so new it would be. It was thus decided that we would build a brand-new bathyscaphe, but we would build it in absolute secrecy in a facility that was itself secret and called, in the parlance of the intelligence community, a "skunk works." The original *Trieste* would be requisitioned by DSSP as a test platform for the Deep Submergence Search Vehicle envisioned by the Stephan committee.

The new, undercover bathyscaphe was built during a period that stretched from September 1965 through August 1966 in the skunk works. A World War II floating dry dock was modified, allegedly for support of diving facilities and experimental small submarine prototypes such as Electric Boat's *Star I* and *II*, Westinghouse's *Deep Star 4000*, Lockheed's *Deep Quest*, and other small craft dedicated to research and development. The floating dry dock *White Sands* was a relic but it was modernized at a cost of $100 million to be a very sophisticated ship for the clandestine support of the new bathyscaphe while it was engaged in secret missions for the DIA. The name of this game was "outwit the KGB." Our initial strategy was to advertise the use of the original *Trieste* for test purposes as a decoy when a significant mission opportunity presented itself and to sneak out to the site with the covered floating dry dock containing the secret bathyscaphe. The old *Trieste* would be used for support; the new bathy-scaphe would do the work.

The third and most ambitious capability under the DSSP program was to be the clandestine deployment of saturation divers from the submarine *Seawolf*. Saturation diving is a technique whereby the diver is acclimated to move freely as a marine mammal moves in the deep ocean at depths up to six hundred feet or more for long periods of time. This revolutionary diving capability was still in development in 1965 in SeaLabs, which were experimental units of the Office of Naval Research and not then a part of the DSSP program. Anticipating the success of this development, we knew that the deployment of divers in such depths would require a submarine modified to include a diver support facility. It was, therefore, not premature to select the nuclear submarine *Seawolf* to be cut in half to allow for the installation of a new section that would in fact be a compartment housing divers who were trained for saturation diving. If these divers were to be employed in collecting intelligence, then this cadre of dedicated submariners would have to be trained in secret and, as a cover, would be placed in a special category of divers in the Navy designated as SEALs. Not all SEALs are saturation divers but all saturation divers involved in the special programs have been designated as SEALs.

Saturation diving requires long periods of time for compression and decompression. The special compartment in the submarine would have to provide for these long periods of compression and decompression and would have to provide a means of egress and reentry for the team and its equipment. The actual equipment to be installed would await the completion of development of the Mark II Deep Diving System (a component of the unclassified programs of the Navy's Supervisor of Salvage and later a joint development of SupSalv and DSSP). This system was made up of three main components—the divers' equipment, a compression/decompression chamber, and a personal transfer capsule (PTC), which moves the divers either from a compression/decompression chamber on the deck of a surface ship or from the interior or deck of a sub to the diving work site. The pressure in the PTC would be the same as the pressure of the ocean at the depth of the diving site.

Seawolf was being fitted out to carry this system and the divers who would operate it. During the construction period neither the shipyard, the officers, nor the crew of Seawolf were to be informed of the nature of the section to be inserted. Various cover stories at various levels were given; most of which were related to experimental tests of new mines or cruise missiles, even the development of a new type of reactor. Seawolf was in the yard being modified from May of 1965 to August of 1967. Her reactor, its liquid sodium problem resolved, was refueled—for reasons known only to a very few of the top brass. She was cut in half to allow for the insertion of the new section to support the Mark II Advanced Diving System and saturation diving operations.

As time passed and history unfolded each of these three separately compartmented programs had very different outcomes. The Halibut was responsible for the success of at least two of the most significant espionage missions of our time. Its tale may never be fully told but I will reveal as much as I can. The Seawolf had a bittersweet story, a tale I will also tell.

The Trieste II would be forced to come out into the light of day when the Navy embarked on the search for and inquest into the ill-fated Scorpion. Until then she, like Halibut, would exist in the silent world and fight the silent war of clandestine operations. The selection of the submarine Halibut as the first vehicle for the first mission was just the initial step in a chain of stealthy steps of submarine technology.

When you are modifying a sub like Halibut to undertake Special Intelligence missions, you have to notify the sub's flotilla commander that his submarine has a new mission at a classified level that limits access only to authorized personnel. He must set up an elaborate and tight security system without knowing the specifics of the mission. The next step is the selection of a contractor to handle modifications and install new equipment. The contractor must have the team and the technical capability to carry out the operation without disclosing the fact that the corporation has a major contract to do work on the submarine. There was no alternative except to choose a contractor already actively engaged with the Special Projects Office in a program of submarine technology.

It was during this time that the Central Intelligence Agency became keenly interested in the Navy's rapidly evolving undersea intelligence program. After he left the Polaris program, Admiral Raborn was briefly Director of the CIA under President Lyndon Johnson and made people in the agency aware of the Navy's capability. But the Navy had no reason to give the CIA its intelligence because the Defense Intelligence Agency was the only agency authorized to handle this intelligence once the Navy had collected it. CIA was kept at a need to know distance.

The CIA thought that Lockheed was our contractor—and we did not discourage them from thinking so. But the company we selected for the work on *Halibut* was already involved in work on Polaris as well as the DSRV, so both of those jobs served as cover for the company's work on *Halibut*. Gradually, from management on through the ranks of technicians required to oversee and carry out the work, personnel from that company and from my own shop were subjected to stringent security checks by the FBI.

Clearances established and the team assembled, I assumed the role of project manager and from the middle of 1965 until I left the program in the fall of 1969 a weekly management meeting was held in classified spaces. Aside from security it was not smooth sailing. There were, of course, technical difficulties resulting from the structural configuration of Halibut and the fact that it was not designed to tow underwater bodies. Some of these difficulties make for exciting reading and are described in the books Blind Man's Bluff and Spy Sub. But I think these problems pale beside the importance and ultimate impact of the intelligence operations that Halibut would be involved in and the grave dangers she would face. Her first mission was the clandestine observation and perhaps collection of guidance, reentry body, and decoy hardware that was deposited in the ocean during Soviet missile tests. For navigational safety reasons we and the Soviets announce the time and location of these tests. Surface ships of both navies arrive on the scene to observe. Halibut's mission was to be there undetected to locate, photograph, and collect other intelligence information with respect to these reentry body parts.

Experience had taught us that there would be a high probability that the first missions would fail but we had to learn whether we could carry out such operations under the enemy's nose without being detected or operationally inhibited. The first scheduled Soviet missile tests that we were supposed to be ready to observe took place in February 1968. This put us on a tight schedule. Only one of our towed bodies, or "fish"—devices towed by a ship or a sub on a wire cable—had been completed on time. On the first day of operational test and evaluation it was launched and slid out of the launching tube into the deep blue sea. Someone had failed to secure the shackle to the towing cable. Another fish had to be transported to Pearl Harbor in time or the elaborately planned operation would have to be canceled. Carefully disguised as an irrelevant piece of hardware, the replacement fish was loaded on the first ship bound for the war zone in Vietnam via Hawaii, but the precious cargo was never unloaded. Instead it was mistakenly carried to Vietnam and offloaded on a dock there with no one to call for it and no one to care. Standard, expedited, and emergency measures for its recovery were to no avail. We could not reveal the significance of the cargo to anyone—and no one, in the midst of that war, with enough authority to retrieve it, could understand why this search would have priority over the war effort.

This was not the only time that intelligence constraints required that a mission be abandoned, sometimes with tragic consequences. On June 8, 1967, Israel launched an air attack against the USS *Liberty* during the Arab-Israeli Six Day War. All U.S. ships had been warned to vacate the war zone. But the intelligence ship *Liberty* had instructions to respond only to orders received through highly secure back-channel communications. The message sent via that channel was too slow in arriving and the *Liberty* was attacked with significant loss of American lives. To avoid repetition, a military officer in the Pentagon was authorized to make direct contact with the Joint Chiefs of Staff when petitioned to do so, if in his estimation immediate action at that level was justified in the interests of national security. I made that petition to try to retrieve our fish from Vietnam and was turned down. Undeterred, I contacted the most senior aide on the staff of the Joint Chiefs, who carried the message to the top, and a directive from the JCS to the commander of the armed forces in Vietnam produced the desired result. The fish was located and shipped to Hawaii in time for the operation.

The mission was not an intelligence success but the operation was not detected by our own forces present in the splash-down area observing Soviet naval activity. The technical defect was traced to the tow cable, whose length was more than twenty thousand feet. It was composed of many strands of wire of shorter length. These wires had welds that snapped when they were exposed to the high stresses of the towing machinery. It was impossible to recover the cable through the hawse pipe. It had to be retrieved by a difficult and dangerous operation on the surface of the sea.

Once again classification prevented us from convincing any manufacturer to produce a cable with seamless strands on short notice. The problem was tossed into the lap of Undersecretary of the Navy Robert Frosch. He contacted a company that made cables for elevators in skyscrapers. The chief executive was persuaded that the immediate production of this cable was in the national interest, so his company set to work. But the CEO asked Frosch if, at the very least, he could tell him what building required an elevator cable of that length. Frosch smiled and said, "All I can say is that it is a tall order."

The first of these cables was ready by January 1968, about the same time that the fish was retrieved from Vietnam. The *Halibut* deployed to the missile splash-down area. The technical problems that invariably plague the first deployment of a complex system were present in almost every subsystem. No missile hardware was found but *Halibut* was not detected. Finally the cable failed again and the ship returned to Pearl Harbor in April. I was present to meet it, to make an inventory of the malfunctions in order to modify the design, and to accompany a new cable and other spare parts that would be required to remedy defects and turn *Halibut* around to return to the silent fray. My mind harked back to the many days of frustration in World War II and to when the *Nautilus* returned from the first investigation of the cause of her near fatal damage with the mission unfulfilled.

There are many who would say that these extraordinary measures to ensure the early completion of *Halibut*'s operational capability were not justified in the interests of national security. But in May 1968 *Halibut* was operationally and technically qualified to carry out its mission. That mission would turn out to be providential. In April, the word had gone out that the Soviet fleet had lost a sub and didn't know where it was. Fortunately *Halibut* was now ready for the most significant intelligence coup of the century. But more on this in due course.

11

Humans As
Marine Mammals

Before *Halibut* could be brought onstream, in 1965 I was put in the middle of one of the most revolutionary and dangerous human performance programs ever conceived. This program, which would place an unprotected human as a free swimmer in the ocean to depths greater than one thousand feet, would also serve as a cover for covert programs of espionage that boggle the mind. How distinctly I remember that bleak September morning when I received the fateful call. The telephone is an inanimate object. Its ring should be the same regardless of the message of the call. But the mind seems to believe that the telephone will, on occasion, have a ring pregnant with meaning for things to come. It was just such a ring and it came from the Pentagon. I was informed that the Man-in-the-Sea program with its related SeaLabs was to be a part of the Deep Submergence Systems Project. The messenger had no time for argument, negotiation, or equivocation. The transfer of authority, responsibility, and accountability was immediate and the paperwork was in the works.

Man-in-the-Sea and its related SeaLabs program offered an unprecedented potential for intelligence gathering, with humans deployed for unlimited amounts of time in the deep ocean tapping cables or retrieving and salvaging sophisticated military hardware.

But those in high places had decided that the first priority was to get a team of wild adventurers under control before embarrassing national disasters occurred. It was in fact a bold stroke of management to initiate this program and allow those adventurers to turn vision into reality. The SeaLab program signaled the occupation of the sea by humans as marine mammals. Whatever the reason the Pentagon chose to reassign this program to DSSP, I now had a new and challenging mission.

As a child, I had immersed myself in the literature of the sea. Was it Jules Verne's wildly improbable fantasy of an undersea habitat named *Nautilus* in *Twenty Thousand Leagues Under the Sea* that had stirred my memory? More likely, it was Commander Edward Ellsberg's book, *On the Bottom*, describing the attempts to recover the sunken submarine S-51. My most vivid recollection was that of the unfortunate diver who suffered an explosive underwater compression. His body and bones were reduced to a mass of jelly compressed into his diver's helmet. The prospect of a repeat of that disaster made me reluctant to accept the responsibility of this extremely high-risk operation.

This experimental program was already well underway under the auspices of the Office of Naval Research. The first experiment in living undersea, SeaLab I, had been completed and SeaLab II was about to begin. The project had been initiated by naval medical captains George Bond, Walter Mazzone, and Robert Workman. My first order to this team was to keep doing what they were doing, but to keep me informed and notify me of any problems that arose that they could not resolve themselves. George Bond was transferred to my staff and was designated SP007. I was SP001. He savored the designation but I was completely unaware of the Ian Fleming novels that made these designations significant.

Among those involved in SeaLab II, only I was aware that the next demonstration project, SeaLab III, was to be a cover for the top secret development of an operational saturation diving capability for intelligence purposes. SeaLab II would be completed in November of 1965.

My thoughts turned quickly to recollections of my first detailed exposure to the service forces (the Navy term for noncombatant ships and facilities that support Navy operations). I was not exposed to them during my battleship days on the *New Mexico*, but I was in it up to the gunwales as soon as I went to work for the David Taylor Model Basin. My first assignment in September of 1951 was the development of techniques for sweeping Soviet-built pressure mines used by the North Koreans to blockade Wonsan Harbor.

The Korean conflict had started a year earlier and, as a reserve ensign in the Civil Engineering Corps, I had expected to be called back into service but was spared because of my combat experience in World War II. Therefore, like many Americans, I had taken only passing note of the disaster that befell our Navy at Wonsan Harbor during the early days of that war. The defense of South Korea had required a massive landing at Inchon and the installation of a follow-up pipeline of logistics and personnel that exists to this day. Wonsan was the port for this logistics flow. Prior to our takeover, the North Koreans had mined the harbor with sophisticated Soviet mines. Mine warfare is known as a measure-countermeasure game. The harbor is initially mined with unsophisticated mines, generally moored floating mines. When the invader introduces minesweepers to cope with this threat, more sophisticated mines are introduced. The first of these may be acoustic mines that are set off by the sound of the ships' machinery. These are swept by noise makers. Then follow the magnetic mines. These can be nullified by what are known as degaussing cables that reduce a ship's magnetic "signature" and by minesweepers towing a long high-intensity magnetic tail. Then may follow the most insidious mines of all, the pressure mines, which are activated by the pressure field of a ship passing above it. These are very difficult to sweep, and, if all else fails, divers are put in the water with mine-hunting gear to locate and disable the mines—an exceedingly difficult and dangerous endeavor.

When in September 1951 I went to work at the David Taylor Model Basin, I was assigned the task of developing new countermeasures for mines and in particular pressure mines. What I heard then about the Wonsan disaster was that two U.S. Navy minesweepers had been sunk with significant loss of life in the process of clearing the minefield. In desperation, the Navy put Underwater Demolition Teams in the water and in one weekend the harbor was cleared without fatalities. Some thirty years later, I would learn that this story was false. The minefield was indeed cleared by these valiant swimmers in short order but in the process a number of the divers had lost their lives or were permanently incapacitated by compression injury to the ears and brain.

My boss at DTMB at the time was Philip Eisenberg, who, like me, had a Ph.D. in ocean engineering. He also had had wartime experience in the Navy in the development of the first sweeps for pressure mines. When a ship traverses shallow water (forty to eighty feet) its bow wave creates a small positive pressure on the bottom at the bow; the hull displaces water and creates negative pressure on the bottom under the hull and the propeller completes the signature with a small positive pressure. The pressure-influenced mine senses this and when it registers negative pressure for ten seconds or more it actuates, exploding under the hull of the ship. Eisenberg's first attempts at sweeping these mines was to tow a large fabric bag, twenty feet in diameter and two hundred feet long, filled with water under pressure. This would simulate a ship and explode the mine, which would do no more harm than squeeze water out of the bag without rupture. The device had been tested in Scotland's Loch Ness and its classified name was the Loch Ness Monster.

My first assignment at the model basin was to test an anti–

pressure mine scheme invented by John Isaacs, the maverick genius of the Scripps Institution of Oceanography in La Jolla and chairman of the National Academy of Science's Mine Advisory Committee. The scheme didn't work but Eisenberg and I traveled to La Jolla to meet with Isaacs. He had a host of new approaches derived from his admirable ability to learn from his mistakes. He had been a fisherman with only a bachelor's degree in physics but he applied all he had learned to everything he did and saw the environment as a whole, generating theories that he later matched against those of his Ph.D. colleagues. I, for one, learned more about pressure mines in one night than in all the years preceding.

On our return to Washington, we initiated new programs utilizing hydrofoils or jets to interrupt ship signatures or, as would later prove invaluable, to project the following waves of a large high-speed ship over a minefield. Our brainstorming session paid off with solid results—new ideas that we could try out in the labs, ideas that would advance countermeasures against sophisticated mines for years to come.

During my minesweeping adventures in the 1950s, I worked with a remarkable collection of Navy mustangs. Now, once again I would have a chance to work with some of the most remarkable people in the "hardhat" diving Navy as I turned to the SeaLab assignment. Diving experience was the key—the essence of SeaLab was pushing the envelope of saturation diving. Bond, Mazzone, and Workman had conceived and developed this technique for humans to live in the sea as though they were marine mammals.

SP007 Bond first came to the Navy's attention as a submarine medical officer who had set the world record of 363 feet for a free ascent from a submarine. One means of escape from a sunken submarine is through an escape trunk. The trunk is located between two hatches on the submarine, one above the other. The escapee enters the trunk at atmospheric pressure and the lower hatch is closed behind him. Then the hatch above him is opened to the sea and he is suddenly pressurized at the depth at which the submarine lies. The sailor who tries a free ascent now has two major hazards to overcome. If he rises too fast, the air in his lungs will expand and rupture the blood vessels attached to the alveoli. Air will enter his bloodstream, lodge in his brain, and he will be permanently paralyzed or killed. If he rises too slowly, the air will exit his lungs. He will involuntarily inhale, and he will drown. The second hazard can be resolved by a device called a Momsen Lung. This is simply a bag placed over the head to contain the air that has been exhaled so that it can be inhaled again when involuntary breathing occurs. Bond made his deviceless ascent accompanied by a diver with a Momsen lung. Bond held his head back and let the air float out of his lungs as bubbles and he followed the bubbles to the surface. He acquired instant legendary status.

Bond had graduated from McGill Medical School in Montreal many years earlier and had been in the Army Inactive Reserve. He opened a clinic for the poor and underprivileged in Bat Cave, North Carolina, and soon he was featured on the network television program *This Is Your Life* as a kindly country doctor from the hills of Appalachia. From that time until as a full-fledged captain in the Navy Medical Corps he made his spectacular entrance rising from the deep, his life had been a mystery, which was the way he wanted it to be.

Captain Mazzone was something of a mystery himself. He had been an enlisted man in the submarine service during World War II, after which the Navy sponsored his studies in human physiology leading to a Ph.D. degree and a commission as a diving medical officer. It was one of our favorite roasts that he had always wanted to be a physician and that he had chosen sea duty as a diving medical officer because that would carry him on long voyages and permit him to legally perform emergency surgery. His skill was legendary, and many a sailor boasted a Captain Mazzone scar as a complement to his tattoos.

Working together, Mazzone and Bond had dreamed up the notion that humans could live at great depth as long as their bodies were saturated with gases—nitrogen or helium—under pressure. In this state, they could make no excursions to shallower depths and only carefully regulated descents to greater depths, which further required long periods to decompress. The SeaLab, an elaborate underwater habitat, would be their base. For the first time in history humans would actually live and work underwater for days and weeks at a time at depths from which divers working at the surface would be limited to periods of duration measured in minutes if at all. With the addition of Robert Workman, the three men formed a perfect team. Workman had a conventional and rigorous career in education and human development as a naval officer, medical officer, and hyperbaric physiologist, a specialist in how the human body behaves under the pressure of many atmospheres. It was Workman who kept a careful watch over the two extroverted innovators.

SeaLab I had been a public relations and technological success, though few knew that it had been marred by a near fatality resulting from a procedural lapse. SeaLab II was conducted near San Clemente Island off the coast of La Jolla at a depth of two hundred feet in extremely cold water. Although the project was now under my direction, there was no time to restructure and it was as disorganized as SeaLab I. The on-scene commander, a captain from the Office of Naval Research, was not required to be on the scene. Captain Bond, known as "Papa Topside," was the de facto leader of the expedition. As a medical officer he was not "qualified for command at sea." The crew aboard SeaLab II had been expanded from the previous complement of master divers from the Navy to include civilian scientists from the Scripps Institution. One of these scientists was a former surfing champion from Hawaii who would go on to a distinguished career as an ocean scientist. Another was Astronaut Scott Carpenter, who had been recruited for the saturation diving experiment as the SeaLab II "aquanaut/astronaut in residence" for a full thirty days. Had there been a disaster of any magnitude requiring a court of inquiry, the court would have found that the authority, responsibility, and accountability chain of command was not in place. Unaware and innocent heads at senior levels would have rolled.

The word was soon out that I was seeking a naval officer to serve as commanding officer for SeaLab III. It was not long before I received a call from Captain William Searle, the supervisor of salvage, recommending Commander "Black Jack" Tomsky for the job. I did not know Tomsky, although I was aware that he was a mustang master diver with extensive wartime and postwar experience, a seaman par excellence. He had all the credentials you could ask for except the one needed most for this job—experience in project management and research and development—and I rejected the suggestion.

A short time later, the telephone rang. It was Tomsky, who asked if we could meet. A few minutes later, a weather-beaten but fit-looking mariner appeared, decked out in all his ribbons.

"Dr. Craven," he asked after we shook hands, "what makes you think I am not qualified to be your project manager?"

I would hear other versions of this question, each made with the same self-assurance many times in the future. "Dr. Craven," Tomsky would say, "what makes you think that I am not holding a full house?" "Dr. Craven, what makes you think I haven't got an ace in the hole?" I didn't know it then, of course, but I had just met my match.

For now, I began to enumerate his deficiencies. To each, he countered convincingly. Once or twice he said, "I must confess I don't know much about that, but I can learn." He got the job but to be sure, I soon put him to the test. As a firm believer that innovation

requires both theory and practice, I told Tomsky that I needed familiarization with diving equipment but I did not have time for formal
certification.

"I think that can be arranged," he said, in a tone that I would
come to learn as meaning: "This will be interesting. We'll get it done
despite the rules and regulations and I will find out what kind of boss
I have."

"Are you in good health?" he asked. That was my medical exam.

"Can you swim?" That was my minimum proficiency exam.

"Report to the Experimental Diving Unit at 0800. Bring your
bathing suit."

I arrived as directed and was taken to the pool. Laid out before
me was every piece of scuba gear in the Navy inventory including
mixed gas. I was to put on each piece of gear and swim two laps. My
only instruction was to breathe continuously so that I would not get
a killer air embolism. A chief master diver swam alongside me with
one fist clenched. If I held my breath he would sock me one in the
stomach with a punch I would never forget. As Tomsky would often
say, "There is no learning in the second kick of a mule."

The morning soon passed and we discussed it all over a bite of
lunch. "Is that it?" I asked, believing I had passed with flying colors.

"Not quite."

Off to a pier on the Anacostia River. Arms and feet thrust into a
bulky rubberized suit. Heavy lead shoes anchored to the pier. The
suit secured, cinch straps tighten it to the body until the bass voice
turns tenor. The helmet is lowered over the head, the bolts secured.
A crane lifts the helpless diver into the air. Tools, nuts, and bolts are
thrust into his gloved hands. The diver is swung over the side and
lowered into the cold, worse than murky waters of the Anacostia. He
is given a task requiring the tools, nuts, and bolts, all of which fall out
of his hands and into the mud. There is no alternative. Honor and
leadership require that they be retrieved. Finally, the job done, the

diver is lifted from the water. His masculine voice restored, he thanks Tomsky for a wonderful instructive day. "Not so fast, Dr. Craven. We are going to compress you to two hundred feet." The compression and decompression must be rapid to minimize the possibility of the bends. First, one must learn to equalize the pressure in the oral and nasal cavity to eliminate the risk of puncturing the eardrum. How? "Swallow. If the pain is too great, let us know." So into the chamber, down to two hundred feet, back up to atmospheric pressure, and at last it's over. The next day I purchased my first set of fins and face mask and from then on I would snorkel or don scuba gear at a test site from time to time, but it would be fifteen years before I took the time to be certified and twenty before I felt fully qualified as a marine mammal.

Experience had to be complemented by knowledge. I would get lots of technically accurate sea stories from George Bond and Walter Mazzone, but my mentor was Dr. Chris Lambertson of Penn State University. He carried out the vast majority of theoretical and experimental studies in diving physiology and prepared the research programs for the SeaLabs. Philippe Cousteau, the son of Jacques, and Commander John Rawlings of Britain (later knighted for his contributions to diving physiology) were also members of the team.

Armed with literature, mentors, aquanauts, liaison with the world of Jacques Cousteau, and a project manager with a lifetime of experience of command at sea for unanticipated missions, I was ready to establish a program leading to an operational capability for saturation diving in the broad ocean.

My very first decision as Man-in-the-Sea project manager concerned the short- and long-range goals for the operational depth. Limits were automatically set by the geophysical characteristics of the ocean and by the two-and-twenty rule employed for other components of the total system. The two-and-twenty rule was based on the fact that a 2,000-foot depth capability gave access to most of the significant continental shelves of the world, whereas 20,000-foot depth capability gave access to almost all of the deep ocean bottom. There are marine mammals that can dive to the very deepest parts of the ocean, so in theory there ought to be a way for humans to do the same.

The realistic limits for saturation diving were set by the effects of the breathing gas on human physiology. At a depth of two hundred feet the use of air results in nitrogen narcosis—a peaceful and often fatal slumber induced by air, which, being compressed, is enriched with both nitrogen and oxygen under pressure. A lungful of air at ten atmospheres (340 feet) has ten times as much oxygen and nitrogen as it does on the surface—and the richness of the oxygen can become toxic with prolonged use. Instead of air, SeaLab II successfully used a mixture of helium and oxygen. Tests on land indicated that helium-oxygen could be used to a depth of six hundred feet with excursions to eight hundred feet. (The operational depths now reached by U.S. Navy divers are classified but the French have publicized successful dives to three thousand feet utilizing a hydrogen-oxygen mixture with a small amount of nitrogen diluent to suppress tremors. It would now appear that the two thousand to three thousand feet useful continental shelf limit is obtainable if not obtained.)

In search of means to go still deeper, we supported studies of fluid breathing at Duke University. Fluid breathing would be sensationalized in the special effects of the film *The Abyss*, but it is in fact possible to completely flood the air cavities of a mammal with a fluid that is then "breathed." The fluid is filled with oxygen in solution, which moves from the flooded lung into the arterial system. As a result there are no additional dissolved gases in the body regardless of the depth. Mammals so flooded can be pressurized at depths up to several thousand feet without fear of the bends or embolism. One of the problems in the application of this technique to humans is an inability to eliminate the carbon dioxide. It would require resurfacing every half hour or placing a shunt in the veins that would filter the blood through a dialysis system. With such a modification, the human could indeed become a full marine mammal equivalent to the whale, which dives to the deepest depth on a single breath hold (although the whale's lungs are not flooded, they are compressed into a bony structure in its body). Humans may yet do the whale one better. With advances in bionic surgery the day that the two-and-twenty rule is met by the human as a marine mammal, truly at one with the sea, may not be too far away.

Once the operating depth capability (still classified but well in excess of 600 feet) had been determined, the heart of this application of saturated gas technology that would give us long-duration deep diving capability was designated, as I have mentioned, the Mark II Deep Diving System, jointly developed by the Supervisor of Salvage and DSSP. The Mark II system consisted of a deck decompression chamber complex and personnel transfer capsules for transporting divers and diver suits and equipment from the chamber to the dive site. The transition would be made from SeaLab II to SeaLab III and then to the classified program in the black (as covert programs are known whose very existence is classified). It was this unknown program that would furnish the saturation divers for the missions to recover weapons from Soviet ranges, to intercept communications from Soviet cables, and a host of others still untold.

SeaLab III was plagued with strange failures at the very start of operations that ultimately led to the mysterious death of an aquanaut. The site, again off San Clemente Island, had been readied several months earlier. Two barges were moored in close proximity and the command and control center was established on the largest of these barges, along with the deck decompression chamber and two personnel transfer capsules.

Each personnel transfer capsule, the PTC, was capable of transferring up to ten divers at the pressure of depth from the decompression chamber to the dive site in a sphere-shaped carrier. The bottom of the sphere had a hatch for exit and entry, either into the open ocean or into an underwater habitat fitted with a hatch with which to mate. On return, the PTC would reconnect to the deck decompression chamber. The divers would transfer and begin the long decompression process.

Around the outside of the sphere were bottles of helium and oxygen to provide the breathing mixture appropriate to the depth of submergence. Inside the sphere were canisters of baralime, a material that absorbs carbon dioxide. From time to time, these PTCs would be "soak-tested" for leaks by closing all hatches and valves and immersing them in the ocean for twenty-four hours or more. I would visit the site routinely when returning to Washington from trips to Hawaii for other missions. On one such occasion, I arrived at a moment when a PTC had just been recovered from the ocean and had been found flooded with seawater, which had destroyed all of its internal electronic equipment. Examination of the capsule's valves and hatches indicated that they were in perfect order and a soak test proved it. An investigation was immediately launched by a senior officer on the DSSP staff. He concluded that a valve had been positioned incorrectly and the culprit had covered it up as soon as the PTC had broken clear of the surface or while still submerged. There was no time for repair before the scheduled start of a series of operations in which aquanauts were ready to be transported to the SeaLab, and the project director decided to proceed with only one PTC.

Some two weeks later, by coincidence, I returned to the site during the initial operations. Anticipating news about them, I boarded the little blue seaplane that would carry me to San Clemente Island. I was greeted at the landing with dismay and grief. Aquanaut Barry Cannon was dead.

The sequence of events, which was later to occupy a court of inquiry, was as follows: The first two aquanauts had been carried down to a depth of six hundred feet, where they were to swim to the SeaLab and prepare it for occupation by another four divers, who had remained in the PTC. There had been a concern about gas leaking from the SeaLab. The packing in the laboratory's valves that opened on the sea, it was believed (and later proved), had been installed in the wrong direction. The first two divers were to repair the valves before the full contingent would enter the laboratory for a fifteen-day stay. In full view of the underwater television camera installed outside the lab, one of the two aquanauts, Cannon, had suddenly been seen to go limp. The other aquanaut promptly initiated buddy breathing but got no response. He quickly towed the unconscious diver back to the PTC where CPR was administered. It was too late.

The divers, now saturated at a depth of six hundred feet, were returned to the deck decompression chamber. They would have to undergo a decompression that would last a week. Their immediate task was to examine Cannon's gear. The cause of death was obvious. The baralime required to scrub carbon dioxide was missing from his canister.

But now, with the repair mission aborted, the SeaLab was leaking gas and would soon be flooded. Millions of dollars of experimental equipment would be destroyed. A simple solution would have been to send down another two divers and have them operate SeaLab's ballast system and return it to the surface, where it could be repaired and redeployed. There were many volunteers, among them Philippe Cousteau and Scott Carpenter.

The medical people, however, were against sending anyone back to the lab, even though the cause of Cannon's death appeared to be known. Commander Tomsky, in charge of the operation, agreed with the doctors. He did not believe that the fatality was in any way connected to the leak, but he recognized that the recovery operation was risky, and that everyone was under emotional stress. He knew he had to find another way to save the SeaLab in a race against time. The senior naval officer in the chain of command had been ordered to return to Washington and had done so. I was now the senior officer present and in a position to head up an advisory group to make recommendations to Tomsky. Captain Gus Eble, from the DSSP staff, who had won the Silver Star for his rescue of crewmen from the submarine *Darter*, formed the core of this group.

The problem we faced was salvaging the SeaLab with equipment available at the site. The lab was leaking a nonflammable mixture of helium and oxygen. In a few hours the supply of that gas would be used up. It would then be possible to shift to compressed air, except that the mixture would now be rich with oxygen under pressure and therefore explosive, ignitable by a spark (from, for example, a short generated in a battery that became flooded with seawater) inside the lab. The air supply was also limited but could be replenished if a submarine were dispatched to the site. This was immediately arranged but the submarine would not arrive for many hours. The salvage would have to be accomplished inside about ten hours or not at all.

Now that the time element was known, the major problem was the lack of a lift capability to hoist the SeaLab to the surface. It had been deployed with a fifty-ton-lift floating crane that had by now been returned to the Long Beach Naval Shipyard nearly one hundred miles away. Moreover, the additional force required to break free of the mud on the anchor was unknown. As for the onboard equipment, there was a winch with a length of cable on the barge alongside the command barge but it was not in a serviceable position. The cable that had been used to deploy the SeaLab was in place and tied to a buoy. We concluded that a salvage was possible with certain modifications of the equipment we had. It would require two sheave installations, one to bend the winch wire at 90 degrees in the horizontal plane so that it could be located over the lab and a second to bend the wire 90 degrees in the vertical so that it could be spliced into the SeaLab cable.

A search of the barges produced the sheaves and pillow blocks, and the welders took up the task of making the apparatus. A major problem now appeared. The maximum stress on the winch cable, as rated by the manufacturer, was insufficient. Eble and I made separate calculations of the expected real strength of the cable, based on our knowledge of the holding power of such materials. Both calculations agreed. A safety consideration arose. If the cable were to snap, it would present a serious hazard to the winch operator. We estimated where and how the cable might snap and Tomsky decided that the risk was sufficiently small. A major positive factor was the presence of the Westinghouse submarine *DeepStar*. It could observe the lab from underwater and signal when it had broken free from the muddy bottom. A step-by-step plan was now worked out.

It was agreed that if the winch's dynamometer, a device that measures the load on the cable, reached a certain value and the SeaLab had not yet broken free, we would terminate. If instead the lift were successful, the lab would be raised to a depth of one hundred feet, where divers could be deployed to blow ballast and bring it to the surface. With procedure established, the race against the clock to build the rig and attempt the salvage was in full swing. The first thing that Tomsky did was to take a time-out and get two hours sleep to sharpen his wits. This ability to act on a self-evaluation during the heat of an operation was one of his finest qualities. He had been through crisis situations before and each experience had added to the grit needed to face the next without the crushing fear of failure or its consequences.

The hours passed. The nonflammable gas ran out and we switched to air. The submarine heading our way reported its position. It would be too close to call whether it would arrive before our air supply was exhausted.

As the drama unfolded, a more sinister development was occurring on the command barge. Captain Mazzone, who had the responsibility of monitoring the condition of the five men being decompressed, suddenly noticed that the mixture going into their breathing masks in the chamber was overly rich in oxygen. He found the problem. A valve from an oxygen tank was open when it should have been closed. He closed it. A short time later he found it open again. He closed it again and tagged it with a wire placed in the valve that would break if the valve were opened again. An hour later the tag was broken. It was closed and retagged and Tomsky assigned a guard to watch over the decompression chamber for the remainder of the weeklong decompression. At the time Tomsky did not reveal this situation to anyone involved with the salvage and we were unaware of the additional stress this had placed on him.

It did not cloud his judgment. When the submarine arrived—just before the air supply was about to run out—Tomsky decided to go ahead with the lift, recognizing that problems might develop in the interface between the submarine and the SeaLab.

The strain on the winch cable continued to build up and soon the dynamometer indicated that the maximum stress was being applied. Suddenly, we saw that we had overlooked an essential factor. The freeboard—the distance between the deck of the barge and the surface of the water—was diminishing. The strain on the cable was pulling the barge down. A few more inches and the water would be pouring over the deck, flooding the barge's compartments. But there was no time to worry. The cable was now approaching the load limit, and Tomsky was about to call it all off when the cry came from the *DeepStar:* "She's broken free!" The load decreased swiftly. The lab was lifted to the hundred-foot depth. A few minutes later it broke the surface.

All of us were choked with the involuntary sob that accompanies the end of a battle won but lives lost. "Once more unto the breach, dear friends, once more."

It was midnight and there were cleanup tasks but Tomsky and I began our postmortem analysis. We agreed that there had to have been multiple acts of sabotage. This was the only plausible explanation of the failure of the PTC, the absence of baralime in Cannon's canister, and the persistent opening of the oxygen valve to the breathing masks of the men in the decompression chamber.

Back in Washington, I conducted my own investigation, which included consultation with SeaLab psychiatrists. One of them identified a suspect, someone possibly afflicted with psychiatric problems that could have given rise to this murderous behavior. We agreed, however, that it would be a violation of that person's privacy rights to implicate him in specific acts without due process. So all of the evidence was turned over to the Office of Naval Intelligence.

A court of inquiry was established to examine the Cannon incident. Named as parties of interest were Tomsky, as commanding officer, and Chief Paul Wells, the diving chief who had certified the presence of baralime in Cannon's canister. George Bond petitioned to be a party of interest as well, apparently to assuage feelings of guilt. It was granted, but the court would find no fault with his behavior. Naval intelligence reported that there was insufficient evidence for concluding that sabotage had played any role in the SeaLab disaster. Wells, a thirty-year man with an unblemished record and one of the most upstanding chiefs in the naval establishment, took sole responsibility. The lethal absence of the crucial substance (baralime) that would have purged carbon dioxide from Cannon's equipment—in spite of clear documentation recording that Wells had dutifully filled the scrubbing canister in that system with baralime—had happened on his watch.

The case coincided with the aftermath of an unrelated event of national embarrassment for the Navy. Another court of inquiry was looking into the high-profile capture by the North Koreans of the spy ship USS *Pueblo*. There were many who felt that in the SeaLab disaster a finding of sabotage would be an additional public relations fiasco for the Navy. In any event, the incident was "resolved" by a letter of reprimand issued to Commander Tomsky and Chief Wells. Both men resigned from the Navy.

I urged Tomsky to seek a court-martial to clear his name, but he preferred not to further discomfit the Navy, and he regarded the outcome as no more than a battle injury incurred in his service to his country. SeaLab III would be considered a failure, acknowledged as such by the Navy itself. The SeaLab III crews were reassigned to Panama City, Florida, a most unlikely venue for saturation diving. Papa Topside, George Bond, saturation diving's most fabled pioneer, would soon die in obscurity.

But the highest echelons of the Navy concluded that saturation diving developed during the SeaLab cover program had been successfully demonstrated as an operational capability for underwater espionage. Saturation diving would be implemented as an essential component of the repertoire of the submarines *Halibut* and *Seawolf* when divers were deployed from them for long-duration missions on the seabed. A secret training facility would be established at a still classified location. Black Jack Tomsky would be called back into the service to help start the classified effort—his pride and reputation eminently restored by the fact that, at the time, there were only five officers in the Navy who had been called back for active duty. Four were admirals, graduates of the Naval Academy. One was a mustang with a letter of reprimand.

12

The Fisherman's Friend

On January 17, 1966, a B-52 bomber and a refueling airplane of the Strategic Air Command collided in midair while crossing the Spanish coastline over a fishing village called Palomares. Our nation's strategic posture at that time required that we keep a significant number of aircraft in the sky with fully capable nuclear weapons. The planes were deployed within range of the Soviet Union. When and if directed by the President of the United States they could penetrate air defenses and deliver the weapons to targets preassigned by the Strategic Air Command in Omaha. I don't know about the precise details of the communication links between the bomber, Omaha, and the Pentagon, but the Air Force must have known within minutes of the accident that one of its strategic bombers was down. Secretary of Defense McNamara and President Johnson must have been immediately notified. Their first concern, of course, was the condition of the crew, how many survivors, how many injured, how many lost, and notification of next of kin. But their overwhelming national and international concern was the fate of the nuclear weapons on board the aircraft.

The first to be aware of the accident were the citizens of Palomares. The sounds of the collision focused all eyes on the skies. As fate would have it the bomb bay was ruptured and four of the most powerful thermonuclear weapons that mankind has ever produced came raining down on this peaceful village. Debris of every kind came out of the sky and many parachutes could be seen. It appeared at first that all the bombs had crashed into the agricultural fields of the community. The citizens were terrified at the thought that one or more might detonate and they legitimately feared approaching any of the weapons because of radioactive contamination.

Six men parachuted into the sea and survived. Another survivor, badly injured because he could not detach himself from his ejection seat, landed on the shore. This was headline news around the world.

In an emergency meeting of the National Security Council, President Johnson directed McNamara to take personal charge of every aspect of the Palomares catastrophe. Ordinarily, in the absence of nuclear weapons or casualties to foreign nationals, this would be a problem for the Joint Chiefs of Staff that would be immediately delegated to the Air Force. But in this instance the direct line of responsibility for the recovery and cleanup of the nuclear weapons was assigned to Jack Howard, the deputy secretary of defense for nuclear matters.

His was an awesome burden. He was charged with keeping track of all of America's nuclear bombs. He had to ensure that every single weapon was under the command and control of the President. He was also required to monitor every single nuclear weapon possessed by other nations and report to the Secretary of Defense and the President any situation in which a foreign nuclear weapon was not in fact under a sovereign state's command and control. Moreover, he was responsible for locating any of the world's nuclear weapons lost on land or at sea and developing techniques and methods for their recovery or disposal. Finally, it was his task to identify and locate any nuclear weapon in the hands of terrorists and to develop strategies and techniques to seize or otherwise neutralize such weapons. If the design, development, and deployment of a nuclear weapon with the intent to use it was a sin of humanity, then Jack Howard was charged with the prevention of the sins, not only of his nation, but of the whole world.

Howard's attention was directed to the recovery of the bombs and securing of radioactive areas. Although he knew that these bombs had been designed fail-safe and could not detonate, the world would not believe this until the United States could demonstrate that it had them in its possession and under its control. It was three days before the Air Force realized that only three bombs had hit the land and that the fourth had fallen in the Mediterranean. It was time to call in the Navy.

When faced with the dilemma of whom to contact in the Navy, Jack Howard had the security clearances that were required to know that I was involved in a project to develop systems to find and recover strategic hardware from the ocean floor. On Saturday, January 22, the first call he made to the Navy was to me. Craven, he said, I have lost a nuclear bomb and I want you to find it. I told him that I was not sure that this was the job of the Deep Submergence Systems Project but I would see to it that the right people in the Navy would carry out his wishes.

I immediately contacted Captain Bill Searle, the supervisor of salvage of the Navy whom I had worked with on SeaLab. Searle was a graduate of the Naval Academy whose eyesight had not met the requirements for an unrestricted officer of the line. He had been relegated to the underwater diving world, where everyone is more or less equally blind. He was an Academy graduate in an undersea world of mustangs. Before long he was more than one of them, he was their leader.

There is no marine occupation more dangerous than salvage. The thing to be salved, to use the Navy's word, has generally been abandoned in a storm in coastal waters. The cause is usually associated with a collision at sea, a fire at sea, a storm at sea, and/or a grounding on a reef. It is also competitive. Once a ship or its cargo has been lost or abandoned, any maritime entity is entitled to engage in its salvage. The first to tie on a line is the salver. The salver's reward is a function of the speed and promptness of his response, the peril to which he has been exposed, and his skill in the recovery effort. In addition to seamanship skills, an intimate knowledge of the law of the sea is required. In this instance, if the bomb had landed in waters outside Spain's declared territorial sea the Soviets would be entitled to recover it and hold it for its salvage claim. Indeed, once they were aware that we were searching, they organized their own search outside the twelve-mile limit. For this reason the SupSalv must be prepared on a moment's notice to gain control of any U.S. property that has been lost or abandoned and is subject to the laws of salvage. The supervisor of salvage is the only naval officer authorized to commit government funds beyond those authorized by Congress. Without such authorization SupSalv would lose out in almost every salvage competition. Bill Searle never lost out.

I told Bill I had this nifty salvage job for him—I just didn't quite know where the bomb was. He reminded me that he didn't have the capability for finding lost objects—finding things was my department. I explained that we had not had time to develop search doctrine or equipment. All that the Navy had were minesweepers and minesweeping doctrine and his salvage and rescue ships. None of them was really equipped for this task.

We fenced back and forth until we realized that SupSalv and DSSP were all that the Navy had, that the Navy now had a mission that required that we go, and that we would have to go with what we had and carry on with skill and dispatch. He had the authority and the money, my staff had the know-how and the ability to collect equipment that could be pressed into service. We agreed to work together and we volunteered our service to the Chief of Naval Opera-

tions. On Monday, January 24, the Chief of Naval Operations established a Technical Advisory Group for the recovery project now
called. SalvOps Med. Admiral Swanson headed the group; Searle
and I were the driving forces. The oceanographer Admiral Odale
"Muddy" Waters and former oceanographer Admiral Stephan, who
had chaired the *Thresher* panel that had established DSSP, completed the group. This was a team that was small, competent, and
could act on a moment's notice. It was indeed already in action.

The criticality of the loss of the weapon was such that the Navy
took action to secure the area and to establish an at-sea task force for
the conduct of the operation. Admiral Guest, an aviator, was put in
command and he placed his flag in the cruiser *Boston*. With permission of the Spanish government he established a security zone
around the area in which the bomb might be located. By virtue of international law he could not establish such a zone in international
waters twelve miles out to sea, nor could he prevent the Soviet
Union from carrying out search and salvage operations in the international waters.

The possibility that the weapon could legally end up in the
hands of a foreign power was a matter of great national concern. Secretary McNamara, understandbly unfamiliar with the nuances of the
design, development, and control of nuclear weapons, would have
been briefed by Jack Howard. He would have learned that the design
of a thermonuclear weapon is beyond the capability of any but the
most technically advanced nations. Obtaining an advanced weapon
such as ours would provide a sophisticated enemy with precise details
of design and materials that would otherwise require billions of dollars of research and development to produce.

McNamara, absorbing this new knowledge, apparently viewed
the seriousness of the possibility that the Soviets might recover the
bomb in terms of his bean-counting frame of reference. To underline
his sense of just how seriously it should be taken, he put a price tag on

it, just the way you'd put a sticker price on a Ford sedan. He stated publicly that the bomb was worth $2 billion. The number would return to haunt him.

Since the Soviets already had thermonuclear weapons, what did it matter if someone else recovered the lost bomb? The political satirist Art Buchwald caught the implications immediately in a column entitled "Move Over World We've Got the Bomb." In it he speculated about the behavior of a tribe of hippies who recovered the bomb and employed it to blackmail the world into nuclear disarmament. What if terrorists recovered the bomb? The lost hydrogen bomb in terrorist hands could be every bit as destabilizing to world peace as the bomb in the hands of the Soviets. A credible threat to destroy any major city in the world could destabilize the balance of terror if it were couched in terms that suggested that the terrorism was authorized by a major nuclear power.

When Admiral Guest arrived on the scene, he asked for advice with respect to the composition of the ships, equipment, and operational procedures that he would need for the conduct of his mission. Before the Technical Advisory Group was asked the question I recognized that there was not even a search doctrine or operational plan for such a mission.

A few weeks earlier, I had attended a lecture by Professor Howard Raiffa of Harvard on the esoteric subject of Bayes's subjective probability. The lecture itself was not esoteric at all. It was based on Raiffa's experiences at the racetrack. He noted that the betting odds on horses were determined by the bets placed by bettors before the start of the race. After much research, he discovered that bettors accurately predict the odds on a horse winning a race. Six-to-one-odds horses won once every six times. One-hundred-to-one-odds horses won once every hundred times. Even-odds-on horses won half the time and so on. Based on these odds he could successfully predict the correct odds not only for win but for place and show—the horses that would finish second or third, respectively—through the mathematics of probability. The probability equations were developed by Thomas Bayes centuries earlier, but the concept as applied to operational analysis and game theory was Raiffa's brainchild.

So on the evening of January 24, I enlisted the help of my most cooperative junior assistant and we worked through the night. As a result of telephone calls to various experts and on-site witnesses, we crafted six scenarios. First, the lost bomb had remained in the bomber and would be found in the bomber debris; second, the bomb was mixed with the collision debris and would be found along the path of the collision; third, the bomb had been separated at the point of collision and had fallen free; fourth, one of the parachutes attached to the bomb had deployed and the wind carried it out to sea; fifth, both of the bomb's parachutes had deployed and the wind carried it further out to sea; sixth, none of the above. Shortly afterward we added a seventh scenario entitled "The Fisherman's Sighting." We did this because of a claimed sighting of a parachute entering the water, a sighting made by a very fortunate fisherman. This scenario was almost identical to the single parachute scenario.

The fisherman in question was one Francisco Ortiz, the most senior fisherman in Palomares. He claimed to have seen a parachute falling into the water with the "entrails of a man attached." With a certain shrewdness, he had then contracted with the Air Force to assist in the location operations. With the unerring accuracy of a coastal zone navigator he was able to return again and again to the point where the parachute and its attachment were seen entering the sea. With even greater perspicacity, Ortiz did not waive his right of salvage in exchange for this information.

My colleague and I plotted the probable location of the bomb for each scenario together with the probable dispersion area around that location. Employing an assorted number of experts, we bet on the most probable scenario. Then we plotted weighted probability distri-

butions, added them together and adjusted the total field of probability to make the total probability that the bomb was somewhere in
Palomares waters equal to one.

We immediately sent this probability map to the commander in
the field with instructions to search in the areas of highest probability. It was continuously modified on the basis of the searches that
were conducted. I called in Robert Wagner, a theoretical mathe-
matician involved in operational analyses, and outlined the technique that we had instituted. We placed him under contract to
modify the search plans to insure that they were mathematically rigorous and would stand up under academic scrutiny in any review of
the operations.

These scenarios gave us three major search areas. One was the
debris field spread out along the linear track of the aircraft flight following the collision. This debris was in relatively shallow water that
could be reached by mine-hunting sonar, by explosive ordnance disposal, and underwater diving teams out to a depth of eighty feet. The
SeaLab II team of saturation divers, in one of its first major missions,
was among those deployed and in theory could conduct underwater
search to a depth of two hundred feet.

The second search area was the location that the bomb would
have reached if one parachute had deployed. This was the same as
the fisherman's sighting but was independently arrived at. Unfortunately, this point lay over a deep canyon with steep side walls that
was filled with tailings from a Palomares lead mine—the tailings
were located at the head of the underwater canyon. There was no
equipment immediately deployable that could operate in this cre-
vasse.

The third area encompassed the site where the bomb would have
been if two parachutes had deployed. Some indication of this location was derived from three crash survivors who had parachuted into
the water. They had been carried out to sea, one to a point nine miles

from shore. The probability of the two-parachute deployment was small and located the bomb between nine and twelve miles from shore. This area was symbolically searched by mine-hunting ships with side-looking sonar and mine-hunting sonar. The search was symbolic, since this gear was optimized for floating or moored mines that were anchored on the seabed and was not effective in finding objects lying on the bottom or buried in the mud. The Soviets deployed mine hunters outside the twelve-mile limit in the hope that the bomb had made it to international waters. If we had searched outside the twelve-mile limit, this would have given the Soviets hope that their own search was more than symbolic.

The general understanding of the search problem, the equipment needed, and the areas to be searched were established early on by the Technical Advisory Group to give guidance to Admiral Guest in the search operation. Because of the national importance attached to recovering the bomb, the task force was probably excessive and hence unwieldy. The search and recovery operations would eventually involve more than three thousand Navy personnel, twenty-five Navy ships, four research or commercial ships, four research or commercial small submersibles, and a host of civilian research and contractor personnel.

Admiral Guest had expected a flotilla of advanced submarine search and recovery equipment to be at his disposal. Instead he was confronted with an array of small, uncoordinated research and development teams whose expertise was limited to their individual equipment. The disciplined conduct of a well-organized search was impossible and the equipment needed for search in the high-probability area was slow in arriving. Like the proverbial drunk looking for his car keys under the streetlight because that was the only place he could see, the only coordinated military activities at the site took place nine to twelve miles out at sea where the bomb almost certainly would not be.

The acquisition, rental, transportation, and deployment of this equipment was my responsibility. Pursuing a chance to establish its credentials in the deep submergence recovery field, the Woods Hole Oceanographic Institution volunteered the services of the mini-submarine *Alvin*, a deep submersible sponsored by the Office of Naval Research and named after the much beloved ocean scientist Allyn C. Vine. Woods Hole proposed airlifting the *Alvin*, expecting to have it in the water in a matter of days. I immediately accepted the offer.

At the same time, I arranged for the participation of the Reynolds Aluminum Company's *Aluminaut*. The Ship System Command had rejected this deep-diving, spacious submersible capable of descents greater than 10,000 feet precisely because it was made of aluminum—a material notoriously susceptible to corrosion cracking in seawater. The *Aluminaut* designers, anticipating this objection, had covered the hull with multiple coats of different-colored paint so that any scratch or scrape would be easily visible and repaired. But Ship System Command declared it out of bounds to naval officers because the boat was neither certified nor certifiable. For my part, I had full confidence in the *Aluminaut*, having gained familiarity in a test dive the previous year off Miami at 10,000 feet, setting my personal deep submergence record. Public perception of the search for the bomb was that there was great danger of exposure to radiation and that its recovery would be an act of heroism on the part of the crew. It would therefore look like a display of cowardice, it seemed to me, if there were no naval officers on board the *Aluminaut* during recovery. I appealed to the Secretary of the Navy, who overruled Ship System Command, certifying the submarine for Navy use for this operation. Overruled but underwhelmed, the bureaucracy, true to its everlasting nature, prevailed. The *Aluminaut* would be a hero of the operation, but there would be no naval officers on board.

The heroism, however, was long in coming. Both *Alvin* and *Alu-*

minaut did not arrive at Palomares until mid-February, a month after the bomb was lost. By this time there was great frustration on the part of Admiral Guest, the Chief of Naval Operations, the Secretary of Defense, and, most of all, the President. Deteriorating relations with the citizens of Palomares compounded the festering crisis. The three bombs that had landed on the ground had spread a great deal of radiation over local farmland. The town's demand for compensation was high, hiked by insistence that the soil be removed, taken out to sea, and replaced by imported, higher-quality soil.

Matters worsened when Admiral Guest ordered curfew for task force personnel and placed some areas of the town off limits. This did not ingratiate him with the shopkeepers, hoteliers, and tavern owners. One of the SeaLab saturation divers also took a dim view of the regulations, and one evening got very drunk, made inappropriate advances to a tavern owner's daughter, and when rebuffed smashed the furniture. He was apprehended by the Military Police, and the Air Force hushed up the tavern keeper with compensation paid under one of his few still standing tables. This did not let the aquanaut off the hook. A major court-martial was averted, however, when the military psychologists attached to my staff concluded that the effects of saturation diving on human behavior were still unknown, and the offender was permitted to resign "for the good of the service."

In the meantime, in order to satisfy the daily inquiries by President Johnson, the first of a number of memoranda were prepared for him with an estimate of the probability that the bomb would be found as a function of the intensity and duration of the continuing search. Neither the President nor Admiral Guest was satisfied with our explanations.

When *Alvin* and *Aluminaut* finally arrived, they were assigned to search the ravine where the bomb had probably settled. Visual search in this area proved effective and the bomb was located by *Alvin* on the fifteenth of March. Nearly sixty days had elapsed between the loss and the location.

Meanwhile back in Washington before the bomb was located, President Johnson's impatience, not to mention his fury, had known no bounds. He had demanded a plan that would guarantee the recovery. He was told that the search doctrine was the best that could be had, but the President had insisted on an immediate review with an eye to a new approach. High-powered academics from Cornell, Harvard, and MIT were put to work reviewing the search doctrine. By this time Wagner Associates, Robert Wagner's firm, had constructed a mathematical model whose complexity defied understanding by mere mortals. On the morning of March 15, 1966, the academic review committee affirmed the beauty and rigor of the search doctrine and went to lunch. On their return they learned that the bomb had been found.

The search was over—or so we thought—and now it was time for recovery to begin. *Alvin's* staying power over the bomb was limited, the water was murky and her navigation equipment inadequate to insure a quick return to the location, so she was relieved by *Aluminaut*. For twenty-four cold miserable hours the *Aluminaut* baby-sat the bomb. The cost of *Aluminaut* and her transport by the floating dry dock *Fort Snelling* was now more than justified. *Alvin* returned the next day with navigation aids so it could return again. It became obvious that *Alvin* could not engage the weapon itself without the danger of a hopeless entanglement with the bomb's parachute.

It had already been decided that no public announcement would be made until the bomb was safely aboard ship. Unfortunately, a reporter had gotten word of the find and headlines around the world announced the discovery as though it was a recovery. A rig was now constructed aboard the task force flagship. It had three lines that *Alvin* was to attach to the parachute shroud. *Alvin* succeeded in attaching only one when concern that the sub would become entangled caused a halt. The lift was attempted with this one line, but it snapped and the bomb slipped down the slope to an unknown location. It would take nine days to find it again, some three hundred feet below its original resting place.

In the competition to enter the deep ocean recovery game, the Naval Ordnance Test Station had developed one of the first robotic devices to recover test torpedoes that had sunk to the bottom of the sea. It was called a Cable-Controlled Underwater Recovery Vehicle, or CURV. Operating on the two-and-twenty rule (that what you wanted to get at was either going to be reached at 2,000-foot continental shelf depth or 20,000-foot ocean floor depth), CURV had been designed for a maximum depth of 2,000 feet. It was made ready for recovery, but it was momentarily stymied when the bomb was rediscovered below the device's operational depth. At the request of the Technical Advisory Group it was modified for 3,000-foot operation and its claw was modified to fit the diameter of the bomb. It arrived at the site aboard the USS *Petrel* at the end of March. Its turn had come. It was lowered in the water but got inextricably entangled in the parachute. Finally, CURV, the parachute, the recovery cables, and, at long last, the elusive bomb were hauled aboard the *Petrel* in a tangled mess. The thermonuclear weapon was recovered.

There was a big celebration in the Palomares town square. Almost every local citizen received an award, most notably Señor Ortiz, the fisherman. The operational task force was disbanded and the Technical Advisory Group dissolved. The Americans went home. All was well that ended well—but not yet.

A few months later, Señor Ortiz appeared at the First District Federal Court building in New York His lawyer, Herbert Brownell, Attorney General of the United States under President Dwight Eisenhower, accompanied him. They were initiating an action in admiralty for the salvage award to which Señor Ortiz was unquestionably entitled. It is customary maritime law that the person who identifies the location of a ship to be salved has the right to a salvage award if that identification leads to a successful recovery. The amount is nominal, usually 1 or 2 percent, sometimes a bit more, of the intrinsic value to the owner of the thing salved. But the thing salved off Palomares was a hydrogen bomb, the same bomb valued by no less an authority than the Secretary of Defense at $2 billion— each percent of which is, of course, $20 million. Ortiz and Brownell were only asking for their due.

The Air Force legal staff, suddenly seeking an education in salvage law, flocked to my office. Surely the Wagner mathematical model would demonstrate that the fisherman's sighting played no role in the recovery of the bomb. Sorry, it most assuredly did. The case was settled out of court. I never learned for how much. Presumably Señor Ortiz became a wealthy man, and perhaps like a mythical figure of the day, learned to stop worrying and love the bomb.

13

The Tide of Destiny

There is a tide in the affairs of men,
Which, taken at the flood, leads on to fortune;
Omitted, all the voyage of their life
Is bound in shallows and in miseries.

—William Shakespeare, *Julius Caesar*

There is indeed a destiny that shapes all our ends—and it brought together two very different men, both of whose lives were profoundly influenced by the relentless force of an ever changing sea.

The course of Admiral Hyman George Rickover's life would intersect with mine in 1965 in a fashion that I as SPO Chief Scientist could never have imagined. On April 18 of that year President Lyndon Johnson announced that the Atomic Energy Commission and the Department of the Navy had undertaken the development of a nuclear-powered deep submergence research and ocean engineering vehicle. Two weeks before that announcement, in early April, I had been contacted by Admiral Dennis Wilkinson, who reminded me of a study that I had conducted in connection with the Advanced Sea-Based Deterrent Program. It was a feasibility study for a small nuclear-powered submersible. Admiral Rickover had been critical of the study. Wilkinson was noncommittal but he told me that he and Rickover knew how to build such a submersible and the admiral wanted to know if I would be the project manager. This was even more astounding than Admiral Raborn's invitation to me in 1959 to be Chief Scientist of Special Projects.

The next week Admiral Smith, Admiral Rickover, and I met with Undersecretary of the Navy Robert Morse. Believing that this was the start of a two-year process leading to congressional authorization, Morse was casual in his questioning.

> *Morse:* How much will this submersible cost?
> *Rickover:* How much money do we have?
> *Craven:* I can make $10 million of R&D money available.
> *Smith:* I am going to turn back $22 million in appropriated ship construction money which the Congress could reauthorize.
> *Rickover:* Good. It will cost $32 million.

This was the only cost estimate ever made for development of this submersible. Morse seemed satisfied and asked Rickover to take the lead.

Rickover called on the morning of April 18 and asked me to tell Defense Secretary McNamara and Secretary of the Navy Paul Nitze that President Johnson would make his announcement that afternoon. The next week Rickover called me to help him with an emergency meeting called by an unhappy House of Representatives Armed Services Committee. He asked me to prepare a justification for this project. I told him that I would have to use my report and that the submarine had to have a thirty-day mission. He told me to invent a mission and after a long and contentious meeting with Congress the authorization was approved. Three weeks from conception to authorization—a peacetime record.

We started immediately but, following his policy, Rickover only communicated with Admiral Smith, the Navy's top man in Special Projects. Therefore preliminary design started with our respective deputies. I knew then that I was not secure in my appointment as project manager until I had my "Rickover interview"—the ordeal by fire endured by anyone who reported to the Kindly Old Gentleman, as he was called (behind his back). It would not take place until the following May, when the Deep Submergence Systems Project became an independent Navy field activity. Thus began the complex relationship between two "outsiders" from Brooklyn, one who made it to the Academy only to have a very storm-tossed career in the Navy, and the other who never made it to the Academy, but found a home in the Navy despite that bitter disappointment.

From the day in 1924 that I opened my eyes in the shadow of the Williamsburg Bridge on the Brooklyn shore, I was taught by my father that I was predestined to be a naval officer and not incidentally an elder in the Presbyterian Church. The roots of my heritage, I was told, went back as far as Oliver Cromwell and the seventeenth-century English Civil War. Among other things, that war saw the British navy divided into a Parliamentary fleet whose captains were Protestant, and a Royal fleet, whose Catholic and Anglican captains were loyal to the crown. Thus a cohort of captains of the sea developed that were linked together by Protestantism, Presbyterians among them. Their ships were built in the Firth of Clyde in Scotland or in the Netherlands, their uniforms made of wool produced by the weavers of Scotland. They believed in Predestination and the Trinity. God's Trinity, the Father, the Son, and the Holy Ghost, and the Devil's Trinity, War, Commerce, and Piracy.

The next century ushered in the Industrial Revolution and the mill technology that caused massive unemployment among the Scottish weavers. The weavers, along with Scottish mariners, set out for a New Scotland, or Nova Scotia, in Canada, and a New England on the East Coast of America. At Harvard, Yale, and the College of New Jersey (later Princeton), my forebears taught navigation and began the tradition of a Craven male child being predestined at birth to be a Presbyterian minister or a naval personage. Thus, side by side with the generations of Elijah Cravens and James Cravens all destined, if not predestined, for the Presbyterian ministry, there were the generations of Tunis Augustus MacDonough Cravens (at least four), Thomas Tingey Cravens (at least three), John Cravens (three, if I am counted among them), and a smattering of Truxtons, Francises, and Fredericks, all destined for the Navy. Some, like the Tunis Augustus MacDonough Craven who was one of the fourteen midshipmen in the first class of the Naval Academy and then commanding officer of the Union's ironclad ship *Tecumseh*, were even destined for footnotes in history. Every American would learn that when the *Tecumseh* was torpedoed and sunk by the Confederates at Mobile Bay, Admiral Farragut cried, "Damn the torpedoes! Full speed ahead!" But we Cravens know that the crew and the pilot escaped while Tunis Augustus went down with the ship, saying, tradition has it, "After you, Pilot."

This long and often repeated family litany had coursed through my mind as effortlessly as it had passed from my father's lips when I sought to enumerate my genetic credentials for acceptance as a member of the Special Projects team. But then there was my beloved mother's side, the Piña side, who had been stripped of their ethnic tilde and arbitrarily renamed Pinna as Hispanic immigrants passing through Ellis Island. James McDougal Craven, my father, in marrying the love of his life, Mabel Consuelo Pinna, had married a girl from the other side of the tracks, or so it was seen in the eyes of the contemporary Navy men Cravens, who called him Mac. Young John, meaning me, would thus lose his Academy-worthy pedigree, a pity. If that were not enough vexation for my father, dear Uncle Eddie Pinna, the bearer of Piña family oral history, never failed to remind him that the Spanish Piña clan descended from a seafaring line, too—pirates of Moorish blood, practitioners of a tine of the Devil's pitchfork Trinity, who had settled in Gibraltar. My father had anointed me with the Christian name of John, as if to signal that I was predestined to be a naval officer. But his father-in-law demanded that Pinna live on in my middle name. He instructed me never to use my middle name, only the initial P., since I was "not one of them." But I was one of them and proud to be one, so I was doomed to a culturally schizophrenic life. By day I lived in the alleyways of floating crap games, speakeasies, street gangs, and the enmities of ethnic diversities. Evenings, after my father returned from his white-collar job on Wall Street for a proper family dinner, we would gather around the piano learning the anthem, chorale, and oratorio music of Bach, Handel, Mendelssohn, and Mozart. This would be followed by a reading from the Bible, a recitation by young John to see how well he had learned a new Psalm, then, kneeling, we would pray. Finally, before retiring, there would be a reading from a great novel, usually one by Dickens. Sunday was observed in utter orthodoxy. It was church worship morning and evening. No movies, no games, no secular activity, not even homework—a regime broken only at midday when we sat down to agnostic Grandma Pinna's pollo con arroz and pot roast.

The annual cultural clash would come on Thanksgiving, with Uncle Eddie seated at one end of Grandma Pinna's table and Presbyterian patriarch James presiding at the other. Father would solemnly open the meal with the Presbyterian Prayer, asking God's blessing on the sinner Franklin Delano Roosevelt, who was otherwise bound for impeachment and hell. Uncle Eddie would then declare that FDR would one day be elected king. Inevitably, he would speak of Piña pirates from Gibraltar and their Moorish origins, and Father, red-faced, would declare that there was not one drop of black blood in the Craven family. I loved and worshiped Uncle Eddie but sided with my father with respect to a future naval career. I was indeed to have a career, but one that would not lead me through the portals of Bancroft Hall at the Naval Academy.

Before the building of the late-nineteenth- and early-twentieth-century bridges across Manhattan's East River, the neighborhood in

Brooklyn known as Williamsburg was the domain of the Victorian gentry of that borough. The Williamsburg Savings Bank, with its gold dome, was the center of Brooklyn finance. St. John's Methodist Episcopal Church replicated the Gothic abbeys of England, with stained glass windows, family pews on red-carpeted floors, and a choir loft where a Cassavant-designed organ held forth as long as the sexton could manage the bellows. The streets were named for signatories of the Declaration of Independence—Clymer, Rodney, Rutledge. Plush horse-drawn carriages from the Wheeler stables waited alongside the four-story brownstone mansions.

Then came the bridges. A steel gash severed the backyards between South Fifth and South Sixth streets. Factories built to spin the bridge cables replaced the houses between South Fourth and South Sixth. Number 79 South Sixth, where I would be born years later, was cut in two, the open wall sealed with cheap red brick. The garden between 77 and 79 became a cement alley that would soon be the home of a permanent floating crap game in the shadow of the bridge, and the swings and seesaws in the nearby park would become the playground equipment for prostitutes plying their trade in a uniquely mobile way.

By then, the Williamsburg elite had long fled to sunnier, leafier realms. In their stead immigrants poured in. Among them were the teeming masses of Orthodox Jews from the Russian Pale of Settlement. So it was that Hyman G. Rickover, born at the turn of the century in Makow, Russia (now part of Poland), settled first in Williamsburg in 1904 and a few years later in Chicago. Whether in Makow, Havemeyer Street at the terminus of the Williamsburg Bridge, or Maxwell Street in Chicago, Jewish ghetto life hardly varied. Although Rickover's biographers, foiled by the admiral, are silent about his childhood, it is certain that he was immersed in the world of Jewish culture, religion, and tradition.

My maternal grandfather, John Pinna, joined with Samuel Gompers, a Jewish immigrant born in London, in the founding of a new, secular religion called the Ethical Culture Society. Both had settled in Williamsburg. Gompers, a cigar maker, came to America seeking freedom and justice for the working man and would become one of the nation's foremost trade unionists. Grandfather Pinna, a militant labor organizer, was a clothing cutter, the son of a tailor from Gibraltar, Peter Piña—a militant himself in his support of Garibaldi's revolution—who had immigrated to Boston and then to Brooklyn. Spearheaded by Gompers, with John Pinna as one of his organizers, the cigar makers and the tailors and other workers in the clothing trades founded the International Ladies' Garment Workers' Union (ILGWU) and the American Federation of Labor (AFL).

What an unmelted pot was Williamsburg in the early decades of the twentieth century! Hispanic, Italian, Polish, the national origin changed block to block—and woe to those found on the wrong block—with the overwhelming majority being Jewish. This was the neighborhood in which I lived from birth until I joined the Navy at eighteen years of age. Although Rickover had left Williamsburg for Chicago at seven, his new neighborhood was similar to the old, until he, too, at eighteen, departed for the Navy.

My father's sister, Sarah Craven, who had graduated from Smith College with a major in the new field of sociology and had come to do social work at the Abraham & Straus department store in Brooklyn, ran a program for underprivileged Hispanic girls. They were taught to hand-crochet silk lamp shades to learn a higher-paid skill. Aunt Sarah saw that Mabel Consuelo Pinna was an intelligent and beautiful young woman who would make a fine wife for her brother James. James was smitten, and without realizing that he would cross the line drawn by the Craven naval family ethnic boundaries, he proposed marriage. Had Hyman G. Rickover had a similar, schizophrenic experience as John P. ("You're not one of them") Craven would have as a boy and a young man? The name Hyman was clearly derived from an Orthodox Jewish tradition meant to immortalize the name and memory of a recently departed forebear. The middle initial

stood for the decidedly gentile name George, but why it had been be-
stowed (was it to honor King George of England and the English
who had rescued the Rickover family from the pogroms of George's
cousins Czar Nicholas of Russia and Kaiser Wilhelm in the Polish
Pale?) remains a mystery. Whatever the reason, both he and I had
been motivated to enter the Naval Academy. Rickover succeeded,
and though I did not, our paths crossed again when in 1935 he was
assigned to the battleship *New Mexico*. It was there, as an engineering officer, that he would play a major role in establishing the *New
Mexico* as undisputed Queen of the Fleet. I would serve as a helmsman on that same ship when she was flagship of BatDiv 38 in World
War II. I would play a small part in the ship's proud tradition, one
which he had done so much to help create.

The *New Mexico*, commissioned in 1918, was the epitome of the
technology and military culture of the battleship era. It was a floating
city, inhabited by two interdependent social classes, officers and enlisted men. All of the officers, except for a few mustangs, were graduates of the Academy, steeped in the John Paul Jones tradition. The
enlisted men were the sons of Irish, Italian, Polish, Spanish, German, and Scottish immigrants. There were no African-Americans,
no Asian-Americans, except as mess "boys," no practicing Orthodox
Jews. Some of the crew were "plank owners"—enlistees assigned to
the ship for their entire naval career.

The culture in which the *New Mexico* crew was steeped is exquis-
itely described in Melville's *White-Jacket*, a fictional but autobio-
graphical account of life aboard a man-of-war. My 1944 wartime
experience resonates painfully with Melville's of a century earlier.
The peacetime rigors he describes were compounded by war in the
1940s. As in *White-Jacket*, sailors on the *New Mexico* stood watch four
hours on, four hours off, twenty-four hours a day. They slept in hammocks stowed in hammock netting during the day, but all hands went
to general quarters for one hour before sunrise. It was at just such an
hour during the Gilberts campaign that the aircraft carrier *Liscomb*

Bay was blown to smithereens off the *New Mexico*'s starboard quarter. Those moments of shock and trauma would live with my shipmates all their lives. In peacetime helmsmen kept the ship on the most favorable course given the wind, sea, and ultimate destination. In wartime, we continuously zigzagged, changing direction every six or seven minutes to make it difficult for a Japanese submarine to torpedo us. All the other routines of an old-fashioned peacetime Navy were carried out. Full-dress inspection in whites was held every Saturday morning even as troops were fighting their way ashore. Holystoning the teak deck until it was gleaming white and then painting it gray as camouflage was a monthly event. All day and all night the boatswains whistled and the buglers sounded reveille, call to colors, taps, mess, and general quarters. We sailors sang a bugle song that to my puritanical ears sounded like, "It's a good ship, it's a good ship for the officers, it's a horseship, it's a horseship for the crew."

But it was a tough ship for the officers as well. Lieutenant Rickover arrived on the *New Mexico* at a time when of fifteen U.S. battleships she was ranked, in terms of engineering efficiency, number eight. The big E pennant flown only by number one was earned, in part, by the amount of smoke that the ship generated on the horizon—less smoke, less over-the-horizon visibility, less vulnerability. Another measure was the efficiency of consumption of fuel and the state of machinery as gauged by a white-glove inspection of the engineering spaces, Rickover's domain. Every bit of brightwork, including the hardware in the urinals, had to shine like the noonday sun. Officers, however, had to be more than masters of discipline. They had to know every aspect of a ship's machinery, its performance, maintenance, and repair. Rickover, both as martinet and Machiavelli, drove the crew to levels of excellence that elevated the *New Mexico* to the coveted E for three consecutive years. At the end of that tour, he was promoted to lieutenant commander and given an assignment as CO of a minesweeper on the Yangtze River. This was, in fact, a devastating appointment. For those unfamiliar with the caste system of the Navy, it consists of "up or out." If an officer is not promoted in rank when it is time for promotion, his retirement is mandatory. The rank of a commanding officer is associated with the size of his ship. In order to reach flag rank an officer must be a captain who has had a "deep draft" command. Minesweepers and gunboats are often commanded by mustangs, who have risen through the ranks to be chief and warrant officer and then attain commissioned officer rank. Rickover now knew that his career in the Navy was over unless he transferred from the line to become an engineering duty officer.

My military colleagues at the David Taylor Model Basin were all engineering duty officers and most were graduates of the Academy. Their version of the Rickover story was that of a young nonteam player who had entered the Academy with grandiose dreams and a disdain for the high jinks of his fellow midshipmen. It was said that he would put the plebes on report for the most minor infraction, and of course he was quickly alienated from his classmates, becoming the target of hazing and ridicule. As a result, they maintained, he graduated with a lifelong prejudice against his fellow Academy alumni. And he continued to make enemies. Nonetheless, he received regular promotions because of his technical skill until an evaluation of his fitness for command found him to be unsatisfactory. This, for a line officer, was a death knell. His career would have essentially been over had it not been for World War II. That was when he became an EDO and, in the wartime dearth of trained technical personnel, assigned full responsibility for the acquisition of naval electrical systems. In a position of power, he rapidly developed his techniques of browbeating contractors, and handpicking ninety-day-wonder junior officers while systematically rejecting Academy graduates regardless of skill or reputation. This more technically complex Navy of radar, sophisticated communications systems, submarine batteries, and electrical machinery was to be Rickover's wartime Navy and he was effective. Rickover was thus admired by the line officers whose lives depended on the reliability of his equipment.

High marks from the line, however, did little to raise the low es-
teem in which he was held by his fellow EDOs. According to them,
EDO Rickover was assigned to the Atomic Energy Commission's nuclear power school as a means of ending his career, but he returned
riding on the success of the Philip Abelson nuclear reactor design.
The Bureau of Ships decided to support the program and chose Rickover to head the effort. That decision had been made by the head of
BuShips, Admiral Earle Mills, who in his autobiography expressed
regret. Rickover's primary motivation, he had come to believe, was
gaining personal power to achieve a boyhood dream of becoming
"monarch of the sea"—a sea that would now be exclusively popu-
lated by nuclear-powered ships. This opinion, shared by many, was
seen by insiders as the reason that Rickover was later denied flag
rank by the Navy. Undaunted, he went on to muster the support of
Congress, which enacted a law in 1953 requiring the Navy to ap-
point a senior nuclear-trained captain to flag rank. Even this was
opposed by some of Rickover's superiors, who sought to thwart
congressional will by naming another man who met the bill's qualifications. Wiser heads prevailed, however, and Rickover was made
rear admiral. Some years later (1963), Congress promoted him to the
rank of vice admiral, and then to four-star admiral (1973) with a
"lifetime" appointment, expanding the pool of bitter EDOs and
other Academy graduates who bristled endlessly at the disdain with
which they were regarded by the Kindly Old Gentleman.

Having attained power, he opened a suite of offices in the old
World War I munitions building in Washington, which would house
his personal domain, the Nuclear Reactors Branch. In one or another of these offices, he relished exercising his prerogative to select
all the officers who would serve on nuclear-powered ships, conducting theatrically bizarre interviews in the knowledge that he, "the
outsider," was thereby establishing a legend.

14

Two-and-Twenty—
The Aquatic Circus

In May of 1966, with the Deep Submergence Systems Project established as a Navy field activity, I retained my title as Chief Scientist of Special Projects. As I have described, there was an agreement that my senior staff could be called back to Special Projects if their services were needed on a priority basis. The events and assignments of 1965 were such that I found myself a ringmaster in an aquatic circus. Some performers carried out their acts in water depths from the surface to 2,000 feet, while more daring performers carried out their acts in water depths as great as 20,000 feet. Each ring of this circus was separately organized and managed, and the performances were, as they are in any great circus, apparently uncoordinated. There were two arenas. One was top secret with admittance only to those with a need to know. Captain Bradley and I were ringmasters for mission and technology. *Halibut* and *Seawolf* had cover stories as research submarines assigned to one of the submarine flotillas operating out of Mare Island in San Francisco Bay. The crews and their families were housed in the associated naval base. There was little need for maximum security with respect to the submarines themselves, since they only transported top secret equipment and teams of industry specialists who would carry out unknown missions in unknown parts of the sea. The performers and the performances were invisible.

Seawolf had been cut in two to refuel the pressurized water reactor, but she was also cut in two to receive other equipment and other men. *Halibut* did indeed have a mock-up of the DSRV on its deck but as far as the crew knew, the mock-up was only a temporary expedient until the real DSRV would appear. But the very existence of *Trieste II* was a secret and nobody thought to provide a home for the crew and support personnel. She would soon come out of the black, and finding a home and mission for this orphan would be one of my major tasks.

In the public arena Admiral Levering Smith was the acknowledged master of the greatest show on earth, the Polaris/Poseidon Fleet Ballistic Missile System. The Poseidon was the next generation of missile after the Polaris A-3. (The Polaris had appeared in three models, A-1 to A-3.) Its offspring were the Deep Submergence Rescue Vehicle, The Man-in-the-Sea Program with its SeaLabs and Advanced Saturation Diving System, and an amorphous Large Object Salvage System, a means of bringing up something as large, say, as an aircraft. Together they comprised the family of the Deep Submergence Systems Project and, as of May 1966, the management of these programs appeared to be under control.

Admiral Rickover was the master of the greatest side show on earth—the NR-1, a new class of submersible—and as usual, he was pretending to be the center of the show. I had been named project manager for NR-1 a year before and I had many concerns about the adequacy of the systems that were being proposed for this submersible.

I knew, of course, that NR-1 was to explore and map the seabed, and to go deeper than our other nuclear subs. That meant that she would require technology that wasn't exactly off the shelf. My deputies had been preparing preliminary mock-ups of the equipment that we would provide for the submersible based on guidelines established by Rickover's shop. I was aware that he insisted that all such equipment must meet "military specifications" (milspecs), which meant that all the equipment was at least two years old and therefore obsolete. I hadn't the foggiest notion of the design principles that were being employed, and most of all, I had no idea what role Rickover was playing in this first phase of design. So I was waiting for the inevitable first interview with the Kindly Old Gentleman. It was not long in coming. On the very first day of the project's independence, legally under my exclusive management but, in point of fact, under Rickover's sole authority, his call arrived.

"Craven, this is Rickover. I am going to hang you from the highest yardarm."

"Why is that?"

"The equipment you are putting on that submarine is crap."

"You're right. The equipment I am putting on the submarine *is* crap."

"What do you mean the equipment you're putting on the submarine is crap?"

"The conditions you've imposed on procurement require me to use obsolete equipment."

At this point he challenged me, naming equipment whose deficiency I described until he named one I did not recognize.

"Admiral, I don't recognize that equipment."

"Craven, what kind of project manager are you, putting on equipment that you don't know. That could sink the ship."

It was time to counterattack.

"Admiral, the equipment *you* are putting on the boat is crap." Then I cited some examples.

He fielded the first two or three but then became silent. "Craven, I don't recognize that piece of equipment."

"Admiral—what kind of project manager are you? You are putting on nuclear equipment and you do not even know—"

"Okay, Craven, knock off the bullshit. Come over here this afternoon and we'll design this boat together."

As I prepared for the meeting I reflected on the admiral's management techniques and the reasons for its successes and failures. As I've mentioned, he personally interviewed and selected each individual who would serve in the nuclear reactor program. He sought out two types. The majority were "boy scouts," who would carry out his directives without question. A much smaller cadre of individuals in his inner circle were the tough SOBs who would stand up to the admiral whenever they thought he was wrong. They would save him from error.

He was also very conservative in his design philosophy. He worked from his unshakable belief that he had a small competent shop and that all others were large and incompetent. He continued, in spite of my attempt to vanquish his invincible ignorance, in his insistence that every piece of equipment which was not under his direct control be one that had been fully qualified to military specifications. He took a sadistic delight in exposing salesmen who did not know the precise details of this process. He told me how he would ask a salesman if his equipment could pass the radiator test or the drop test. If the answer to the first was yes he would smash it against his radiator until it was destroyed—no matter how delicate or valuable the equipment. If they said yes to the drop test he would open his second-story window and drop the equipment onto the pavement below.

It was this slavish insistence on milspec standards that led to his dissatisfaction with the equipment we were to provide. When I pointed out that all the equipment we were furnishing was at the leading edge of technology and there had been no time to put it through the rigorous milspec procedure, he wanted to know how we could insure that it was effective and reliable.

I told him about the equipment we had designed for the DSRV, the *Trieste II*, and, without describing the programs, for the classified projects. I told him of the many new pressure tanks we had designed and built in secret in connection with these programs. I expounded on the two-and-twenty rule, how all equipment external to the hull was ideally designed for depths of 20,000 feet so that it could be used anywhere in the ocean and for future deep submersibles. But when restricted by cost or technology, external equipment had to be designed for at least 2,000 feet to cover the world's continental shelf. He seized on this and decreed that all items of equipment (thrusters, motors, manipulators, wheels, sonars, lights, and so on) be tested at the pressure associated with 20,000 feet and that each should be cycled 15,000 times to simulate a forty-year life. He wanted the works. The cost would be staggering, upped suddenly from the $32 million that had been budgeted to $60 million or more.

The Kindly Old Gentleman was unfazed. "Craven," he said, "go get the money. Beg, borrow, or steal."

I did everything but steal, aware of the many who were ready to pounce on anything untoward to shut down a Rickover project. Indeed, there were moments of glee when the Ship System Command reported that, on the basis of the proposed components, the *NR-1* would sink at the pier at launching. The reactor was far too heavy because of the shielding requirements. A decision was made to remove the shielding from the back of the reactor and substitute a tail cone full of water. From the standpoint of physics, this was a rational and safe solution. A simplified description of what happens is that water speeds up the neutrons in the reactor but as a result their energy decays. Thus water serves as a shield. It is not as effective as lead but twelve feet of water is the equivalent of about one foot of lead. Thus the radiation outside the submarine would be the same as it would be if the lead shield were in place. Since no humans would enter the tail cone, there was no additional hazard to the crew but in the view of environmentalists, then and now, water is not an acceptable shield. Lead had become a shibboleth for reactor safety.

With the design problems resolved, construction proceeded at a rapid pace, but not fast enough for the KOG. By 1968 I was involved in both the search for the lost submarine *Scorpion* and a top secret mission in the Pacific about which he knew nothing. Instead, he thought that I was not spending the appropriate amount of time on the NR-1. The telephone rang.

"Craven, I am taking over the project as project manager. Is that all right?"

"Of course. My people will await instructions from your people."

A week of dead silence went by. The telephone rang.

"Craven, I'm giving the project back to you. You have a large incompetent shop, I have a small competent shop, but we need a large shop to manage the program."

"Admiral, my shop is more competent than your shop, but that is irrelevant. If I am to be the project manager my people will chair all the meetings."

He wasted no time trying to rewrite a report that my people had written, but they would not budge. There was an agreement between us that all reports of significance would be signed by both the KOG and me. Would he sign this report? I waited a few days and then called his aide to find out. A few minutes later the phone rang.

"Craven, this is Rickover. Do you know why I am calling you?"

"Yes, sir."

"In this business you have to be a son of a bitch. You are learning but you are not good enough. I want you to go home tonight and stand in front of the mirror and say 'son of a bitch' seventeen times. Will you do that?"

"Yes, sir."

It was true, I knew why he had called. He had signed the report unchanged. That night I stood before the mirror, said "son of a bitch" once, and burst out laughing.

We soon got into the practice of having a private meeting after every staff meeting. He told me many "Rickover stories" that I had already heard. He delighted in challenging me.

"Craven, what is this crazy hammer you are putting on the sub to be used by the crew to beat out a message on the hull if they are ever stuck on the bottom?"

"Not crazy, Admiral. The hull is a perfect resonator and the sound of that hammer can be heard for hundreds of miles."

"You are right, Craven. I should have known that. You know there was a night that I stayed on board a tender. At about 3:00 A.M. I wanted a basket of fruit delivered to my cabin. I called the quarterdeck—no answer. I called the exec—no answer. I called the captain—no answer. I called at random until I got an answer. It was the blacksmith. I had him bring a sledgehammer to my cabin and I beat it against the bulkhead until I had awakened the entire crew."

I had heard that story before.

He did not trust my designs or those of my people and asked me to find a qualifed consultant to review them. I suggested MPR, Inc. (Mandel Panoff and Rockwell), a team that had worked for the admiral for more than twenty years.

"Those ungrateful bastards," he said. "They left me to make money after I taught them everything they know. I will not give them a single dollar."

I took him literally and gave the contract to Westinghouse, with an instruction that they should subcontract it to MPR. The admiral was pleased. He got his review and he didn't give them (directly) a cent.

One day I expressed my concern about the psychological makeup of the crew of the *NR-1*. Six men cooped up for thirty days in a confined space, standing watches four hours on, four hours off, twenty-four hours a day. We had to minimize the size of the crew in order to give space to the equipment required to let the sub operate deep and for very long duration. Still—two men on watch to operate a complex nuclear submarine was unprecedented. The admiral said, "Don't worry, if I choose them they will perform."

I did worry. I commissioned the Office of Naval Research psychologists to run tests with volunteers in a mock-up of the *NR-1*. They were given tests to calibrate their need for dominance, need for social affiliation, need to achieve, and level of dogma. Two men with matching profiles were kept in the mock-up for periods as long as ten days and were observed through one-way glass. Whenever there were two individuals with a high need for dominance the tests would end in violence in just a few days. We learned a lot. Rickover refused to read the report—but his captains did and that is all that mattered. They too had a role in selecting the crew.

At the end of every staff meeting, he would admonish the participants that there was no escaping his directives. He would never retire, the litany went, he would outlive, outwork, and outlast all. After one particularly grating tirade about his immortality, when we were alone, I chided him.

"Admiral, I know who's going to be your relief."

"Relief? I have no relief. Who's my relief?"

"Your relief is Midshipman Dole" (a pseudonym, since Dole is still on active duty).

"A midshipman? No midshipman is going to relieve me."

"Of course not. He will relieve you when he is an admiral and you are eighty-seven."

"Why eighty-seven?"

"That's when Michelangelo cashed in his chips."

The admiral leaned back and laughed. "That's good, oh, that's good. Who is this Midshipman Dole?"

Dole was a brash young man who skipped the mandatory summer Naval Academy midshipmen's cruise in order to ride the Westinghouse *DeepStar* submarine to a depth of four thousand feet—where he planted a flag on the bottom that said, "Beat Army." I told him a lot more about Dole and he said, "Good. You and I must follow this young man's career and make sure that he has the toughest, most onerous seagoing experiences. You do your part, Craven, and I will do mine."

Ensign Dole reported to the *Trieste* unit and was told he would be the docking officer of the bathyscaphe *Trieste II*. He demurred because he had obtained alternate orders to go to the Navy diving school. When it was time for him to apply for nuclear power he chose the oceanographic Ph.D. program instead. When he got his Ph.D. he was ordered to meet with Admiral Rickover, who asked why he delayed his application for nuclear power. Dole replied that he had no intention of entering the program. The admiral flew into his best rage, castigating and browbeating the young lieutenant (as he was by then). He ordered him out of his office, vowing never to talk to him again. As Dole was retreating, Admiral Rickover ordered him to report the conversation to the chief of personnel. Alas, Rickover had briefed the chief, who informed Dole that he could go into nuclear power or command a minesweeper in the most obscure backwater the Navy could put him in. Dole was baffled and mystified as he was sure that Rickover regarded him as a miscreant. Dole was surprised (as was I) when he was named a commanding officer of the SSN *Hyman G. Rickover,* the only Navy ship named after a living naval hero. Shortly thereafter he was given a prize command of a submarine tender. When Rickover died I met with Dole for the first time and told him of our prophecy. He was flabbergasted. He had believed that Rickover held him in low regard and that his career was independent of any Rickover action or influence. As of 2000 Dole was named chief of naval research, a position that will influence the future of the new information age Navy much as Rickover, the father of the nuclear Navy, shaped the Navy of his day.

But I wonder, as Dole wonders, how and why Rickover decided to play God with our lives. He must have known the Craven brothers Fritz and Frank in his class at the Naval Academy. He must have known of the brutal game of Craven volleyball (or hernia ball) played with a sixteen pound medicine ball on the deck of a pitching and heaving ship on the high seas. Did he know of my duty as helmsman on the *New Mexico* or our mutual experience growing up in

Brooklyn? I do not know, I will never know. I do know that up to the day that Rickover died he took steps to ensure that his prophecies would be fulfilled. The Kindly Old Gentleman fathered his own Navy, selected its personnel, developed the first nuclear-powered submarine, controlled the development of the entire fleet of nuclear submarines, ranging from the attack boats of the *Skipjack* class to the newly commissioned Trident missile subs and intelligence submarines. He fathered the first and most enduring of the mini–nuclear submarines, the *NR-1*, operated by a crew of only two men on watch; he had forced the Navy's hand to acquire its first undersea capital ship; he advocated the production of the *Seawolf*, the Navy's newest class of submarine and the latest vessel to bear that name—and he had, perhaps, chosen his own relief.

As for me, I am not privy to the career of the *NR-1* except by hearsay and current publicity. If I were I would imagine that I would be required to remain silent, and I do not wish to burden my aging brain with any more information that I cannot reveal. It is as of this moment the oldest nuclear submarine in service with an unsurpassed record of reliability. It still has its original motors. It must have carried out its original mission, since the famed oceanographer who created the most complete and detailed map of the Atlantic seafloor, Dr. Bruce Heezen, was its science observer when he died of a heart attack in the middle of a cruise. A technical paper reports that it played the major role in the recovery of the *Challenger* debris. But all that is, of course, hearsay.

But I am proud of its first operational test. It submerged with a crew of six and one scientific observer, and planted a marker buoy on the ocean floor. For the next thirty days it conducted a transit of the seafloor without recourse to external navigation and then returned to within one hundred yards of its point of departure.

But I am most proud of my project team. I grew bold enough to go the extra step—telling Rickover that DSSP was the most competent shop in the nation. That was not a boast, it was an objective statement of fact. The core of the DSSP team was the innovative core of the Special Intelligence team, which, in turn, was the innovative core of Special Projects. These teams built the systems that deterred a war and won a peace. The names of most core members will be anonymous until they die. They will have no memorial and they won't be buried in Arlington. But at that final day each one can say, "Glad did I live and gladly die, and I lay me down with a will."

15

The Hunt for Red September: A Tale of Two Submarines

An ambitiously subtitled, groundbreaking book called *Blind Man's Bluff: The Untold Story of American Submarine Espionage** appeared in 1998 and soared to the top of many best-seller lists. My family, friends, students, and former professional colleagues were amazed to the point of disbelief to learn from reading *Blind Man's Bluff* that I was the flamboyant mastermind of two searches for missing submarines in 1968—the USS *Scorpion*, an American submarine lost in the Atlantic, and a Soviet submarine lost in the Pacific.

Blind Man's Bluff asserts that the *Scorpion* search was conducted with as much public exposure as security would allow, whereas the Russian submarine search, which began while the Soviets were hunting for the lost sub themselves, was extremely classified. "What if the United States could find the sub first?" the book asks. "There in one place would be Soviet missiles, codebooks, a wealth of technological information." The operation had a code name that itself was top secret, and the material that was recovered and analyzed is today still classified as special intelligence that can only be revealed

* By Sherry Sontag and Christopher Drew with Annette Lawrence Drew (New York: Public Affairs, 1998).

within the four walls of high-security facilities and only to those with a recognized need to know.

Since the publication of *Blind Man's Bluff*, I have been besieged by friends, journalists, and complete strangers seeking to learn the truth. What is the real story? they ask. I tell them that nobody truly knows and nearly all of those who knew the most are now dead. The vast majority of the people involved in the search for the subs knew only a single aspect of the entire matter and, by design, would never see the forest for the trees. *Blind Man's Bluff* suggests that my intimate role provided knowledge of the big picture as well. It is hard to know what is meant by "the big picture," but this is probably true. Therefore, most readers of that book believe that I was the major informant for this material. Although I am the only person cited by name among sources the authors refer to as their "main interviews," nothing could be further from the truth.

Security investigators have informed me that they have been covering me closely for the past three decades and are covering me still. But these young and presumably dedicated and competent investigators probably would not recognize a transgression if it occurred because they do not know any of the classified facts, let alone "the big picture" of this case and do not have a need to know. Indeed, there does not appear to be anyone alive who has the authority, knowledge, and need to know to declassify for public airing these old but enormously significant espionage tales.

Yet someone must have told the authors of *Blind Man's Bluff* something. The facts recited in that book have such a ring of truth and credibility that they must have been provided by an informant or informants who were knowledgeable to some extent and were either divulging this information because they personally believe that the time is ripe for the public to know or they had been officially encouraged to do so with a sufficient amount of obfuscating disinformation added in the name of protecting national security. In any event, there has now been enough factual information released one way or another to whet the thirst for more on the part of the media, and the danger that goes along with this is that some may dream up and publish scenarios that are sensational, inflammatory, and otherwise ill-advised and thereby undermine the public's legitimate right to know.

Indeed, as a private citizen who no longer possesses the requisite security clearances, I believe that the public now has a right and its own need to know the true story before it is lost forever. At the same time, I am reluctant to arrogate to myself the generation of history when I cannot be absolutely sure that I am correct. For as the Good Book says, "We know in part, and we prophesy in part."

Therefore I propose to tell my tale of two submarines as one might testify in an unclassified court of inquiry where the court is in full possession of the material that has appeared in the public media. I am still constrained by security neither to confirm nor deny the material that has now appeared in the media. But if you accept the verisimilitude of the reports contained in *Blind Man's Bluff* and in other responsible publications, I can lead you, without violation of national security, through the logic of the search for and the investigation of the Soviet submarine, and I can also lead you through the logic of the search for and the investigation of the lost U.S. sub *Scorpion*. Let us begin.

In an almost unbelievable coincidence of fate, the Soviet Union and the United States both lost submarines at sea at about the same time, in the spring of 1968. The losses were also contemporaneous with the establishment of the Deep Submergence Systems Project, under my direction, with its mission to develop the hardware and techniques for search, rescue, salvage, large object recovery, and undersea espionage. As a result, I was appointed chairman of a Navy task group charged with conducting the search for and investigation of the submarine *Scorpion*. At the same time, I had full responsibility for the search for and investigation of the lost Soviet submarine as part of a Special Intelligence program. The very existence of this latter effort was known to only a handful of individuals. The Soviet sub was the first to vanish. Her fate was certainly of considerable interest to us and we began clandestinely to search for her. But soon we had a much more pressing problem.

In the evening of a beautiful day in May of 1968, I was driving on the Virginia side of the George Washington Highway along the Potomac when I heard on the radio that the USS *Scorpion* was missing with ninety-nine hands on board. I immediately turned my car around and headed for the war room of the Pentagon. When I arrived, the Commander Submarine Forces Atlantic and his senior officers were already there as well as senior representatives of the Chief of Naval Operations and other naval officers concerned with operations and communications. I probably recognized several officers who were involved in the top secret Special Intelligence search that had just been initiated for the lost Soviet submarine. Though a civilian, I was legally a commanding officer of a submarine research, development, and operations command. My initial duty was to muster equipment for deployment to locations where the submarine might have sunk and might lie at a depth where men could still be alive and recoverable. My first question, therefore, was: Where might the *Scorpion* be?

She had been returning from operations in the Mediterranean and her last message had come from the Atlantic in the vicinity of Rota, Spain. There was an uncomplicated great-circle track across the Atlantic that subs followed, and she was presumed to be somewhere along that track. I knew of course that she might be engaged in Special Intelligence operations and I also understood that that was a question I could not ask. But since I was engaged in such operations myself, I was aware of someone present who would know, and I received a reassuring shake of his head that told me that *Scorpion* had simply been heading home. There was not a bit of shallow water along the great-circle route until the sub arrived in the waters of the

East Coast continental shelf. There was plenty of rescue capability in the vicinity of Norfolk, Virginia. But the deep submergence program had constructed a highly mobile, "fly away" version of a conventional submarine rescue chamber based at Pearl Harbor. Against the remote possibility of an uncharted shallow seamount on the Mid-Atlantic Ridge, I had the rescue material flown to the Azores, where it could be loaded on a Navy ship if needed. I then asked whether the *Scorpion* had been located on the Navy's SOSUS (Sound Surveillance System) acoustic net.

The Navy's number one expert on SOSUS was Captain Joseph Kelly. He had grown with the development of the system from the time I first met him as a young lieutenant. He was one of the finest men I have known, proud of all the Irish blood within him, yet humble and good-humored. He was dedicated first and foremost to the Navy and to his specialty, and knew more about the localization of sound in the sea than anyone else. It was he or his representative who was there that evening, and they had found no trace of the *Scorpion* on the SOSUS records.

The search thus became one of air reconnaissance along the track, hunting for the aftermath of a tragedy—an orange submarine-sunk-here buoy or orange life jackets in a location relative to the track where flotsam and jetsam might be carried by the current. No attempt was made to hide the search effort from the Soviets even though by doing so we could betray past operations or operational areas.

The task seemed hopeless, since the track was about three thousand miles long. I realized that if we were going to find the *Scorpion*, the sounds of its collapse—the implosions that occur at collapse depth—would have had to have been recorded on some remote scientific or military hydrophone (i.e., an underwater microphone). I immediately called civilian scientist Gordon Hamilton at an Office of Naval Research Laboratory in the Bahamas. He in turn told me of a research station that he had in the Canary Islands with a research hydrophone. The voluminous records accumulated there were regularly destroyed every week or so. He contacted the station and luckily the scientists there had not yet disposed of the records of significance. Examining them, they found about five separate trains of acoustic events that could have been associated with a submarine breakup. Matching the times of these events with the expected track of the *Scorpion* gave us five areas in which to concentrate the air search for surface debris. But this was still grasping at straws.

Kelly came to the rescue with his awareness of super-secret hydrophone installations in the hands of another government agency. The sounds of *Scorpion*'s death might be buried in this organization's records. The records were given to Wilton Hardy of the Naval Research Laboratory and he located "blips in the noise" that correlated with the Canary Island tapes. We now could triangulate on a position that had generated a sequence of sounds that could be interpreted as coming from *Scorpion*. We could see from that position that the events had occurred along the expected track at the time she was scheduled to be in that position. We now felt secure that no other nation was involved with the casualty. The highest probability was that the sinking was caused by an accident on board the submarine. President Johnson was given this very significant news. There was now no national security crisis. He could sleep more soundly even though the self-inflicted-sinking scenario was only a circumstantial probability.

Compare this phase of the *Scorpion* investigation with the opening scenes of the Soviet drama. Our first awareness of the Soviet loss, which preceded the *Scorpion* sinking by a few weeks, had come by way of observing an intensive and open search on the part of the Soviets that was similar to the activities that we would undertake in the loss of *Scorpion*. Like us, they would have known the mission profile of their own submarine and would have searched along its track. (As Russian subs left their ports, we could track them by getting directional fixes on their radio transmissions, and through satellite photos of any subs running on the surface.) If their lost sub was a ballistic missile submarine we, too, well knew what that track would have been.

The search started in Kamchatka, a Soviet peninsula in the Pacific, in a geophysical environment that suggests a latitude of about 65 degrees. This latitude is a crucial item. Then the track continues eastward and crosses the international date line. Apparently the submarine, which we presumed to be a diesel-powered Golf-class ballistic missile boat with about one hundred hands on board, was to patrol a region some 750 to 1,000 miles northwest of Hawaii. The deterrence mission of such a patrol, routine but fearsome, is graphically depicted in William J. Broad's *The Universe Below*: "The stagnant air and cramped quarters of the sub were home to about one hundred men ready for the possibility of war with the United States, ready to target Hawaii, the heart of American military strength in the Pacific. If the Kremlin had sent the coded message the sub would have fired its missiles skyward to precipitate a rain of thermonuclear ruin." If its mission was as we suspected, we could assume a great-circle path that had the submarine crossing the international date line at a latitude of about 45 degrees north. The Russians had been searching along this track. They continued east as far as the date line and much farther.

Unfortunately for both the Soviets and ourselves there appeared to be no radio location after it had passed Kamchatka. Thus, there was no precise fixing of the submarine's position by either the Soviets or the United States. At best, there was only a very generalized location, which we could glean only by observations of the Soviet search.

We knew nothing more except that the Soviets had lost one of their conventional, early-generation missile subs and that they had not found it. If, somehow, its position could be precisely determined, one of our submarines, *Halibut*, was configured to find it as long as there were no other higher priority mission to carry out.

Initially only Captain Kelly was called in. His SOSUS people were looking for the telltale signs of a submarine loss, i.e., the power-ful implosions associated with collapse of the hull and its compart-ments. They had not found any. Shortly thereafter Kelly got in touch with me to disclose information that was mystifying and inexplicable to him. He had discovered an isolated, single sound of an explosion or implosion, a "good-sized bang." He had found lots of recorded sounds. The ocean is filled with isolated sounds from every closed container that is thrown overboard and eventually implodes, but his one had a unique characteristic. It had occurred at a precise latitude of 40 de-grees north and a longitude of 180 degrees—the international date line. That particular point on the globe is no accident of nature. Dol-phins and whales, which make all kinds of recordable noise in their oceanic peregrinations, know nothing of latitude and longitude, nor does anything else indigenous to the sea. Forty degrees north on the international date line is a construct of the human mind. What a strange coincidence it would be if nature or random chance had con-spired to produce a good-sized bang at precisely 180/40. The highest probability was that some human instrumentality chose that precise position for some activity that resulted in the "good-sized bang." Could that single bang have come from a sinking submarine? If so, where were the sounds of collapse from implosion?

I immediately started considering the scenario and subjective probability technique I had employed in the search for the H-bomb. There were only three plausible scenarios. First, that the sound had nothing to do with the lost submarine. Second, that the sound was made by the submarine but that it did not sink, and like Jules Verne's *Nautilus* was still gliding beneath the sea. Third, that this was the sound of a sinking submarine where for some reason all of the water-tight doors were open and the submarine was completely flooded with water (which meant there would have been no implosion, since the sub would have flooded completely well before reaching implo-sion depth). Because of security only I, Admiral Philip A. Beshany, then the Pentagon's top submarine admiral, and Captain Kelly were involved in the formal speculation. We all agreed that the highest probability was that the sound was unrelated to the lost submarine. What about the second scenario, that the sound had been made by the sub? What made us think that the submarine sank? Indeed, we had no reason to believe so; we knew only that it was lost. Our intuition was based on the Soviet search and the continued silence of their submarine. If it had not sunk, however, it could clearly be a missile-bearing conveyance on the loose, and we did not want to entertain such thoughts. But it is precisely conventional assumptions that blind reality. A scenario that had to be accorded a high degree of probability was that the submarine had made that recorded sound and then took off. But if it were not a nuclear submarine, it would have had to surface and reveal itself in a short period of time. Kelly and I gave this a very low probability.

Admiral Beshany doubted that the sound was that of a submarine, but he had nothing else to go on.

But if we could dream up an operational scenario in which the submarine had all its hatches open and was hit by an explosive event that incapacitated the crew, then the third scenario would make sense.

Moreover, if that explosive sound recorded at those coordinates, 180/40, had come from that submarine, *then it was indeed not where it was supposed to be*, which was why the Soviets could not find it. When it passed 180, it should have been farther north, at a latitude of 45 degrees, or more than three hundred miles away. If that was a navigational mistake it would be an error of historic proportions. Thus if the sub were not somewhere in the vicinity of where the Soviets supposed it to be, there would be a high probability, if not a certainty, that the submarine was a rogue, off on its own, in grave disobedience of its orders.

At this point, even if the probability were considered to be small by most experts, the decision to search for the submarine became the responsibility of the President of the United States. If it was, or even could be, a rogue, he must try to find it, dead or alive, and learn what it was doing at the moment and what it was doing when the bang occurred.

What about the Soviet leader, Leonid Brezhnev? He and the rest of the Soviet navy probably had no idea that their lost submarine might be a rogue. They had apparently not recorded a signal at ·180/40; they knew only that they had lost a sub and were unable to find it. Finding lost submarines is far more difficult than finding the proverbial needle in the haystack. Since the Soviets didn't know how far off course their sub had been, the *Soviets would have had no idea that their ship was a rogue unless we told them*.

It may be useful to refer to a study I had conducted as Chief Scientist of the Polaris program. In designing Polaris's communications system, we needed to know as much as we possibly could about its requirements during times of crisis. The political science faculty at MIT had developed a crisis simulation game to test such needs. Three teams would be assembled and meet for about a week at MIT. The teams would be segregated from one another, housed in different motels. One team would consist of individuals playing the role of the President, his foreign policy adviser, his military advisers, and other staff personnel. The actual players were drawn from the White House staff, the State Department, and the Pentagon so that they could predict what their bosses would do. A second team consisted of those in the roles of their Soviet counterparts. This team was composed of scholars and analysts who were specialists in Soviet political and military policy. The third team played the role of God and devised the scenarios and the communications that informed each team what was transpiring.

The MIT game most relevant to this case—our real-life, mysteriously vanished Soviet sub—was one in which the American President was informed that one of his Polaris submarines had not returned from patrol and was missing. The Soviet leader was also informed by his naval commanders that one of his ballistic missile sub-marines had not returned and was missing. Neither had the slightest inkling of the other's problem. Both chief executives had an immediate first response. They insisted that all boats on patrol be contacted and required to report their condition and whether they were under surveillance. This was the first game-engendered answer that my office was seeking because there had been a furious debate as to whether this communication would be permissible, since such contacts could reveal the whereabouts of the boats at sea and, as a consequence, increase their vulnerability to attack. We had gotten our answer and our design principle—namely that the one condition most dreaded by both chief executives was the loss of command and control of their strategic forces—and, in particular, their strategic deterrent. The U.S. President or the Soviet leader must have continuous assurance, particularly in time of crisis, that he is the de facto, and not just in name only, commander in chief of his armed forces.

The second phase of the game, as played out by the team called God, was to have the respective searches carried out in the same part of the ocean. The General Secretary and the President are now in a state of near panic (great chiefs never completely panic). Are the Americans—and are the Russians—searching for theirs or ours? Was there some kind of interaction between their sub and ours? Did they collide? Did they kill each other? Or is this just a coincidence, a case like the loss of Scorpion and the Soviet sub at more or less the same time? Whatever the private thoughts of the players in the game, they both immediately activated the hot line between the President and the General Secretary. Both leaders had the same messages for each other. "We don't know what is going on, but if it's bad it wasn't us."

What did this game teach us with respect to our real two subs?

At this juncture both the United States and the Soviet Union were perfectly comfortable in the belief that Scorpion was an accident. Scorpion was an attack submarine armed with torpedoes, not a ballistic missile submarine, and if she were involved in a track-and-trail collision with a foreign sub, it would have been a serious international incident but it would not have been, as it might have been for a ballistic missile submarine, the end of the world. As for the Russian submarine and the debate as to whether the evidence justified setting out on a costly and dangerous search, Admiral Beshany and others were skeptical that the signal at 180/40 was from a dying submarine. But those few knowledgeable individuals were convinced, on the basis of the location of the blip and the unsuccessful Soviet search, that if it really were a signal from a dying submarine, then the highest probability was that it was a rogue. National security demanded that we use all reasonable means available to discover the truth.

The search was authorized. Its purpose—unlike the one described in *Blind Man's Bluff* and all of the other media reports—had nothing to do with recovering Soviet code books or weapons technology or missile technology. It had everything to do with whether the submarine was where the explosion occurred, why it was there, what it was up to, and who had authorized its mission.

In our tale of the search for two submarines, we have now come to a convergence. We thought we knew that *Scorpion* sank as a result of an accident and where it lay.

We also thought the highest probability was that the Soviet submarine was a rogue and if it, too, sank we thought we knew where it might be.

But before we went on what was possibly a wild-goose chase, we wanted to extract from the acoustic record everything we could that would help us precisely locate *both* submarines on the seafloor and get some insight as to the probable causes for the failures so that we could prepare our investigation tools. The *Scorpion* presented the first enigma. The relative position of each implosive sound from—we assumed—*Scorpion* suggested that she was heading in the wrong direction. The Naval Research Laboratory's Wilton Hardy and his colleagues disagreed. They believed that some of the signals were just multipath, i.e., echoes of one or two collapse events. The indication that the submarine was moving in the opposite direction, they maintained, was simply a product of the variations in the velocity of sound at different depths.

Civilian scientist Gordon Hamilton and I put this hypothesis to the test. We sent a ship to the probable site of *Scorpion's* sinking and had it drop charges at different depths. To our surprise, the size of the charges we used was inadequate to create the signals recorded—at least not until we increased the explosive force to eight times higher than we had anticipated. This, in turn, also provided an important clue with regard to the Soviet submarine. The blip on the Soviet acoustic record was *not* that of a moderately substantial implosion. It was a good-sized burst—and *if* it was not an undersea implosion at all but an explosion that took place in the atmosphere when the sub was on the surface, then it was really a very good-sized burst indeed. Remember, the magnitude of the explosion, if it took place on the surface, would not be truly reflected by the amount of sound that got into the water from the surface interface and then, in attenuated form, reached our electronic ears.

We did tests to determine what happened to our sub and to confirm the hypothesis that *Scorpion* was traveling in the opposite direction—east—to the track it should have been taking, west, to home. This sudden and unexplained reversal of course—a reciprocal—is consistent with the classic method for deactivating what is known as a hot-running torpedo.

In World War II, there were several instances in which torpedoes would miss their target, change direction, and come back and strike the launching submarine. To confirm this as a high-probability scenario, we ran a computer simulation, with the former executive officer of *Scorpion*, Lieutenant Commander Robert Fountain, Jr., acting as skipper. Given no hint of our theory, Fountain was told only that he was heading home at eighteen knots at a depth left up to him. When he was well underway, we asked him to check his torpedoes and moments later sounded an alert with the cry, "Hot-running torpedo!" With barely a blink of his eye, Fountain shouted, "Right full rudder!"—the command to initiate a 180 degree turn. When the simulated *Scorpion* had completely turned around, a simulated explosion took place in the torpedo room, and the skipper, made aware of rapid flooding, issued a series of commands aimed at rescuing the boat and bringing her to the surface. But instead she continued to plummet, reaching collapse depth and imploding in ninety seconds—one second shy of the acoustic record of the actual event.

Thus the hot-running torpedo scenario was now the highest priority but not the only priority. The designers of torpedoes are dedicated and skilled engineers who spare no effort to anticipate and test every contingency to avoid failure. There was an understandable reluctance to accept the idea that one of the *Scorpion*'s own torpedoes was the cause of the accident. Some twenty years after her loss, however, it was revealed that the torpedo batteries on the boat may have been defective and could have accounted for the loss. Tragically, the defect had been identified at the time and the batteries had been recalled from the fleet but *Scorpion* was still on patrol and a decision was made to change her batteries on her return. In the face of the risks and demands of war and Cold War missions, who can fault a decision to trade one risk for another in order to complete a mission?

A very different result comes from the analysis of the Soviet acoustic signal. For that submarine the only explanation for her silence—except for the one big bang—would be that all her watertight compartments were open when catastrophe struck. Moreover, the disastrous event must have taken place with such rapidity that watertight integrity could not be established for any compartment. If every compartment were open, the boat would have flooded as it sank and there would be no implosion. But apart from the compartments, there are many small tanks of various kinds on a submarine, such as the bottles of compressed air used for ballast, that would normally be pressure tight and thus would implode and, in theory, make a recordable sound. The physics is relatively simple: The energy of implosion is equal to the pressure of depth at the time of implosion multiplied by the volume of the tank. A sphere two feet in diameter would generate eight times more acoustic energy when it implodes than a one-foot-diameter sphere. The frequency of the larger sphere is lower and carries farther.

But these calculations were no substitute for empirical evidence. So, to re-create what might have happened to the Soviet sub, we requisitioned an old submarine, sank it in the open sea with all its hatches open—and to our surprise it went down without a sound from the small pressure tanks being detected on any of our acoustic systems. We therefore concluded that the Soviet submarine was not underway when the single sound was generated, that she must have been dead in the water on the surface and must have had a reason for all compartments to be open. If so, in the wake of whatever event sent her down, she would have filled with water and would have sunk like a rock—and we would find her at exactly 180/40.

We were now ready to find both subs. The submarine *Halibut* was secretly dispatched to the Pacific in April and the surface ship *Mizar* was sent to the Atlantic in early June. The *Scorpion* search was protracted, since it initially took place on the more comfortable assumption that the *Scorpion* did not turn around but had continued to move west on her anticipated track. The director of the search, Chester "Bucky" Buchanan, was a civilian scientist with the Naval Research Laboratory. He was an expert in finding lost objects on the seabed. He had a stylish habit of letting his beard grow at the start of a search and then he would communicate success by shaving it off. He did not expect to be pressed for time. Thus he did not resist his initial directive to search in front of the last recorded signal and be-

lieved, as I did, that he was in hot pursuit when he detected underwater magnetic signatures. When these leads proved false—they
were large, hull-shaped rocks—the Navy felt we had exhausted the
possibilities, but Bucky was not one to give up. He asked me to try to
find ways to continue for a few more weeks. I asked the Navy for time
to calibrate the area, whatever that meant, and one week later we received word that Bucky Buchanan had shaved off his beard. Studying the submarine with the care necessary to determine the cause of
the loss would be deferred for one year until the *Trieste II* could be
completed, tested, and transported to the site in a floating dry dock.
This will be described in greater detail in the next chapter.

The search for the Soviet sub was easier—we knew *where* it disappeared and our scenario indicated it had sunk there. Once again,
to avoid security violation, I have to turn to *Blind Man's Bluff* for evidence that I can neither confirm nor deny. Nevertheless, there are a
number of elements in that story that I can indeed confirm without
crossing the line. It was certainly true, for example, that hardly anyone aboard the *Halibut* knew what her mission was. True as well is
the story of the *Halibut*'s photographer bursting out of the tiny dark-
room overcome with emotion by his perfect picture showing that at
last the sunken submarine had been found—three miles down in the
target site, says *Blind Man's Bluff*. The photograph, the first of
22,000, again according to the book, displayed the sail with its call
numbers clearly legible.

Friends and students immediately asked me what those numbers
were. The numbers on the submarine's sail (and I cannot tell you what
they were because of security classification) would remain as engraved
in my mind as the numbers 180/40. Family members of the Soviet
sailors who went down with the ship, interviewed in 1999 by *60 Minutes*, speak of it as the *K129*. I can honestly say without any breach of
security that it was news to me when I heard that on *60 Minutes*, just
as it was news to me the first time I heard the boat described as a Golf-

class submarine in a 1978 book on the *Glomar Explorer*. (The *Glomar Explorer* was a huge surface ship constructed for a top secret CIA operation. Under a cover story that the boat, ostensibly owned and operated by Howard Hughes's Summa Corporation, was engaged in a commercial enterprise to mine manganese nodules from the seabed, the *Glomar* attempted to raise the Russian sub in 1974. The effort failed in terms of complete recovery and continues to be considered by the media a colossal boondoggle, but remains highly classified.)

When I first came across the Tom Clancy novel *The Hunt for Red October*, I was jolted by my recollection that the CIA had referred to our mission as "the hunt for Red September." Or was I confusing this with a decision not to search for a Soviet November-class nuclear submarine that sank in 1970? If my recollection is correct then it implies deliberate disinformation on the part of the authorities and even suggests that such disinformation might have found its way into an immensely popular novel. But such speculation is frowned on in intelligence circles, and it can be argued that the specific title and class of the submarine is nearly irrelevant, particularly when one recalls that *Halibut* retained its designation as a cruise missile submarine long after it had been completely modified for very different missions.

Of far greater significance is the vivid description given in *Blind Man's Bluff* of one of those many photographs: that of a skeletonized Russian sailor lying on the seafloor, "dressed in foul-weather gear, a brown sheepskin coat buttoned up to his neck, thick wool pants, and heavy black military boots." The conclusion is almost inescapable. The so-called Golf-class sub was on the surface when the fatal event took place.

What should we look for now that we have found the submarine? First we should seek evidence of explosive damage that would account for the single loud bang. *Blind Man's Bluff* reports "a hole blown nearly ten feet wide just behind the Golf's conning tower." It then surmises that the hole "probably came from a hydrogen buildup that could have occurred as the crew sat charging the diesel submarine's 450-ton sulfuric acid battery."

When I read this I could not restrain my sardonic chuckle. I have never seen or heard of a submarine disaster that was not accompanied by the notion that the battery blew up and started it all. This is such a classic error that I must tell an old World War II Rickover story to explain why this speculation sooner or later appears.

Shortly after Lieutenant Commander Rickover was put in charge of fleet electrical systems, one of the old S-boats operating in the Philippines was in need of a new battery but spare parts were in short supply. Adopting extreme measures to extend operational life was the order of the day. Rickover instructed the submarine personnel to give the dead battery a maximum overcharge and then a "flash discharge," which it was hoped would add a few more months of life. By a flash discharge he meant simply throwing the cables of the overcharged battery overboard. The highly conductive seawater would cause the most violent short circuit imaginable, thereby cleaning the battery plates and extending its life. The procedure was carried out with gusto and the battery promptly exploded. The sub was towed to port and given a brand-new battery. Rickover's failed solution was not resented. The crew now had a new battery and if the technique had worked they would have been popular with the rest of the fleet. This story was especially edifying to me in my role of hunting for lost submarines. Naive investigators, examining the damage in salvaged battery compartments, invariably blame the sinking on battery explosions until they learn that any fully charged battery suddenly exposed to seawater will explode. It is an inevitable effect of a sinking and almost never a cause.

In the real world that hole in the Soviet submarine's sail was caused by some other exploding component. Fortunately there is a clue. Each of its missiles' warheads has a high explosive component—and two of the sub's nuclear warheads were missing. One was obviously torn from its missile and the other was completely out of sight. No mention is made of the missile to which this second warhead must have been attached. A Discovery Channel documentary suggests that this missile fell out of the tube when the *Glomar Explorer* tried to raise the sub. No evidence for this assertion is cited in the program but the show does have a colorful bit of animation showing how it might have happened.

For my part, I can add a piece to solving the puzzle that has never appeared before, a detail obtained on an unclassified basis many years ago. While the Russian submarine was presumed to be at sea, an oceanographic ship of the University of Hawaii was conducting research in the oceanic waters off Hawaii's Leeward Islands. The researchers discovered a large slick on the surface of the ocean, collected a sample, and found that it was highly radioactive. They reported this to George Woolard, the director of the Hawaii Institute of Geophysical Research. Although Woolard was unaware of my role in intelligence operations, he knew that I was Chief Scientist of Polaris and informed me of this find. He asked whether the Navy already knew about it and if the information was of any consequence.

Fearing that the university would release this to the press, I replied quite incorrectly that the Navy was fully informed. It was the result of a minor spill of no significance, I said, and the Navy would be embarrassed by it being made public, as it would create much ado about nothing. Furthermore, I deliberately withheld this intriguing report from others who were cleared for the Soviet submarine investigation. They had no need to know. It did not in any way alter the analysis of the event. If *Blind Man's Bluff* is correct (and since I was privy to all of the photographs I will not dispute its conclusion), two warheads were outside the sub and the one that could be seen had suffered violent mechanical damage, probably caused by an explosion. The probability that a detonation of high-energy explosive in that warhead was the cause of the damage was equally high—the radioactive sample wasn't required to prove that. The repercussions of the release of that additional information to the public—or, the more likely event, the attempt to suppress it—would have been very grave because all hell would have broken loose. And not for justifiable reasons.

At this point, it seems logical to examine the implications of the disappearance of the two warheads and the uncertainty regarding the existence—or absence—of a missile in the launching tube.

A highly probable scenario is that the submarine was a rogue and that it was probably a Golf, a diesel-powered, not nuclear-powered, submarine. At a time when the development of the ballistic missile was progressing so rapidly, this sub could have been armed with a liquid-fueled missile with a range of 350 miles or, according to the accepted authority, *Jane's Fighting Ships*, a liquid-fueled missile with a range of 750 miles and a one-megaton warhead. Polaris had a one-megaton warhead that was reputedly very much lighter than the highly inefficient Soviet warheads. But a 1,700-mile range (the distance from 180/40 to, say, Honolulu) could have been achieved with a lighter warhead, and if we credit *Jane's Fighting Ships*, the Soviet Union had already engineered rockets with 1,500-mile ranges. At the time I conducted a Bayes subjective probability assessment and concluded that there was a small probability that the Russian submarine, whatever its name and class, could have reached Hawaii with a nuclear warhead.

To put it succinctly, there existed a possibility, small though it might be, that the skipper of this rogue submarine was attempting to launch or had actually launched a ballistic missile with a live warhead in the direction of Hawaii.

There is also a small possibility that this launch attempt doomed the sub. Whatever happened, something in the missile's warhead may have exploded, causing the initial damage and possibly kicking off a chain of other events. Given the fact that the sub was armed with highly flammable liquid-fueled missiles, an explosion was certain to produce a conflagration in the command and control area. It would certainly have killed everyone in the vicinity. The surviving crew members would have made efforts to get on deck and put out the fire or, failing that, abandon ship. And those fighting the fire would be dressed in protective garb—like the clothing and boots on the skeleton.

The Soviets, like us, have certain mechanisms designed to prevent the unauthorized launching of a missile or the unauthorized arming of its warhead. Nothing that has been invented through man's ingenuity cannot be circumvented by equal ingenuity. And a little good luck. Here may be a case where both ran just a bit short. The unauthorized attempt to launch or arm the missile and its warhead may have triggered a mechanism in the warhead, which in turn triggered the high-explosive component in the warhead—because such precautionary mechanisms are designed to do just that to prevent such unauthorized use. The possibility of defeating these precautionary systems is small.

How small is small? If we take as the yardstick of being close to World War III the events at the height of the 1962 Cuban Missile Crisis—where in spite of all that happened there is something akin to zero probability that anyone attempted to launch, let alone launched, a thermonuclear missile—then even very, very small looms large. I communicated this personal conclusion to Gene Fubini of the DIA Scientific Advisory Board and later I communicated this conclusion to Carl Duckett of the CIA.

This line of inferential reasoning was so disturbing that few wished to contemplate it. This was news that General Secretary Brezhnev would not want to hear. It was news that President Johnson did not want to hear. Johnson had been hearing so much news that he did not want to hear that he had decided he would not run for reelection that year. The new President, Richard Nixon, and his National Security Adviser, Henry Kissinger, however *did* want to hear this news and were in fact briefed almost immediately after Nixon took office. So impressed was he by this briefing that the new President flew to Hawaii—on an unannounced trip that does not appear on the official record—and presented the Presidential Unit Citation to the *Halibut*—the highest award of its kind and the first time it was awarded in peacetime. The crew had performed a great service for their country, the President told them. He could not, however, reveal what it was, he said; neither were they to speculate nor could they ever expect to know. He did not fly to Hawaii on *Air Force One*, nor did he meet with any officials of the state of Hawaii, and the ceremony was conducted in secret.

To my further surprise, I was given the Department of Defense's highest civilian award, the Distinguished Civilian Service Award. That ceremony was conducted by Secretary of Defense Melvin Laird and Secretary of the Navy John H. Chafee, and the only attendees were my completely mystified wife and ten-year-old son. This is not the type of award one can hang in one's den. I have never even seen the citation.

At about the same time, I was cleared for the CIA project to recover the Russian submarine from the ocean floor. I immediately volunteered my team for this operation. It is a fundamental principle of intelligence operations that the successful team in a highly compartmentalized operation be retained for subsequent phases in order to limit the number of people cleared for top secret or Special Intelligence operations. I was turned down and advised that the operation would be conducted from a surface ship.

As the entire world would learn in due course, this "clandestine" operation would be mounted by a ship then still to be built—the future *Glomar Explorer*. When I learned that the proposed cover story for this operation would be the harvesting of manganese nodules from the seabed for the commercial recovery of nickel, copper, and cobalt, I strenuously objected.

The primary reason for my objection was that cover stories have to be true. I was aware that metals refined from such manganese nodules would not be commercially viable for scores of years, if not a century. The cover was sure to be blown. The second reason that I objected was my awareness that we had made very substantial advances in deep ocean technology and a covert operation conducted completely beneath the sea would be simpler, cheaper, and could be carried out in complete secrecy. *And we had the capability to do so!* But apparently that was not the game.

Why should Nixon go to all that trouble, fly all that way in a discreet aircraft, just to hand out a citation? Any number of admirals could have done that. One might reasonably speculate that the other purpose of Nixon's trip was to meet with a person or persons unknown—and not necessarily in Hawaii.

After the sub was discovered and photographed and Nixon and Kissinger were fully briefed, there was a telephone conversation between Brezhnev and Nixon. Nixon publicly announced that he had "personally rescued flagging arms control talks" in a conversation with the General Secretary. But what preparatory conversations or discussions took place before that phone call? And what helped him "rescue" the arms talks?

The key to understanding Nixon's shift from use of Navy resources to the still controversial CIA *Glomar Explorer* project lies first in the recognition that Kissinger was the architect of Nixon's foreign policy and national security policy, just as Haldeman and Ehrlichman were the sole overlords and gatekeepers of his domestic policy. Nixon would never on his own initiative make a secret visit to Hawaii in order to honor the *Halibut* and its crew—not solely for that purpose.

The second key to understanding is in the strategy pursued by Henry Kissinger. There was a fundamental difference between the deterrence philosophy of the Special Projects community and the Kissinger philosophy. A hallmark of Kissinger's approach was deterrence through the communication of uncertainty. In his 1960 book *The Necessity for Choice*, Kissinger devotes a section to "Deterrence Through Uncertainty." Uncertainty, he writes, "has a certain utility. It makes the calculations of the aggressor more difficult. . . . Uncertainty about the nature of our retaliation may be the best means of producing certainty that some retaliation will occur." The discovery of a high probability that the Soviet submarine was some sort of rogue and that at the outset the Soviets had no idea that its loss was not just an accident, was a situation made to order for Kissinger. Moreover, our disclosure to the Soviets of what we had learned about their submarine would likely raise an unanswerable question in Brezhnev's mind about his command and control of his armed forces.

As in the MIT games, in which the hot line between the American President and the Soviet leader was immediately activated in a crisis of uncertainty, we can now understand why Nixon immediately communicated with Brezhnev and made a public announcement with respect to that communication. Against the backdrop of the Kissinger strategy of uncertainty, the *Glomar Explorer* strategy of the CIA, far from being the $500 million sand castle for which it has become famous, made a good deal of sense. It was a form of blackmail that said to the Soviets, "If you do not play ball, and negotiate steps leading to détente we will retrieve your submarine and demonstrate to the whole world what it planned to do." Of course we were not sure what we would find or whether we could demonstrate anything, but neither were the Soviets, and they were afraid to acknowledge the existence of the operation or to interfere in any way. If this was the scenario, the *Glomar* recovery operation *had* to be one that could be observed by Soviet intelligence. The CIA and the DIA knew that the Soviets could and would observe every phase of the construction and deployment of the *Glomar*.

I had my own mischievous opportunity in September of 1974 to unmask the clandestine nature of the operation. In connection with a purely scientific mission, I and some of my colleagues spent several days in the middle of the week at a remote location on Catalina Island. One night we yearned for beer and I remembered that there was a bar open on the weekends to meet the thirst requirements of the weekend sport sailing community. We walked expecting the bar to be closed but it was not. Lights were on and a big crowd of men were at the bar. When we walked in the bartender was dumbfounded. "Where did you guys come from?" "Oh," said I, tongue in cheek, "we were driving down the coast highway and we got lost in the fog." While he was recovering from his apoplexy I recognized and greeted several workmen I knew from Hawaii's Dillingham shipyard. They pled with me not to reveal that they had met me at the bar. Of course not, because the *Glomar* was anchored in the bay— and they were working on her. She was obviously engaged in manganese nodule recovery (a cover must always be true!).

In the meantime, the CIA took charge of this operation, actively excluding others. The agency did not coordinate its strategy with the State Department, the DIA, and other government authorities who had a need to know. The false cover story about the manganese nodules would wreak great damage. It would, as will be seen, result in worldwide misunderstanding of the limits of ocean resources and the waste of precious development resources. Gagged by security restrictions, my inability to reveal the truth when the truth would have made a difference would become an albatross around my neck. I did not know that my future professional activities would place me in positions where my oath of silence would make me an unwilling participant in the distortion of America's foreign policy, obstructing its ability to develop ocean resources, and hurting its accomplishments in inner space. But all that was coming.

16

Pensate Profundus

On January 23, 1960, the strange-looking craft called *Trieste* was lowered into the water above the deepest part of the ocean in the Mariana Trench, a few hundred miles from the shores of Japan. It consisted of a large float filled with high-octane aviation gasoline, beneath which was a sphere designed to resist the pressure of this deepest ocean. There is no mountain on earth that is as high as this deepest deep. More than seven miles down is a barren wasteland where no photon of light, no electromagnetic signal, can be seen or heard. Biological life, if any exists there, depends upon nutrients falling from above, dissolved oxygen in the water below, and the presence of a few fish. Elsewhere in the deep ocean geothermal vents pour out the heat from below the earth's crust. This environment produces strange life forms based on hydrogen sulfide as the molecule of life. But on this day in the deepest point on our watery planet, life as we know it was confined to this single pressure-tight sphere. As described earlier, curled up inside was six-foot-five Jacques Piccard, the designer and builder of this craft that he called a bathyscaphe, and Lieutenant Donald Walsh of the United States Navy, who was assigned to the Office of Naval Research. This office had funded the development and testing of this submersible.

Much like the Apollo moon landing that would follow later, this mission would succeed only if man reached the deepest abyss and returned to the surface. Critical to the success of the mission was the design of the metal sphere that housed the pilots. At a depth of 36,800 feet it would have to resist an external pressure of eight tons per square inch. This is a pressure that is hard to conceive. It is more than one thousand times greater than atmospheric pressure.

Structural engineers will tell you that such a sphere can be built to sustain the pressure—provided the wall is perfectly spherical and appropriately thick. But the slightest deviation in shape can induce buckling, which will cause catastrophic failure at very high pressures. An implosion at depth will have more punch than the most powerful TNT on the surface.

There was no way that the *Trieste* bathyscaphe's gondola could be perfectly spherical, given the necessity for hatches and ports, various protrusions for connections to the float, lights, tools, and other instrumentation that were attached to the exterior of the sphere. There were no pressure tanks on land capable of testing spheres of this size at this pressure, and computers did not then exist that could carry out the detailed structural calculations. Thus the ability of *Trieste* to resist buckling was unknown, success or failure riding on the intuitive sixth sense of the designer.

Imagine the psychological stress on these two pioneers as the sphere reached its record depth. Without warning there was a sharp clink or crunch as the sphere suddenly adjusted its structural config- uration in response to the weight of seven miles of ocean above them. At the sound Don Walsh and Jacques Piccard could only cringe, knowing they were alive and well at that moment but might still have only a fraction of a second to prepare for the lights-out shock of instant violent death. Then came blessed relief. The sphere had not buckled and in fact it had deformed so that its maximum stress had been reduced. Piccard and Walsh returned to the surface destined for long lives as world-record-holding heroes—but the sphere was deformed beyond repair. This first *Trieste* was placed in the custody of the Naval Electronics Laboratory in San Diego. The original sphere was replaced with a new sphere conservatively de- signed for shallower depth. Here it languished under the control of Lieutenant Don Keach, a maverick nonnuclear submariner with a penchant for button pushing on untried experimental vehicles just to see what might happen. Then came the call in 1963 for a vehicle that could find and inspect the lost submarine *Thresher*, whose loss was described earlier. The call was a hopeless plea for help and hope but Keach and the *Trieste* with the shallower depth sphere re- sponded. *Thresher* was about two miles down. *Trieste's* descent from the surface was not a simple thing. At the surface weight must be added until the vehicle is fully submerged. As soon as the vehicle is below the water it begins to sink, but too fast, so weight must be re- moved. If it encounters a density layer at depth, i.e., a layer of water that is denser or heavier because of increases in salinity and/or tem- perature, it will float in the layer until more weight is added. If the Fathometer that is used to measure distance from the surface by look- ing up to the surface is inaccurate in measuring the thousands of feet of water above, and if the Fathometer that is used to measure dis- tance looking down is inaccurate in measuring how many feet there are to the great depths below, there may be no way of knowing whether you are rising or falling. I have sat on density layers in *Aluminaut* for several hours gingerly changing ballast and waiting for some indication of whether the craft is going up or down. This elemental *Trieste* had almost no way of navigating and almost no means of maneuver. It had limited battery power and battery life for the illumination required to see out the ports to determine from the "biological snow" whether you were falling down or rising up.

Skillfully and miraculously, Keach finally made a landing on the hull of *Thresher*, but we could see and learn nothing except that it was there. Then came equipment failure and the smell of an electrical fire in the *Trieste* sphere. What had happened? It was expected that some cables would leak and that the salt water would cause a short circuit, but *Trieste* was equipped with many fuses that would cut the current to a circuit when it was drawing excessive amperage. One or more fuses had failed and now the electrical machinery acted as if its own fuse was burning up—the unchecked current was shorting out and causing an electrical fire inside the sphere. Would the fire spread and what would happen when the *Trieste* returned to the surface and the large tanklike float of high-octane gasoline came in contact with the oxygen-rich atmosphere? One spark or one flame from the electrical fire and disaster would be inevitable.

A longer period of danger of fatal portent no less than that experienced by Walsh and Piccard now awaited Keach and his copilot until they vacated the sphere, secured the power, and emptied the float. *Trieste* had accomplished one more heroic, if only symbolic, mission and once more would not return to the deep ocean without substantial redesign and reconstruction.

It is with full knowledge of this perilous history that Bradley and I considered the possibility of utilizing *Trieste* for Special Intelligence missions. Because of the unique surface craft required for support of the bathyscaphe, the Soviets would spot it immediately. Because of its elemental design, it had no search or observation capability. It was not possible to use the craft on covert missions or in fact on any mission. So we thought, why not requisition *Trieste* and announce to the world that we would use it as a research and development test vehicle? Why not at the same time build a brand-new competent, capable bathyscaphe in secret, then deploy it using *Trieste* as a decoy to convince the Soviets that the only known Deep Submergence Search and Recovery Vehicle was fully occupied and no other capability existed.

Done—without knowledgeable congressional authorization, without preliminary design, without cost effectiveness studies, without a steering task group, two individuals who had authority, responsibility, and accountability—and a mission and a budget—could now proceed.

Construction of the "phantom bathyscaphe" started in a skunk works in September of 1965 and was completed in August of 1966. There was no cover story for this construction. The bathyscaphe had no name. We referred to the phantom as *Trieste II* as a cover if it was ever mentioned outside classified spaces. Indeed, we now referred to the original *Trieste* also as *Trieste II*.

Two barriers to successful completion of the task existed: First, we had to find a way to quickly and rapidly test the design of the new equipment, which had to operate reliably at a depth of at least 20,000 feet. Second, we had to find the cause for the electrical fires on the original *Trieste*. There were not enough pressure-testing facilities at the Navy laboratories to accomplish the task. The pressure-test facilities are hemispheres with heavy flanges and large bolts around the periphery. The item to be tested is placed inside the hemispheres and they are bolted together. It takes many hours to bolt and unbolt these flanges and more than a day to carry out a single test. We called up the experts at the Southwest Research Institute. This nongovernmental organization had carried out all of the design and development work on *Aluminaut*, the submersible built by Reynolds Aluminum Company in the late 1950s despite government refusal to sponsor the design. Could the institute design a pressure tank that could be loaded and unloaded in a short period of time? A novel and innovative design was immediately produced. I had to make the decision to build or not to build. Everything I learned at Cal Tech about elasticity under Professor Hausner was brought into play. Circular rings of differing diameter replaced the flanges and acted as ring fingers so that the two hemispheres could be assembled like hand in glove. The precisely machined holes around the periphery were fitted with tight pins. Assembly and disassembly took about an hour. The one tank did the work of twenty. This tank, built and assembled in absolute secrecy in 1965, was a major reason for the success of NR-1, the DSRVs, and the phantom *Trieste*.

Components designed and manufactured for the DSRV would be the components for the phantom *Trieste*. They were built in the open. They were stored in the DSRV warehouse and passed out the back door by night to be delivered to the skunk works where the phantom *Trieste* was to be assembled. A more difficult problem was maintaining the fiction that the project managers and technicians for these covert activities were not involved in any way with these nonexistent programs. The size and magnitude of Polaris and the Deep Submergence Systems Project was such that one system provided the excuse for an individual's apparent failure to complete important assignments in some other cover program. This fiction could not always be maintained.

For example, one morning in San Francisco there was a DSRV task force meeting. Remarkably, the meeting wound up in the morning and I, along with one or two participants, announced that we were going to the ball game at Candlestick Park. We arrived at the front gate and watched the first inning, and then departed for the skunk works. We got to the skunk works and did our thing and then returned to the ballpark in time for the last inning—since our cover had to be true and we had to know what had happened at the game. Our associates, of course, grumbled at the amount of time we spent playing golf (first tee, eighteenth hole) or poker (all-night sessions that made us late for work the next day). Our cover commandment for these activities was Admiral Raborn's admonition, "I want you guys to work hard and I want you to play hard or you'll never last in this program." All cover stories were true enough, of course, to preserve national security.

In the midst of all this cover subterfuge we were spending a lot of time trying to determine the cause of the bathyscaphe fires and finding out that that was difficult to determine. The fuses that were used were simple metal strips that would melt with current overloads. To keep them out of contact with the salt water they were encased in a small cylinder filled with nonconducting hydrocarbon oil. We failed to remember that the density of hydrocarbons, in either solid, liquid, or gas form, changes dramatically with the application of pressure.

At about 6,000 feet of depth (for most hydrocarbons) comes a point called the "triple point." Here the density of the solid, the liquid, and the gas are the same. Above 6,000 feet, when a fuse blows, the oil vaporizes and carries the heat away. Below that depth the gas does not expand, and the oil gets very hot and breaks down into charred carbon and hydrogen gas. The carbon will conduct electricity. It is like the old gimmick of putting a penny in the fuse box—it doesn't blow and, quite dangerously, doesn't do the job of breaking the circuit before excess current overheats and destroys the mechanism protected by the fuse. The solution seemed simple—we replaced the hydrocarbon oil with silicone oil, which breaks down into nonconducting silica. As we shall see, we were wrong.

The first event of significance in our project to get the phantom *Trieste* operational was the selection of officers and men to man her, and to link support facilities and their assignment to an appropriate naval command. I was greatly surprised, however, by the arrival of a contingent of naval officers and enlisted men, qualified submariners of the line. They were led by Lieutenant Commander Bradford Mooney, who announced that they were reporting for duty. Mooney was probably unaware of the specifics of the intelligence projects and believed he was reporting as his orders specified, to operate the small submersibles, bathyscaphes, and diving facilities that were to be developed by the project office.

I could not reveal to anyone who was not on the list of cleared individuals that this contingent was, as yet unknowingly, a part of a covert operation. Without revealing this fact I had to get these officers assigned to an operational command.

The reader will now understand my command dilemma. When Lieutenant Commander Mooney and his contingent of small-submersible operators reported to me for duty only a few of their superior officers knew that they were to be the operators of the phantom *Trieste*. Everyone else believed that they would be operators of the small submersibles developed by DSSP. Because of security no operational command structure could be established and, again because of security, most of those responsible for establishing such a structure had no reason to believe that one was necessary. I was going to have to fabricate the need for a command structure out of completely unclassified whole cloth.

Having discovered that an East Coast facility called Submarine Development Group Two had no counterpart on the West Coast and that none was foreseen for at least a year, I arranged to rent a dilapidated barracks at the Ballast Point submarine base in San Diego. Stepping into the role of commanding officer, I told Mooney to go west. For the next month, I ordered, the men were to sand the decks, scrape all the paint off the walls, repair the lavatories, polish up the brightwork on the urinals, and in every respect make the outpost worthy of description as a naval facility. Furthermore, I told him to have an appropriate logo designed and to cast a brass submarine command plaque with the motto *"Pensate Profundus,"* Latin for "Think Deep." When these tasks were completed he was to arrange for the commissioning of the facility with all hands in dress whites and officers with swords—plus a Navy band to provide the appropriate music and a congressman to give the commissioning speech.

Mooney was aghast. He said, "Surely, we're not authorized to conduct such a ceremony. This will mean the end of my career."

"Maybe so," I said, "but this is an order."

It was carried out letter perfect in July of 1966 and ended in great fanfare and publicity, all favorable to the submarine Navy and its new mission. The next day I received the expected call from the Pentagon brass.

"Craven, what the hell have you done?"

What else could I have done? said I. If our operations were in the Atlantic, these men would have been under the command of Submarine Development Group Two, but since our operations were in the Pacific we had to attach to Submarine Development Group One. Unfortunately such a group didn't exist, so we invented it.

Our San Diego site, Submarine Development Group One, was headquarters of a submarine intelligence command that would be home for the *Trieste, Halibut,* and the DSRVs and would become a sure route for fame and senior commands in the submarine service, the Navy, and the Department of Defense. The first tasks of this group were the completion of the construction and deployment of the phantom *Trieste* and the completion of the construction and deployment of its supporting dry dock. The dry dock modifications proved to be the most difficult of all the ship modifications undertaken by DSSP. Because the program emanated from the Special Projects Office, it automatically enjoyed the highest priority in the Navy, BrickBat01. We could not explain to the shipyard that this was a fixed budget item for an intelligence decoy. Nor could we explain our desire to employ an old World War II floating dry dock to eliminate Soviet curiosity about a new design. The major design problem revolved around the docking and undocking of the *Trieste*. It had a float that consisted of eighty tons of high-octane aviation gas contained in a light eggshell structure. There was always the possibility of a rupture during the docking process and a spill of an explosively flammable fluid. Everything on board had to be made spark-proof. Every member of the crew as well as visitors had to wear spark-proof rubber-soled shoes. Not only was smoking prohibited in all but a few designated spaces, carrying matches or cigarette lighters was banned.

The modifications of the dry dock and the construction of the phantom were carried out without a specific mission in mind until the submarine *Scorpion* was found in October of 1968. A detailed examination of the *Scorpion*'s hull was required to determine the cause of failure and, most of all, to provide an explanation for what happened—and thus closure—for the families of the crew. Only the phantom could do this. It was thus an opportunity for a new cover mission that would convince the Soviets that all of our deep submergence capability was tied up in domestic operations. But on the premise that all cover missions had to be true we could not pretend to use the original *Trieste* for the operation—and we did not have a current mission in the Pacific for a radically improved bathyscaphe that was still a phantom. We decided to ease the phantom that was built in secret out of the closet as, ostensibly, a modification of the original bathyscaphe with a new float and a new sphere and apparently little else. We called it *Trieste II*. In point of fact it was a very sophisticated vehicle, with integrated controls and displays, a sophisticated manipulator, lights, cameras, sonars, precise navigation, and as much of the equipment that we were manufacturing that could be usefully employed. The reader will recall that the equipment employed on the NR-1 was tested to twenty thousand feet. The wisdom of that decision was made evident in the capabilities of *Trieste II*.

Thus the phantom, now called *Trieste II*, was openly and honestly dedicated to a mission of compassion to find out for the families of the lost men the reason for the ship's demise and to reassure submarine crews that whatever destroyed the *Scorpion* would be discovered and that such a tragedy would never happen again. This did not placate the researchers at the Naval Electronic Laboratory, who were blissfully unaware that the original *Trieste* had no operational capability. They believed that they had lost their deep submergence laboratory capability to a nonmilitary mission. To quiet this unrest at the lab the Navy released a story about another cover mission, not realizing that this information would be the first disclosure in the premature exposure of the Navy's role in Special Intelligence.

At this point, in May of 1968, the ARD (floating dry dock) was on the West Coast and the *Scorpion* was resting on the seafloor in the Atlantic, south of the Azores. The speed of the ARD under tow by a Navy tugboat was at best four knots. A journey of ten thousand miles would take a hundred days. It was arranged that the ship would leave San Diego in November 1968, would pass through the Panama Canal, with a stopover for Christmas leave at a port in Florida, and then it would proceed, again under tow, to the *Scorpion* site. Here it would be joined by a destroyer escort that would ferry men and supplies between the site and the Azores. Captain Harry Jackson, the engineering duty officer for the ill-fated *Thresher*, volunteered to be the on-scene investigator of the wreck as observer on every dive of *Trieste* and photo interpreter between dives. He boarded the dry dock in Florida.

Because I had been involved in the original search for the *Scorpion* and in the investigation of the cause of its loss, I was privileged to participate in the on-scene investigation. As the reader can well imagine my multiple assignments were such that I could not participate in any of the legs of the sea journey. Therefore in July of 1969 I journeyed by commercial air to the Azores, after which I would travel by military air to the island of embarkation of the destroyer escort assigned as courier for the mission. In the Azores I had my first opportunity to actually fly a Navy DC-3 from the commercial airport to the U.S. Air Force base. The Navy pilot was unaware that I was not qualified to fly until he asked me if I wanted to land the plane. Thank God I demurred.

It was less than a day's journey by sea to the site. It was the eve of the big day. The next morning, *Trieste* would make its first dive on *Scorpion*. In a few days the Apollo astronauts were scheduled to make history's first manned landing on the moon. As I've mentioned, our dive to the floor of the Atlantic was at least as difficult technologically as Apollo touching down on the moon, if not more so. We felt that our *Trieste* pilots were as heroic as the astronauts, our mission as spectacular and as significant to humanity. Meanwhile, however, I happened to be right on time for the officer-contractor evening poker game. Detecting more than a little resentment over my arrival just in time for the first dive, considering the months everyone else had been away from home, I had to establish some credibility as "one of the boys." I lit up a cigar with the rest of them in the spark-proof smoking room and played my best.

As Polaris Chief Scientist, I was actively involved in the poker games of a number of naval circles. Each had its own mystique and culture. The high-stakes players were the contractors, and in particular the original designers of the famous Douglas DC-3. Donald Douglas was their hero and Donald Douglas, Jr., was the organizer of the games. Another group consisted of the navigators associated with the MIT Instrumentation Laboratory and North American Aviation. Most professional of the poker players were the officers and senior enlisted men of the service forces, the minesweepers, the salvage ships, the submarine rescue ships, the SeaLabs, and the SEALs. Games would last well into the night or early morning. We played in pre-smoke-detector-equipped spaces and the smoke of preference was the cigar. All of the skippers of the first Polaris sub-marines were inveterate cigar smokers. Captain Osborne of the *George Washington* and Captain Pappy Sims of the *Abraham Lincoln* were never seen without a cigar. Although I never smoked at home, at the office, or in the Washington domains where admirals and cap-tains had need to dominate the scene, I, too, was never seen without a cigar at meetings where my presence was symbolic of the Special Projects Office.

My most flagrant use of the cigar was in conferences with Admi-ral Rickover dealing with the *NR-1*. The admiral did not smoke, so I always showed up with the cheapest, most obnoxious cigars I could find. He would never show signs of annoyance. One day, however, he leaned across the table and asked if the cigar I was smoking was a good one.

"No sir," I replied, "it is a rum-soaked crook, one of the worst ci-gars made. It was given to me by the supervisor of salvage."

"Well, Craven," he said, "what's a good cigar?"

"An Uppman," I said.

"All right, when the *NR-1* is a success, I'll buy you a box of Upp-man cigars." The Kindly Old Gentleman could not bring himself to add, "If you will put that one out." He never did supply the promised box but I'm sure he would have had I not later been replaced, at my request, as the director of the Deep Submergence Systems Project. I requested replacement because as a civilian with the legal status of a commanding officer I was charged with preparing the fitness reports of the naval officers under my command. Their careers depended upon those reports and I did not believe that I had the institutional savvy to prepare them fairly. I was the only project manager who was not a naval officer and the success of DSSP was now producing aspi-rants for the postion. When I was replaced I retained all of my Chief Scientist roles, my unique clearances, and my technical responsibili-ties; I divested myself of a mountain of paperwork.

When Rickover heard of this decision he called me up and said, "Craven, is that what you want? If you don't, I can fix it so that you stay in charge."

I replied, "Yes sir, it is what I want."

He hung up the phone and, except through his aide, he and I never spoke again.

Game by game and story by story my reputation as a poker player grew, but my triumph was to be achieved right here, during the *Trieste II* dives on the *Scorpion*. That first night of poker in July 1969 I won about a hundred dollars. We quit early because of the big day ahead. The excitement of the first dive by *Trieste II* was quickly tempered by a short circuit and an electrical fire. The fuses had not worked again. How could that be? Commercial-grade silicone oil is a mixture of silicone oil and hydrocarbon oil. Not knowing the reason for the change to silicone oil the California shipyard had used commercial-grade oil. New fuses were built in California in a matter of hours and shipped by commercial air to the Azores, then dropped at the site by Navy air. In the meantime the navigation transponders that had been placed on the seafloor for navigation purposes suddenly and unexpectedly came bobbing up to the surface. I knew what was wrong immediately. The transponder beacons had been tethered to their anchors by stainless steel wire. We already knew that stainless steel at the bottom of the ocean must never be scratched. If it is, electrolysis takes place between the parent material and the stainless coat and in a few days the wires will part. The manufacturer had assured us that the cables were not scratched and would not be scratched. Alas a Navy chief, not knowing this fact, had tightened every cable before deployment just to be safe. His strong arm made sure that each fitting cut into the wire to make it secure.

By the time we had replaced the cables and redeployed the navigation net, the new fuses had arrived. Once more we were excited as the *Trieste II* disappeared beneath the waters, and once again our excitement was quickly tempered by a short circuit and an electrical fire. How could that be? Alas, the cases of the replacement fuse were made with a hydrocarbon plastic. Below the triple point the heat from the fuses produced a charred path of carbon on the case, which once more closed the circuit.

This time we had lots of silicone oil and innovative machinists on board and we manufactured new fuses on the site. The next day, July 20, 1969, our excitement was greater than before because, at the same time that *Trieste II* was diving, the astronauts were landing on the moon. It was thus by chance and circumstance that two great moments in history occurred simultaneously. They were, however, observed simultaneously by only a favored few. Our ears were glued to the acoustic transmissions from the *Trieste II*, but we could listen simultaneously to a radio broadcast of the moon landing. *Scorpion* was in fact spotted about the same time that the Apollo landing module was nearing the moon's surface. In the meantime, *Trieste II* could see that *Scorpion*, when it had plunged to the bottom, had created a large mound of seabed material around its bow. *Trieste II* had a chain attached to its tail, resting on the bottom. This was used to fine-tune its height above the seabed. Rising, she lifted the chain from the bottom, adding weight, compensating for an excess in buoyancy. She was thus always in a neutrally buoyant position. But the chain also stirred up the seabed, and the *Trieste II* pilot was concerned that this might release an avalanche from the mound around *Scorpion*. Thus he proceeded slowly and cautiously, which almost precisely paralleled the cautious landing on the moon. Indeed, the *Trieste II* touched down in front of *Scorpion* as Neil Armstrong set foot on the moon. Hearing the astronaut's historic words, "That's one small step . . . ," we all reacted by raising our arms to the sky. Someone shouted, "No, dammit, no! *Two* small steps!"

But there was no envy, only pride in our own achievement. Over the next week or so, *Trieste II* obtained a series of partially successful and partially frustrating results. It collected many photographs, but we were unable to inspect the torpedo doors. As we have learned since, that particular inspection might have been crucial and determinative. Almost nothing had escaped from the hull except the ship's sextant, which was recovered by *Trieste II*. It is the icon for seamen navigators, who are guided by the stars. It is now displayed in the Naval Museum in Washington, D.C. Ancient Mariners who view it and know its tale will hear in their mind the impassioned plea of the seaman's hymn:

> *Jesus, Savior, pilot me*
> *Over life's tempestuous sea;*
> *Chart and compass come from thee*
> *Jesus, Savior, pilot me.*

Soon we had gotten all that we could underwater, and I had won all of the money at the poker game that I dared. When it came time for me to go, I recognized that I would be departing with a substantial sum extracted from individuals who had sacrificed months of their lives to be part of this historic mission, so I gave the major portion of my winnings to the commanding officer to be used for a party in the Azores when the job was done.

I learned later that the CO called in all the poker players and, informing them of my gesture, suggested that they do the same. The story is probably apocryphal but legend has it that there was open bar for all the officers, crew, and contractors for two days after their return. Probably not true, but man's capacity for sea stories should exceed his reality or what's a legend for?

17

MIT Days

On June 17, 1966, Congress established, in the executive office of the President, a National Council on Marine Resources and Engineering Development. Vice President Hubert Humphrey was its chairman and eight members of the President's cabinet were its members. On January 9, 1967, the President appointed a Commission on Marine Science, Engineering, and Resources under the chairmanship of Julius A. Stratton, former president of the Massachusetts Institute of Technology. The commission, reporting to the council, carried out a two-year study called "Our Nation and the Sea," leading to a recommendation for the establishment of a national "inner space" program comparable to the nation's program in space. The commission report, "A Plan for National Action," was released on January 9, 1969.

I had expected Hubert Humphrey to be elected President of the United States in 1968 and to initiate a major program of ocean development leading to the occupation of inner space. I had been promised a major role in NOAA, the new National Oceanographic and Atmospheric Administration. My missions for the Navy, I had thought, were complete, and I was eager to involve myself in what I regarded as one of the major problems that now faced society, the

239

impact on ocean resources of the population explosion and migra-
tion to the coastal zones. But Humphrey, of course, was defeated. As
an inveterate liberal Democrat, I saw little prospect of a role in the
Nixon administration, and I gave some thought to spending a year in
academia. Once again fate intervened, and politics, playing its
strange tricks, made me a bedfellow of the Nixon administration.

In January 1969, I received a call from John Calhoun, president
of the University of Texas and an old friend from the ocean technology community. His first words were a caution, reminding me of the
Hatch Act forbidding political activity by government employees. I
was not to tell him whether I was a Republican or a Democrat.
"Okay, John," I said, "I won't tell you" (he already well knew my liberal proclivities). There had been a major oil spill off Santa Barbara,
he continued, and he had been appointed chairman of a presidential
commission to investigate. He was seeking members for the commission but the ground rules were that no commission member could be
associated with either the oil industry or any environmental group.
Each member had to be an expert in the technology of offshore oil,
and most important of all, each had to be a loyal Republican. "If you
tell me you are a Democrat," he said, "I may not have a commission."

I played along. I was already aware from inside information that
the Nixon administration was developing an enemies list in early
1969 and I had presumed that I was an automatic candidate for that
list. I did not know that there was a list of conservative Republicans
who could be counted upon to loyally support the administration in
its many secret agendas. I did not imagine that, thanks to a bizarre bit
of administrative bungling, my membership on the Santa Barbara
commission placed me on this list of conservative Republicans. Be
that as it may, everyone on the Santa Barbara oil spill commission
.was well aware that we would be politically pilloried by both the oil
industry and the environmentalists. We were also under siege from
the Santa Barbara press simply because of the presumption that the

commission had been appointed to keep the finger of blame from pointing at the federal government, which had approved the drilling of the well that resulted in the spill.

Worse, we soon discovered that we were up against a near hopeless situation. The spill had come from a well drilled by a subcontractor that had never built an offshore platform before. All my students know how to respond to the question "What happens when you use land-based technology in the ocean?" They learn from day one to answer in unison: "You die."

Sure enough, the platform designer had not realized that while oil on land flows downhill, oil in the ocean flows uphill. Nor had he known that if you drill more than one hole in the well to recover oil from more than one strata, the oil from the lower strata, which is under pressure, will enter the upper strata and, if the pressure exceeds the weight of the soil above, the entire formation will crack open— with the oil pouring out along the crack.

When we arrived at Santa Barbara such was the case. The crack in the seabed was about a half mile long. The Coast Guard had attempted to place a floating boom around the spill but there were not enough booms in the nation to encircle this spill. Besides, the oil company had refused the help of the Coast Guard and had called in the famous Red Adair, whose legendary skill at plugging runaway oil wells had been given national prominence. Red, however, was at a loss. Obviously it did no good to plug the drill pipe. The oil was spilling unabated. The beaches of Santa Barbara were black with oil. Environmentalists were photographing dead oil-soaked birds. The highway was clogged with rubberneckers and protesters. Reporters looking for a new angle and a new twist were everywhere.

The new Secretary of the Interior, Walter Hickel, sought an audience with President Nixon, but was denied the meeting by Haldeman and Ehrlichman, the President's aides. Hickel went public, furious that a cabinet member could not talk to his President when-

ever he was so motivated. Santa Barbara had become an environmental, technical, and political disaster for the Nixon administration, still in its early days. What then to do? The commission was not
empowered to take charge of the operation or even give advice to
the oil company. But the oil company had no idea how to clean up its
mess.

John Calhoun and I, ocean technologists, thought the solution
was simple. Install tents underwater, we advised. One half mile of
impervious canvas tents anchored to the seafloor over the source.
The oil will flow into the tents, its buoyancy will make the tents balloon, and a simple hose at the top can direct the oil into a tanker
without so much as a pump. No oil spill, no stopping the oil flow, no
loss of oil revenue for the company. Impossible, said the land-based
company engineers. The water was two hundred feet deep at the site
and divers can only operate at that depth for a few minutes at a time.
Hadn't they heard of saturation diving? we asked. No they had not,
but they agreed to give it a try. They tried, failed, tried and failed
again because of their inexperience, but in the end finally got it
right. Tents and saturation divers ended the spill and as far as I know
that is how the oil continues to be collected at that site to this day.

As I anticipated, the commission was reviled by both the environmentalists and the oil industry, but praised by the Nixon administration. I, alas, was branded a Republican, and placed on the list of
White House friends. The implications of this had yet to sink in. I
proceeded with my plans. I took a leave without pay from my official
position as Chief Scientist of the Special Projects Office. My office
furniture, my mahogany desk, and my flag were placed in storage and
my administrative assistant was in demand for temporary assignments at the executive level. I applied to the Massachusetts Institute
of Technology and to the Scripps Institution of Oceanography.
Scripps sent me a pile of paper to fill out. MIT sent me a one-page
letter telling me when and where to report. Draper, the founder of

MIT's Instrumentation Laboratory, was enthusiastic about the prospect of my sabbatical and volunteered to rent the guest house on his Victorian estate to the Craven family. An office was provided as well. On the first payday I stood in line waiting to initiate the laborious bureaucratic process that I was certain I would have to endure, since I had yet to be asked for my Social Security number or any other documentation. But I got to the window, gave them my name, and they handed me my check. Here was an institution in which I could get my work done.

I had been given a half-time appointment in political science, where apart from teaching I could revise a paper on sea power and the seabed that I had written for the Naval Institute *Proceedings*, and a half-time appointment in naval architecture, where I would give a course in the design of ocean systems. The students in that course were exclusively engineering duty officers of the Navy or civilian employees of the Ship System Command. I welcomed these appointments but the MIT community did not welcome me. The campus was in ferment over the war in Vietnam and anything military. There were three "evil empires" on the campus: the political science department, because it had advised Kennedy on counterinsurgency; the school of naval architecture, because the students were naval officers proud to wear their uniforms to class; and Draper's Instrumentation Laboratory for its role in the development of the MIRVs for the Polaris and other missiles. As Chief Scientist for Polaris, as professor of political science, and professor of naval architecture, I was an embodiment of all three evils. To make matters worse, I was living in the Draper guest house.

The stage had been set the previous spring. MIT had been contemplating divesting the Instrumentation Laboratory of military contracts and there was even talk of closing the lab. The Defense Department rallied to Draper's support, documenting the importance of his contribution to the nation. As part of this effort, Admiral Raborn had given me the task of assembling an account of the professional life of this remarkable man.

Draper was born into an affluent family in 1901. The Wright brothers were his childhood heroes, and his adolescent heroes were the flying aces of World War I. Even as a young man he owned his own airplane, studied aeronautics, and experimented with stability and control, technical terms for daredevil flying. Flamboyance and technical proficiency were his hallmarks. He soon learned how vulnerable the airplane was to gyroscopic forces and realized that the gyroscope itself could be used as an instrument to measure these forces and manipulate the control surfaces of the plane.

His first experiments were manned demonstrations and, on one flight, he took the president of MIT along, put the plane into an apparently uncontrollable spin, and brought it out just before hitting the ground—or so it seemed to the president. Draper's Ph.D. thesis was on the role of the gyroscope in controlling manned flight. (In his thesis he inserted a page that offered a case of scotch to any professor who would call his attention to that sheet of paper during his oral exam. None did.) He never stopped mixing technology with pleasure. For as long as anyone could remember, he kept a bar in his office with a sign saying, "No Drinks Before 5:00 P.M." But when occasion warranted, Draper's impish grin would suddenly appear. He would push a button under his desk and the hands on the wall clock would move to five o'clock.

His opportunity to apply his technological genius came soon after his appointment as a professor at MIT. The attack on Pearl Harbor was followed three days later by the sinking of the British warships *Repulse* and *Prince of Wales*. Early widespread pessimism about the war's outcome was nourished by the dreadful inadequacy of the antiaircraft guns on Allied ships. If the gunner kept his sights on the incoming attacker, the plane would be out of harm's way before the shells fired would reach its altitude. A mechanism that would aim the gun, not where the plane was but where it would be, was lacking. This "lead angle" estimation was beyond the ability of even the most skilled gunners.

The Navy and its gun sight manufacturers Norden and Sperry were at a loss until young Doc Draper somehow entered the picture. He had theorized that a gyro set in a very viscous fluid would rotate at right angles and come to a halt at an angle proportional to the rate of rotation. That meant that the lead angle of the gun barrel could be set in a way that the gunner had only to aim at the target and the gyros would do the rest. Testing this theory, Draper took an ordinary shoe box, went to a brand-new parking lot at MIT while it was still being tarred, and collected soft asphalt, which behaves like a viscous fluid. He filled the box with this gunk, mounted a gyro inside, and attached it to a gun sight. The contraption was taken to a naval laboratory at Dahlgren, Virginia, and tried out against a plane towing a target. It worked.

The Draper gun sights were hastily manufactured and installed on the battleship *South Dakota*. In its first engagement with Japanese aircraft, she shot down every attacking plane. The sights were rapidly deployed for the entire fleet.

During the Cold War, Draper was in at the beginning, working on both the Ships Inertial Navigation System and the Polaris guidance system for the Special Projects Office. The Draper lab also worked with the other services and with NASA. Computers were still in their infancy, but Draper delivered the advanced model required for the Apollo mission to the moon. The docking problem for the DSRV, though far less publicized, was twice as difficult as the moon landing—and solved by Draper with the use of two Apollo computers.

In spite of all these accomplishments in the national interest, Draper was now on the hot seat. Defense Secretary McNamara had decided that the Polaris missile needed MIRVs. Each Polaris missile would then be capable of carrying sixteen independent hydrogen bombs. Draper's Instrumentation Laboratory had been the contractor. The students protesting the war were also protesting the proliferation of nuclear weapons. Many, if not most, of the faculty joined them. Moreover, they argued that classified research was incompatible with academic freedom and the movement to divest the nation's universities of Defense Department research was in full flower.

Hearings were to be held by the MIT board of regents in the spring of 1969. As (still) Chief Scientist of Special Projects, I was scheduled to give testimony. Immediately before my appearance at the hearings, an MIT professor called to ask if I would meet with a few of the students afterward to discuss their concerns. I agreed, though another professor, learning of my acceptance, questioned my sanity. The day of the hearings coincided with a teach-in, and my willingness to talk with the students had been advertised far and wide. The meeting room was transferred to the gymnasium. When I arrived, it was overflowing with hostile students and teachers. The professor who introduced me was brief. He said, "Here he is."

I asked if someone would tell me their concerns. Secrecy was the first one. They wanted to know the number of MIRVs, their yield, and their accuracy. Those were indeed secrets, I said, and I was bound by security not to reveal them. But there must be somebody in the audience who thinks he knows, I said. Information was volunteered and a consensus reached and we all concluded that it was probably correct. Let us see, I said, what is inappropriate about this many warheads. How many of you, I went on, believe in some sort of deterrence? Nearly all believed. The crowd began to warm. A lot of give-and-take ensued. After three hours, the professors who had organized the encounter announced that they had had enough and asked everyone to join them in walking out. Some did, but the vast majority stayed for a dialogue that lasted for about five more hours. I don't know if I changed anybody's mind, certainly not my own, but at the end of my academic year appointment (Fall 1969–Summer 1970), the professors presented me with a plaque bearing a citation lifted from an editorial in the paper of the militant student group SDS, Students for a Democratic Society. It said, "Although Professor Craven wins all his arguments with fantastic logic, he is obviously out of his mind."

In that same year the Instrumentation Laboratory was in fact divested of its defense contracts and reconstituted as the Draper Laboratory. The political science department was bombed; no one was hurt. I was picketed and my children were ostracized at the Newton public schools, but I still accepted every invitation to discuss the issues and defend deterrence and the Draper Lab's crucial role in deterrence.

My year at MIT, in spite of the political turmoil, was very productive. My class in ocean systems consisted of sixteen engineering duty officers and one civilian from Ship System Command. As a class assignment each officer had to design a naval system for some new mission. I would lead them through the design process on the basis of my own experience. Their class studies would ultimately be published in a text on ocean engineering systems. One of my cardinal principles of design is that the designer have an actual sea experience that would replicate the problems he would encounter when his own system was deployed. I soon discovered that although my students were Academy graduates, few of them had an experience that I believed would qualify. So I arranged for the Navy to bring a motor torpedo boat to Boston from a new class of vessels called "nasty" that was being deployed in Vietnam. The Navy had already lost six of them in combat.

Fortuitously, for demonstration purposes, a furious nor'easter appeared on the day that we deployed. Cold sleet enveloped the ship, the sea was fully arisen. It was necessary to head into the sea tacking just enough on each heading to make advance along the chosen course. Safety lines were rigged for officers while they were outside on the deck. No one was seasick, since the slamming and pounding were so great that we were outside the seasickness motion window. I then gave each officer some tasks that involved manual dexterity. Most were unable to execute them. Class dismissed! Our post-voyage seminar addressed the changes in design required to minimize loss in combat and to maximize mission performance. Almost all the members of that class went on to distinguished careers in system design to the level of captain. At least two made admiral.

My MIT year also provided new opportunities for shaping the nation's destiny at sea. To my surprise a letter from Republican senator Edward Brooke of Massachusetts offered me an appointment to the Defense Intelligence Agency Scientific Advisory Board. The Nixon administration, he said, had asked him as a condition of this appointment to verify my political "correctness." The senator thought this to be inappropriate. Political affiliation should play no role in appointment to a committee so intimately involved in national security, he said, and he therefore hoped that I would understand why he had taken the liberty of vouching for me in advance to insure my appointment.

Since I had come to MIT convinced there was no place for me in Nixon's Washington, the senator's letter was quite ironic. But I was now, as I wanted to be, reenrolled in shaping the nation's intelligence strategy and programs as we sought to contain and win the Cold War.

In December 1969, I received a call from James Wakelin, who had been assistant secretary of the Navy in the Eisenhower administration. He had been appointed chairman of a presidential commission to look at the government's relationship with the ocean and ocean activities. He asked me to be a member of this commission. We went through the party affiliation routine, but this time my name had been provided to him by the White House. He wanted me to be on his commission whichever party was in power, and I agreed to serve.

Now my teaching assignments had to be interspersed with surreptitious trips to the Pentagon to advise the DIA on national intelligence and with publicized trips to the executive office of the White House to advise on ocean policy.

Service on the DIA Scientific Advisory Board was frustrating for all. I was not the only one who had been disturbed by the CIA's taking over underwater intelligence. The DIA was very upset. Its Scientific Advisory Board had as complete a survey of all the intelligence projects in the Defense Department, their technology, and their results, as any group in the United States. Although I was not then a member, the board had relied on me for briefings on submarine intelligence. But I had been cut off from detailed knowledge of the CIA's undersea program, and both the board and I were deemed by the CIA as not having a need to know. I was, however, in touch with someone who had such a need. It is too late to indict the late intelligence officer Gary Lang (the Air Force intelligence officer assigned to ride on *Halibut* during its missions) for the "heinous crime" he committed within the precincts of Special Intelligence: keeping me, and thus the DIA, informed of the progress of the CIA program.

As for the Wakelin commission on ocean policy, our first White House meeting in January 1970 boded well. An enthusiastic young staffer told us to conduct our study for the good of the nation without restraint. The Stratton commission report "Our Nation and the Sea" had just been released and we decided to adopt it and convert it to a Republican document. Rewriting assignments were made. One month later we returned and were greeted by one of Nixon's top echelon deputies. I can't recall whether it was Haldeman or Ehrlichman, but one being the same as the other was a given. There had been some changes in our instructions. Our report had to match the conclusion of the executive office, which he then wrote on the blackboard: "The oceans are not of commercial importance to the United States." Whereupon he walked out.

The Republicans of the committee, not to speak of the sole Democrat, were thunderstruck. Almost all of them were involved in the commercial exploitation of the ocean and they had anticipated strong government support. No one but I was aware of the CIA decision to incorporate underwater intelligence, employing submarines, saturation divers, and other undersea machines as a major source of global intelligence. It was all too clear to me that the advances we had made in ocean technology were to be held under wraps as long as possible for espionage purposes and that superiority was to be maintained by a deliberate undercutting of support for nonmilitary ocean technology. Only this can explain the deliberate attempt, in the name of the *Glomar Explorer*, to persuade the world that the major resource of the oceans was manganese nodules, rocks lying on the inaccessible seabed. I suddenly realized that I had been a participant in wounding, if not killing, programs in ocean technology. I would carry that responsibility for the rest of the century thanks to the mistaken assumption that I was somehow involved in the *Glomar* caprice. I hope the publication of this book will relieve me of that burden.

18

A Sea Lawyer in Hawaii

Blessed is that man
Who with scorners sitteth not
But delights in law.
He shall be a supple tree,
His leaf green, fruit in season.

—Psalm 1
(Metrical version)

In the hysteria that prevailed after Pearl Harbor, American citizens in Hawaii of Japanese ancestry faced the same shameful internment that was imposed on Japanese-Americans on the mainland. But had the military shunned them, it would have decimated its civilian workforce. John Burns, a detective on the Honolulu police force, chaired a commission to decide the matter. Burns declared that all but a very few Japanese-Americans were loyal citizens of their country and asked the Japanese-American community to identify the few who should be interned. Only a very small number were.

Burns also recommended that the Army establish an infantry battalion composed entirely of Japanese-American recruits. Thus was born the 442nd "go for broke" Regimental Combat Team. They would fight valiantly in the front ranks of the American Army from Anzio beach in Italy, and across the fields of France to the gates of Berlin. They would be the bravest, most decorated battalion of the war; the fiercest fighters, with the highest percentage of casualties of any American unit in the European theater.

These brave men came home after the war, went to college, married, embarked on careers—and worked with John Burns, who became governor of Hawaii, to make the American dream a reality in multiracial Hawaii. Their goal was to dominate the political process in the territory of Hawaii, to achieve statehood, to send representatives to Congress, not for personal gain but to serve their country one more time. They insisted on doing their part to insure Hawaii's participation as equals in the deterrence of nuclear war, in the winning of the Cold War, and in the assurance of a permanent and lasting peace.

They succeeded. They are disappearing now, but one of their number, Congressional Medal of Honor winner Senator Daniel K. Inouye, remains active in the United States Senate in shaping the size, composition, deployment, and missions of the armed forces of the United States. He has had Top Secret, Q, and Special Intelligence clearances longer than almost any individual and his memory goes back to December 7, 1941.

During my work with *Halibut* I made numerous visits to Hawaii. It was during one of those that I was asked to meet with Governor Burns. That day I met the man who would supplant Admiral Raborn and Admiral Smith as the major influence shaping my destiny. Even in those first moments, I knew that I was in the presence of a most unusual politician. He was physically trim with a weather-beaten face. In his right hand he held a cigar, which he used as a pointer and as a baton to conduct the flow of conversation and thought. He himself was more thought than conversation; he spoke mostly in grunts, grimaces, and gestures. Although unusual for a politician, the taciturn demeanor served him well, for he could rarely be quoted—or misquoted—by the press or his opponents.

I also discovered how persuasive he was. He first astonished me by suggesting that I locate SeaLab III—at that time a highly publicized national and international program—in Hawaii. He argued that all the resources were in place. Tripler, the large military hospital, was a perfect facility for a staff trained in hyperbaric physiology and human physiology in stressful environments. There was the huge sub base at Pearl Harbor, deep water for operations. When I objected that Hawaiian water was too warm for SeaLab's activities, he pointed his cigar at me and growled.

"That's a mistake, Dr. Craven. The first time you do anything in the ocean you want to do it under the most ideal conditions."

As it turned out, he was right. I promised to send my team out to look over Hawaii but our decision was already made. Hawaii was the land of surfboards, hula dancers, and mai-tai's, and the Navy was there because there was no other alternative.

A few years later word reached me from the governor that I was a candidate for president of the University of Hawaii. I sent back my thanks for the honor of being considered but felt, given my military connections and the anti–Vietnam War mood on the university's campus, that I was not the right person for the job. But Burns was determined that someday I would agree to play some role on his team.

That day came scarcely a year later. At that time, in 1970, when the Nixon White House was quashing any nonmilitary ocean technology activity and I had all but given up hope, Governor Burns called. In the wake of Vice President Humphrey's orphaned report, "Our Nation and the Sea," Burns had established a Hawaiian state commission that had drawn up a similar document called "Hawaii and the Sea." Now, the governor told me, the state legislature had implemented the program. Among other things, it provided for a new position at the university, dean of marine programs. In the meantime, he reminded me, a former colleague of mine, Harlan Cleveland, had been named president of the University of Hawaii. Cleveland had been America's ambassador to NATO and after that, head of the State Department's Policy Planning Board under President Kennedy. He was an outspoken critic of U.S. involvement in Vietnam and had therefore been acceptable to the faculty and students despite his military and diplomatic past. Cleveland and he, the governor said, had decided that I should be the marine programs dean, and the post was mine if I wanted it. It was an offer that thrilled me, but I demurred, saying that my roots and my family's roots were in Washington.

"Doctor," he said, "you know that the Nixon people will do nothing with the ocean until they learn the hard way and that'll take at least two years. We won't ask for a commitment of more than two years, and if the administration wants you back, we'll let you go."

That made perfect sense to me. I promised that I would consult with my family and colleagues. I can now confess that I also consulted with Gene Fubini of the DIA Scientific Advisory Board, since I was now an overseas member. Gene reminded me that most of the intelligence operations were in the Asia Pacific region and curiously enough most of the military units that operate even in the Persian Gulf were headquartered in Hawaii. Thus it would be of great advantage to the board to have a member resident in the state. My other colleagues said, "Go—and take me with you." My family was less enthusiastic, but two weeks after we relocated my twelve-year-old son, David, came out of the surf one day and said, "Dad, don't ever leave this place." My wife and our seven-year-old daughter, Sarah, concurred.

Before anything else, I made a courtesy call to the governor accompanied by Harlan Cleveland. He greeted us with his usual aplomb and his animated cigar. One item we discussed was the upcoming appointment of a state official under the "Hawaii and the Sea" program, a marine affairs coordinator. This would be someone I presumably would have to work with, and I asked whom he had in mind for the job. He grunted—and pointed his cigar in my direction.

Once in the job, I soon took my first major initiative. In early September of 1970 in a speech to the American Institute of Architects, I stole a page from Martin Luther King and said, "I have a dream." My dream, I told the group, was of a floating city that moved serenely three miles off the shores of Waikiki. I challenged the architects present to begin design studies of floating cities to meet the needs of our planet's burgeoning population, which had just passed the three billion mark (half of the six billion it reached in the fall of 1999). It was a dream rooted in the reality of a just completed study by the Navy on mobile oceanic floating bases. I had been a member of the three-man concept development team leading up to that report.

Burns had an even grander vision. He called me in and told me to proceed at flank speed. When I asked why such haste was required his answer nearly floored me.

"Archipelago, gotta establish the archipelago." He opened a desk drawer and handed me a sheaf of paper. It was a chronology and history of Hawaii's use of the ocean that had been prepared for the governor by a group of Hawaiian scholars. There was a section entitled "Exercise of Political Control Across the Inter-Island Channels."

Somehow the governor had learned that I, wearing my lawyer's hat, had been advising the Navy on the significance of a newly proposed archipelagic waters regime and the need to preserve the right to submerged submarine passage through straits and archipelagic waters. I was amazed to discover that political and legal leaders in Hawaii had long claimed jurisdiction over the interisland waters despite the federal government's assertion that such jurisdiction did not exist. A floating city under Hawaii's jurisdiction more than three miles offshore would, in international law, be a demonstration of

Hawaiian sovereignty over interisland waters. The governor was right. Hawaii's "gotta have it."

The Hawaii Floating City Project was underway. Renowned Japanese architect Kiyonori Kikutake signed on. I was the project director and engineer. Many departments of the University of Hawaii joined in. But the new worldwide interest in the law of the sea made it likely that Hawaii's archipelagic aspirations would be ignored or denied in the battle between the superpowers for control of the seas.

The first meeting of the United Nations–sponsored Law of the Sea Conference would take place in 1974. The U.S. Congress had authorized a State Department Technical Advisory Group consisting of international lawyers, representatives of the fishing industry, the marine minerals industry, environmentalists, and scientists concerned with freedom of scientific research in the ocean. The Navy, the state of Hawaii, and the intelligence community wanted their special interests represented on the advisory group. The governor pulled a few strings and as Hawaii's marine affairs coordinator, who was both a lawyer and an ocean technologist, I was appointed to this group. Given no specific portfolio, I was able to act as a roving representative among the lawyers, technologists, environmentalists, and scientists.

In preparation for the conference, the Soviets quickly identified a two-hundred-mile, so-called Exclusive Economic Zone in which the resources of the ocean would belong to the coastal state. All the principal maritime powers—the United States, Great Britain, France, and Canada—supported this concept. A division of opinion arose as to the resources of the ocean beyond state jurisdiction. There was a split between those who believed that the resources of the ocean water itself—the so-called water column—were the most significant and those who attached the most significance to the minerals of the seabed.

This issue was up for discussion in the earliest days of the conference when into my roving purview came the representatives of the Summa Corporation, the holding company of the far-flung enterprises of Howard Hughes. They were leading a seminar open to all the delegates on the promise and prospects of mining the seabed's manganese nodules. These nodules were so commercially valuable, they said, that Hughes was building a huge mining ship called the *Glomar Explorer*.

Displayed were numerous pictures of the ship and a device called a "moon pool" through which the mineral ores would be conveyed into the ship. The project, they said, had been carefully researched and a picture was shown of a "mud pit" said to be used to determine the force required to free the nodules. Were I not inured to the tactics of international intelligence my blood would have boiled. This was, of course, not a privately funded endeavor, but the taxpayer-supported, top secret facility whose design I myself had sketched as project manager of what had become the CIA project to raise the lost Soviet missile submarine from the Pacific.

Constrained to be silent, I was seated next to a mining engineer who voiced skepticism. "The crazy fools," he said, "there's no mud like that anywhere near manganese nodules."

Although I was more certain than ever that it was only a matter of time before the cover would be blown, I had no doubt that my mining engineer neighbor would not now make the leap that this was instead a CIA operation. More likely he was thinking that it was some lamebrained project put together by a bunch of land-based engineers who couldn't tell the seabed from a flower bed.

"I wouldn't know," I said. "I've had no experience with magnesium nodules."

He looked at me as though I were one of the Summa "crazy fools." "Manganese, not magnesium," he said. "If it were magnesium, it would have dissolved into the ocean."

"I wouldn't know."

The Hughes presentation set off a tremendous, wide-ranging response. Another seminar was held and presentations were given by three groups. A delegation of ocean miners led by the United States presented a study by MIT that indicated that manganese nodules could only be marginally profitable even when mined with sophisticated technology. A second group, mineral-poor nations at the poverty level, concluded in its study that deep sea minerals, notably gold, silver, and platinum, would prove to be a bonanza and called for the establishment of a United Nations entity to mine the seabed for the benefit of the poor nations. A third study proffered by mineral-rich Third World countries such as Zaire (now Congo) decided that the entire affair was a capitalist plot to put them out of business and that protectionist provisions needed to be adopted to assure their survival.

The net result of the U.N. conference was a treaty in which 35 percent of the text is devoted to a mindless code for manganese nodule mining—replete with recondite formulas that few understood then, fewer today, and fewer still bother even to read. Moreover, the prospect of a mine site on the seabed spurred many nations and private companies to build expensive Glomar-like mining ships and conduct wasteful research and development. International Nickel of Canada, for example, had already concluded that the exploitation of ocean nodules would not develop for decades but began now to test whether they had overlooked something. Other companies, such as U.S. Steel, entered the field for the first time, expecting to reap profit only to learn that the most optimistic assessment of seabed mining was nothing more than a plan for economic ruin. The French, the Germans, and the Japanese also made substantial research efforts. The Soviets, who had reason to believe that the Glomar Explorer was pursuing a hidden agenda, made none.

In the meantime, Hawaii's Floating City Project was progressing. With the help of the Navy and the Air Force, Hawaii built an eighty-five-ton model and tested it in Kaneohe Bay. I wondered whether this Defense Department help was to provide a cover for continuing clandestine activity in mobile ocean basing, but I had no need to know. Instead I helped adapt technologies from submarines such as the DSRV to apply to large structures floating in the sea, with adjustments of ballast, thrust, and springs that would maintain the relative position of each module in the structure. This would allow the city to be easily disassembled or modified, module by module. The design was documented in a book published by MIT entitled *How Big and Still Beautiful* and was featured on the cover of *The Saturday Review of Literature*, but the rest of the media paid no attention to the project until the "unsinkable city" in Kaneohe Bay sank.

The sinking had less to do with the floating city's floatability than with its shoestring budget. There was no money to pay for hatches and other closures on the above-water parts. The Navy had been towing it from one area of the bay to another when a rope broke and the remaining tow began to pull it underwater. The more the tugboat pulled, instead of stopping, the more the floating city model flooded. The press had a field day.

We had to recover as soon as possible. As it happened, my old friend Commander Black Jack Tomsky, of SeaLab and Navy salvage fame, was working as an instructor in marine technology at the university. He was placed in immediate charge of the salvage effort and the Navy volunteered its salvage forces. In spite of this major mishap, the floating city was resurrected in three days. By then, however, the media had lost interest and remained unimpressed.

But Kiyonori Kikutake, the designer, was impressed. The Japanese were preparing an ocean fair at Okinawa for 1974. Kikutake envisaged a floating city as its centerpiece and believed it ought to be a joint project of the United States and Japan, which could later be towed to Hawaii for the planned celebration four years later of the bicentennial anniversary of Captain Cook's discovery of the Hawaiian Islands. I discussed this with the governor and he thought it a great idea. A summit conference had been scheduled in Hawaii between Japanese Prime Minister Kakuei Tanaka and President Nixon, and Kikutake assured me that Japan was ready to place the floating city project on the summit agenda if I could persuade the Nixon administration to agree. I knew how difficult it was to penetrate the Haldeman-Ehlichman protective screen but I decided to give it the old college try. My efforts were most illuminating regarding the true nature of the administration's ocean policy.

I tried people in the Commerce Department, the President's science adviser, even Henry Kissinger, to no avail. Nixon's host in Hawaii for the summer, Claire Booth Luce, managed to introduce me to the President when he visited.

At the private reception given at her estate, my wife and I were standing on the long welcoming line when, queued up to shake the Presidential hand, Claire caught my eye before we reached the President and gave me the thumbs-up sign.

"Mr. President," she said when it was our turn, "this is Dr. Craven whom I told you about last night who has this wonderful idea."

"Oh," said Nixon, "so you are the ocean man, are you?"

"I suppose so, Mr. President."

He reflected for a brief moment and then, in those often-impersonated, mellifluous tones, he said, "Don't you think the ocean in the Bahamas is much nicer than the ocean in Hawaii?"

I gasped. I was speechless. Didn't the President know that he was in Hawaii, his host's home, his host's state, a state of his own country?

The issue of the floating city was not raised at the summit, although Governor Burns and Prime Minister Tanaka talked about it informally. Nevertheless, the floating city, named Aquapolis, was built. The American exhibit at the fair, produced by Lockheed, featured displays of what the United States would do if it ever decided to build a floating city, too. Japan honored my role in the program by making me the Suntory Whiskey international man of the month in the Japanese edition of *Reader's Digest*. But by then Nixon had gone the way of Watergate and Tanaka soon succumbed to scandal in Japan as well.

Governor Burns did not live much longer, but he had one last major contribution to make to ocean technology.

The oil crisis of the mid-1970s precipitated worldwide concern over energy supplies. In the United States, a federal Department of Energy was established; a national program for the development of alternative energy was instituted. The threat of global warming began to loom on the horizon. Interest in energy and the environment revived a hundred-year-old project, ocean thermal electric energy. Studies showing it to be an environmentally sustainable and virtually inexhaustible resource spurred its development. As Hawaii's marine affairs coordinator, I was approached with a proposal to start a natural energy laboratory utilizing deep ocean water. Our office funded a study that identified a site on the big island of Hawaii. It was, however, already occupied by the new Kona Airport, on land that was adjacent to the coast. Obtaining authorization from the state legislature to establish such a facility in that location would be unthinkable without divine intervention or the next best thing. So I called the governor.

He was now confined to the governor's mansion by illness and didn't have long to live. I told him of the plan. He was enthusiastic. "Write up some legislation," he grunted, "and give it to the speaker of the house and the president of the senate tomorrow morning." By Hawaiian law any bill had to have three public hearings in each house, separated by at least three days, but the following day was the last day in which both the house and senate could act, let alone observe the three-day gap. When I reminded him of this impossibility, he growled and said he was governor, not me, and, as Admiral Raborn had growled so many years before, was I going to tell him what he could and could not do?

Without consulting the authorities, I wrote legislation that cut the Kona Airport in half. The bill I drafted established a state corporation called the Natural Energy Laboratory of Hawaii. I delivered it in the morning. By afternoon it had gone through three hearings in the house and senate and in the late afternoon the governor signed it into law. He died shortly after.

His legacy to me was the presidency of a state corporation devoted to the development of ocean resources for the betterment of mankind, a role at the executive level for the coordination of all marine activities in Hawaii, access on behalf of the governor for coordination with state and federal agencies on all matters pertaining to Hawaii and the sea, and appointment as the University of Hawaii's senior dean for the coordination of all oceanic education, research, and public service activities of the university. For the next two decades I would be acknowledged throughout the state as Hawaii's "ocean man."

My residency in Hawaii did not diminish my role in the Cold War, but transformed it in ways I could not have imagined. In 1970 I was elected president of the Marine Technology Society, a newly formed national organization to promote commercial applications of ocean science and technology. I was also elected to the National Academy of Engineering, a newly formed offshoot of the National Academy of Sciences. Election included the tacit obligation to actively participate in the various study programs of the academy. I was still a member of the Defense Intelligence Agency Scientific Advisory Committee. My obligations in Washington made me a more-than-once-a-month commuter for the first decade of my Hawaii residency.

At one memorable meeting of the DIA we learned that one of our members was on an airplane that was hijacked in the Middle East. We were concerned that the hijackers would discover the member's affiliation and would hold him hostage. Fortunately, he was released, but the security people, fearing a repetition, stripped us all of every vestige of identification that indicated we were in any way associated with the Department of Defense. This was the ultimate paradox of tight security; we were to prove to the guards at the gate of the Pentagon that we might be Special Intelligence agents because of the absence of any identification in our wallets or on our person. We were also instructed that, for the time being, we were to travel by land transport and not by air. Thankfully an exception was made for Hawaii.

I was asked by Senator Hiram Fong, the lone Republican in the Hawaii congressional delegation, if I would accept a presidential appointment to the newly formed National Advisory Committee on the Oceans and Atmosphere (NACOA). Its mission was to evaluate the state of the nation's oceanic and atmospheric health and report on it to both Congress and the executive. Once again I demurred on the basis of my Democratic stripes, and once again I was informed that the senator got my name from the White House. Fong told me that if I would not politically embarrass him, he would be delighted to sponsor the appointment.

I was again forced to confront my dual roles as a public ocean advocate and covert intelligence adviser. I discussed this with Fubini. He was of the opinion that I could be of greatest help to the intelligence community if I now divested myself of the stringent security restraints. Thus I could knowledgeably interact with the national and international ocean community and acquire information whose relevance to national security I was in a unique position to assess. Fubini advised me to resign from the DIA committee and accept the NACOA appointment.

The wisdom of this advice was almost immediately evident. Admiral Levering Smith, director of the Special Projects Office, informed me that the Soviet oceanographic ship *Vityaz* would be visiting Honolulu in 1971. This ship, as I have mentioned, was part of the fleet of the Soviet Academy of Sciences, ostensibly engaged in pure scientific research but no on• in Washington believed that. There was the suspicion that what the research was all about was finding new capabilities to conduct the cat-and-mouse game of tracking and trailing our submarines, as we did theirs. As a member of the National Academy of Engineering, I now had the credentials to warrant a courtesy visit to the ship in the name of exchanging views on coordinating international science and technology. Admiral Smith was hoping that I could gain insight into the actual mission of the Vityaz.

On her arrival, I introduced myself as a member of the academy to the chief of the Soviet scientific party. I was cordially received, invited to meet the scientists who were aboard, and promised an extensive tour of the ship. To my great surprise, I discovered that Andrej Kolmogorav, the world's leading expert on ocean turbulence, and Mikhail Lavrientiev, the number two man in the Soviet Academy of Sciences and also an expert on turbulence, were members of the party. Almost at once, I sensed what the Vityaz was up to. We are all familiar with turbulence, that chaotic motion of currents that causes aircraft to bounce crazily even in an apparently unperturbed sky. Turbulence takes many forms. In a ship at sea, the vortices induced by the propeller, the separation of water at the stern, and the effect of the rudder give a unique aspect to the turbulence associated with a ship's wake. Scientists always have a fancy name for any phenomenon, and perfectly random turbulence is called "isotropic turbulence," while skewed or directional turbulence is called "anisotropic turbulence."

Lavrientiev was famous for his work with Mstislaw Keldysch, the president of the Academy of Sciences, on the flow around airfoils and hydrofoils. I was familiar with an obscure paper they had authored, having to do with hydrofoils and fins operating close to a free surface. That's a pretty obvious clue—submarines have fins and foils and operate close to the free surface. Kolmogorav, on the other hand, was known for his measurements of turbulence. While on board the *Vityaz*, it wasn't long before I spotted the Pisces II mini-submarines that the Soviets had purchased from Canada when we would not sell them *Star I.* I noticed certain technical equipment mounted on the bow of these submersibles, and I also saw computers fitted with multiple tape recorders that could carry out the correlation functions involved with measuring the direction of turbulence. My report to Admiral Smith was already written in my mind. When he heard my report Admiral Smith and the Navy realized that I had spotted the first serious track and trail tactic with which we might have to cope.

In the late summer of 1974 the Soviets returned in a new oceanographic ship, the *Mendeleev.* I paid her another of those courtesy calls. This time the ship was prepared for my visit. In each compartment there was a map of the voyage. Close inspection revealed that each map had been traced from a master. The CIA had furnished me with the track of the ship prior to her arrival in Hawaii. It had no relationship with the track that was shown to me. She had in fact been following a hurricane, crossing and recrossing its path. These experiments, it seemed clear to me, were meant to study the turbulence characteristics of natural wakes associated with storms and to differentiate between those wakes and the wakes of submarines. It was equally clear that the earlier work of the *Vityaz* had been neutralized by our side. Dodging tactics, including the use of the environment—such as hiding a submarine wake in a natural wake or crossing wakes with a decoy submarine—had undone the Soviet track and trail techniques based on measurements of turbulence alone. In the meantime, the United States was developing other high-technology approaches to its surveillance of the sea.

The chief of the *Mendeleev*'s scientific party was Anatoly Sagalevitch. He was not a theoretical scientist but a superb ocean technologist. As I have described earlier, he was my Soviet counterpart and the guiding force behind their acquisition of the Mir submersible from the Finns. I had met him previously at an international meeting on deep ocean technology. He was ready to show me his new computers and his modifications of the Pisces but he was preoccupied with a morale problem of his crew because the U.S. Navy had barred them from going ashore. He asked for my help. I checked with the authorities, who were legitimately concerned about visits to Pearl Harbor or the Navy base. The Navy finally consented to a bus trip to Sea Life Park on the other side of the island. Other than the very significant realization that the Russians were attempting to enhance their track and trail prowess, there was little else I could learn of the mission, but my efforts in behalf of the *Mendeleev's* crew saw the beginnings of a friendship with Sagalevitch that would later open my eyes to a significant change in the nature of the Cold War.

Sagalevitch and the *Mendeleev* reappeared in the early 1980s. At that time, I was in charge of a laboratory on the Big Island of Hawaii that was studying ocean thermal energy. We had just succeeded in producing net energy, but were unable to recover a pipe that carried the water from the deep ocean. Sagalevitch had somehow heard of the problem and had volunteered the use of his submersible to inspect the pipe. When this suggestion was communicated to the Navy and the CIA, a fury erupted. Sagalevitch was told in no uncertain terms that no Soviet submarine was going to operate in American territorial waters no matter how benign the mission. He was also told that his crew would again be denied shore leave. Once again Sagalevitch called me, pleading for my intervention.

"Dr. Craven," he said, "these young people are not here to spy. They have been at sea for months and just want a look at the scenery." I called my Navy and CIA friends without success. I then remembered that the *Mendeleev* was not commissioned as a ship of the Russian navy but rather of the Shirshov Institute of their National Academy of Sciences. An inquiry made to the State Department by our own National Academy of Sciences brought an offer from undersecretary of state James Buckley (brother of the famous columnist William Buckley)—with strings attached. If I were to find out what the *Mendeleev* was "really doing," he would allow the crew to go ashore.

My heart sank. I was being asked to dangle shore leave in exchange for Sagalevitch's secrets, if any. It smacked of blackmail. I drove down to the pier in a quandary, but as I approached the gangway, I saw the crew pouring out of the ship, heading joyously for the nearest Hawaiian entertainment. Sagalevitch rushed toward me, threw his arms around me in a bear hug, crying, "Thank you, Dr. Craven. Thank you, thank you!"

I would later learn that Buckley had made an inquiry locally that had been misinterpreted as permission to allow the crew to disembark, but in the meantime, Sagalevitch was expressing his further gratitude, saying, "I know you must have made a lot of promises to get this favor, Dr. Craven, so I invite you to the ship tomorrow morning and we will tell you everything we are doing."

The next morning, after several obligatory vodka toasts in Sagalevitch's cabin, he showed me some photographs of coral reefs taken, he said, by his submarines. He gave me copies of everything, knowing that this would keep our security analysts busy for some time. After another round of vodka, Sagalevitch demonstrated how well he played the Spanish guitar. Since I knew some Russian songs myself, I could not resist going through my repertoire. At last we staggered onto the deck to crawl through the mini-submarines. All the panels had been removed but I had a good idea of the significance of the holes. They matched some cable penetrations on the hull. After this and a few other observations, I had fulfilled my obligation to Secretary Buckley and the intelligence community, even as I cemented my bond of friendship with Sagalevitch.

Not long afterward, an intelligence incident took place involving Sagalevitch, which I later realized indicated that we were at the beginning of the end of the Cold War.

In 1983, a civilian aircraft, Korean Airlines flight 007, was shot out of the sky by the Soviet Air Force as it proceeded on a mysteriously errant flight over far-eastern Soviet territory. All 269 passengers and crew were killed and the wreckage plunged into the waters of the Pacific. We and the Soviets accused the other of duplicity. This was accompanied by an undersea hunt by both sides for the "black box" flight recorder, which, if recovered, would, it was hoped, disclose the truth.

The event was also contemporaneous with an upcoming, unrelated international conference on submarine technology. I was to be chairman of a session on saturation diving, and Sagalevitch was scheduled to talk about plans for the Mir submarines. Prior to my departure for the conference, the CIA asked me to see if I could find out what Sagalevitch knew about the flight recorder. There was a possibility that we already had the recorder, but I knew better than to ask. The agency, I later concluded, was seeking to acquire whatever intelligence it could to help answer a growing conundrum: To what extent was Moscow losing command and control of its armed forces? The seeds of doubt that had been planted by the renegade Red September submarine incident had never ceased to sprout. In this case, the agency was asking whether the distant shootdown of the KAL plane had been decided independently of or, worse, in direct disobedience of orders from Moscow. If we could prove "direct disobedience," then we could once more remind Moscow how tenuous its control of strategic weapons was.

If, on the other hand, Moscow was in control, then Sagalevitch would be in charge of the hunt for the errant flight recorder. If it was not, then he would have been prevented from carrying out the search. Setting off for London, I wondered how I would approach Sagalevitch. There was not much time for speculation.

It wasn't necessary. Sagalevitch was not allowed to come to the conference. The CIA could only infer that he was not allowed to search for the recorder, and Moscow wanted no part in the play. Nearly fifteen years later, with the Soviets, as Soviets, gone from the face of the earth, the Russians declared that their Soviet predecessors had had the black box all along and that Moscow was now releasing the results. This evoked the swift charge from others that the results released were fabrications. More likely, the recorder still lies on the sea floor while both sides claim possession as the standard procedure against unwelcome disinformation. The larger question of the Soviet loss of command and control of its "Republics," however, had long been amply answered.

That was not the last of Sagalevitch. Not too long after his no-show in London, the new ship *Keldysch* came to the big island of Hawaii with its new submersibles, the Mirs, along with Sagalevitch and his Spanish guitar. He was piqued because his crew was left in Hilo on the remote big island of Hawaii and he was pressured to meet the press in Honolulu. When asked about his mission, he told the crowded press conference, "I am here in Oahu, to meet and sing with my friend John Craven." And sing we did:

Two guitars are calling me, calling tenderly,
bringing back from memory's shore
happy days we knew of yore.

It was a news-lite day for Hawaii local television that evening, but at least it rhymed. But it was a signal to me that the Soviets were tired of being seen as the enemy and that the olive branch would soon be extended.

19

The Man Who Was Not There

Last night I saw upon the stair
a little man who was not there.
He was not there the other day.
Oh how I wish he'd go away.

While I was working on SeaLab I learned that nobody knew who had criminal jurisdiction over individuals who were wandering around on the seafloor in ostensibly international waters. I commissioned Louis Sohn of Harvard to study the problem, and on the basis of his report, concluded that any SeaLab would have to extend the jurisdiction of its nation's flag to a zone around the laboratory, on the seabed, and up the water column above it to the surface of the sea.

The United States had already been embroiled in many problems concerning the law of the sea, including disputes with other nations over fishing rights, the rights of one nation to carry out scientific and oceanographic research on the continental shelf of another country, and many other wrangles. It was then that a declaration from the tiny island nation of Malta triggered a massive international effort to resolve these law of the sea questions.

The United Nations immediately set up a seabed committee to

establish guidelines. A series of conferences was held around the world and a number of national and international sea law institutes were born. In the course of attending conferences at such institutes I began to evolve a legal theory that disagreed with the general idea that vast areas of the ocean are manageable, or subject to control or sovereignty. Invited to express my views at an international meeting in Rome in 1969, I gave a paper with a long title and a short thesis garnered from the poet Byron. "Man marks the earth with ruin—his control / stops at the shore." Almost no one read my paper and it has hardly ever been referred to. But there was one man in the Soviet Union who did read it because it was his job to follow me wherever I went and to read whatever I wrote.

This man was Vladimir Pisarev. As a young member of the Soviet elite he had studied nuclear physics and nuclear weapons design. On completion of those courses, he was sent to a different school to learn about submarines and submarine design. He was then given a KGB assignment to monitor all the literature in the open press that he could find on Polaris and the Polaris Fleet Ballistic Missile System. This included the tracking of the senior executives in the program. When I became involved in deep submergence, the scope of Pisarev's activities widened but his focus narrowed to me. All of a sudden his interests included my papers on the interaction among ocean technology, maritime strategy, and ocean law. This was seen by the KGB as an opportunity to move in even closer, so Pisarev was now turned into a political scientist with an academic cover at Georgi Arbatov's Institute for the Study of the U.S.A. and Canada.

When I was appointed director of the Law of the Sea Institute in 1976, Pisarev became a member and attended nearly all of its international conferences. His activities would eventually converge with those of the CIA, Soviet mini-submarine expert Anatoly Sagalevitch, and the alternative energy scientists of the post-Soviet Russian Republic. The Defense Intelligence Agency, through Gene

Fubini, and the Navy, through Admiral Smith, saw an opportunity to have me engage in a form of counterintelligence. But first I would have to disengage myself from active participation in intelligence operations and knowledge of specific intelligence operations.

Early in March of 1975 someone else was interested in my knowledge of a specific intelligence operation. I received a phone call from Seymour Hersh, the *New York Times* Pulitzer Prize-winning investigative reporter, who had his teeth in a very juicy bone and wasn't about to let go of it. I was about to pass through a period when the U.S. media and Soviet intelligence were both wondering just who the real Craven was—the benign oceanic philosopher (Dr. Jekyll) or the sinister intelligence sorcerer's apprentice (Mr. Hyde). Well, as Pascal said, man is neither beast nor angel, but a mixture of both.

A few weeks earlier, the CIA, in a damage control operation, had revealed that the manganese nodule research ship, *Glomar Explorer*, had been engaged in nondescript intelligence operations. According to the agency, top secret documents had been stolen from the Hughes Corporation by thieves who were unaware of their significance. Shortly afterward, the *Los Angeles Times* reported that the *Glomar Explorer* was attempting to recover a Soviet submarine. The story had few details and was filled with errors, including the wrong ocean. There was also not the barest hint that either the Navy or I was in any way connected to this operation. Now I was concerned that Hersh and the *New York Times* were on to the bigger story. I felt that I had to do whatever I could to protect the classified material.

I'd barely put my foot in the door when the phone rang. I picked up the phone and the voice said, "I am Seymour—"

"Yes, I know. You're a reporter for *Ramparts* magazine."

Taken aback, the caller protested, "That was a long time ago!"

He sounded indignant, and I couldn't blame him. After all, Hersh was now the *Times's* top investigative reporter. My first thought was of a troublesome article he had written years earlier on my "violation" of the seabed treaty culled from a cover story leak that had brought him dangerously close to a penetration of intelligence projects. I asked what I could do for him.

"I am calling you about Project Jennifer," he said.

"Project what?" I asked.

"You know, the Hughes ship *Glomar Explorer*."

"Oh, yes, the manganese nodule ship."

"You know it is not a manganese nodule ship. It's a CIA ship that's out to recover a Russian submarine that sank in the Pacific."

At least he had the right ocean. "I guess I did see a story to that effect," I said, "but why in the world are you calling me?"

"Because I think you were involved."

I reminded him that I was just a college professor. At this point he said, "Let me tell you a story."

He recounted the substance of the article he said he would publish. I assumed that he was testing me for reactions to incorrect information, and having learned that trick long ago, I did not react. Interesting story, I said when he concluded, but of no relevance to me, my past, my present, or my future. With some exasperation, he asked if we could meet, and when I told him that I would be in Washington the following week, we made an appointment.

Before the interview, I visited the security people in Washington. They asked me to find out, if I could, the source of what appeared to be the leak that had led Hersh to link me and thus the Navy to the *Glomar*. With that instruction in mind, I met with Hersh at the appointed place, the Cosmos Club, where I would later witness Edward Teller yelling over the phone at Ronald Reagan. Hersh began by repeating his upcoming *Times* story, but this time some details had changed. I again told him that it all sounded interesting, but, I said, I was still puzzled why he thought I was involved. He told me that all his sources were CIA-linked, shared with him by the CIA's Director on the condition that he would not release any information until he received the agency's nod. I asked him again why he had brought me into the picture and from his reply, I finally concluded that someone in the CIA had used my name without indicating any connection. I was satisfied that he knew nothing more than what he had told me and decided to terminate the interview by telling him, as pleasantly as I could, that his story was so intriguing that I was going to tell all my friends right away. I knew that, in any event, his publication was imminent and I wanted to force him to publish it without opportunity for further research.

"You can't do that!" Hersh cried.

"Why not?" I asked. "You have no clearances. I have no clearances. What you've told me must be unclassified. It is certainly worth repeating."

Dismayed, Hersh got up and left abruptly. Undoubtedly he went directly to his newspaper's Washington bureau, since the next morning his story appeared on the front page of the *Times*—with no mention of the Navy or me. Our end of the secret was safe—or so we thought. It was not very long before the first book appeared, in late 1975, purporting to tell all about the CIA and the *Glomar Explorer*. There was only one incriminating sentence in the entire volume: "The mysterious Dr. John P. Craven," it said, "was seen observing the construction of the *Glomar Explorer* from a railway car on the tracks at the Camden shipyard." No other reference was made that suggested Navy participation, but this single reference, though technically incorrect, was more than enough.

From then on, hardly any journalist writing about the *Glomar*—and they would be legion—would fail to ring my doorbell one way or another and seek to dig into that "mysterious" observer in the railway car. From 1975 on, Soviet intelligence would try to learn the relationship between the Navy and the *Glomar* via the "Craven connection." British and German intelligence, and many others in the international intelligence community who believed that they were betrayed in the law of the sea negotiations, began similar investigations. As a result, U.S. intelligence services put me under surveillance, fearing that I would inadvertently identify other people or operations currently active in the collection of intelligence, thus further exposing the existence of the submarine intelligence system.

This was a great moment for the little man who wasn't there, Vladimir Pisarev. In 1975, he was sporting a crew cut and learning how to snorkel, preparing to visit Hawaii. A year earlier, he had published a book in Russian describing U.S. ocean technology and ocean science programs. He would deliver it to me in our first face-to-face meeting in 1976. American intelligence was as unaware of Pisarev's book as were American libraries. Yet it contained evidence of his KGB mission to discover the links, if any, among the CIA, the Navy, and me at about that time.

With the information he already had, Pisarev could have done some research and found much more. The first place he would have turned would be *Jane's Fighting Ships*. This remarkable British publication attempts to document all of the world's navies in as much detail as possible. The 1974–75 edition contains 646 pages of pictures and text obtained from many sources. *Jane's* thoroughness makes this book a bible for intelligence officers. Pisarev would almost certainly have scanned the pages in *Jane's* covering the submarines of the United States Navy. There he would have found a picture of the submarine *Halibut* with what appears to be the Deep Submergence Rescue Vehicle mounted on the fantail. The text says that *Halibut* is no longer considered a first-line submarine and is employed in experimental work. As a first-class intelligence officer, Pisarev would have immediately noted major inconsistencies between the DSRV on the *Halibut* fantail and all the other pictures of the DSRV. He would have been able and undoubtedly eager to report to his superiors that this was not in fact a DSRV. He might have also reported that since the DSRV was indisputably linked to Craven, there was a high likelihood that Craven was linked to the *Halibut*.

The *Halibut* is also fitted with what appears to be a duct

thruster. This is not shown in the 1974–75 *Jane's*, but appears prominently in earlier editions. The thruster was not in evidence when *Halibut* was a Regulus submarine; technologists would know that it was certainly not needed while the submarine was underway. Instead it was obviously used while *Halibut* was in a hovering mode for some kind of mission requiring hovering. *Jane's* also notes *Halibut's* Ships Inertial Navigation System, developed by the Special Projects Office. This is a major giveaway. Only first-line submarines were so equipped, which further links *Halibut* to the Special Projects Office and to Craven. Pisarev would certainly have recognized *Halibut* as a prime candidate for use as an intelligence submarine, and probably a prime candidate in the hunt for the Golf submarine that I call the Red September.

The *Jane's* text also cites the USS *Seawolf* as a "mother submarine" for the DSRV. The photograph of *Seawolf* is old, but the text cites the pressurized-water nuclear reactor that was refueled in a major overhaul from 1965 to August 1967. Pisarev would almost certainly point out in his report that such an overhaul and refueling would belie *Jane's* statement that "she is no longer considered a first-line submarine and has been engaged primarily in research work since 1969."

In thumbing through the book, he might come across the arresting picture of USS *Hawkbill*, a submarine of the *Sturgeon* class. There is a DSRV mounted on its stern and distinctive black-and-white patterns on the sail and sail planes. Other ships of the same class are not so clearly marked. Pisarev knew that the DSRV had been designed to mate with any submarine and that there was no need for special markings unless the *Hawkbill* was specifically designed to support the DSRV on other than rescue missions. He will probably conclude that the DSRVs did not stay in the firehouse until needed, but might well be used in intelligence operations. He would not have imagined any use for them in the hunt for the Red September because of their depth limitations.

His great dilemma would be the bogus DSRV on the *Halibut*. Is it a saturation diving chamber or is it some other kind of DSRV? The original Deep Submergence Systems Project called for a Deep Submergence Search Vehicle and one was designed by the Westinghouse Corporation. Pisarev would have found no evidence anywhere that this vehicle or anything like it was built and, in any case, the *Halibut*'s vehicle did not resemble the published Westinghouse design.

Pisarev would have probably concluded that the Navy does have a sophisticated DSSV in the form of *Trieste II*. The earlier *Trieste*, according to *Jane's*, is a completely different bathyscaphe, but comparisons with *Trieste II* make it more than obvious that these are two different submersibles. Pisarev would know that *Trieste II* had been deployed from a floating dry dock in the *Scorpion* investigation. He would have probably concluded that the Navy DSSV capability was limited to *Trieste II* and that its operation required surface ship platforms. Not to worry, he would have reported. Such activity could have been easily tracked by his side.

If he suspected that the *Halibut*'s fantail vehicle was a saturation diving facility, he would have matched that with the unclassified information that the U.S. Navy's saturation diving program was sharply truncated, if not terminated, following the 1969 death of aquanaut Barry Cannon in SeaLab III. He would have further noted that the only ships fitted for saturation diving are the rescue ships *Pigeon* and *Ortolan*. These are catamarans that can carry the DSRV and are outfitted with the Mark II diving system, capable of supporting saturation diving operations at greater than 600 feet. Pisarev would have probably gone astray and conclude—incorrectly this time—that the rescue boats would be fully visible in any intelligence operation and that saturation diving development had been deferred and was not an element of the U.S. Navy intelligence system.

The conundrum of the structure on the *Halibut* would therefore remain unsolved, but Pisarev would plod on, leaving the identifica tion of the structure to other Soviet intelligence officials to argue over for some time to come. Thus, as long as they argued, the existence of an extensive sophisticated saturation diving capability would be safe—until the KGB succeeded in recruiting American submariner John A. Walker in 1967 and NSA cryptologist Ronald W. Pelton in 1980. Walker would betray the existence of a submarine intelligence capability and Pelton would betray how the Navy had tapped Soviet underwater communications cables, including the crucial role of saturation diving in those operations.

Finally, Pisarev's report would have most likely noted that I had left the Department of Defense. Based on his own cultural background, he would have concluded that the Pentagon would not have given me up so readily and that my academic appointment was merely a cover for participation in submarine intelligence activities that deployed from Pearl Harbor. Pisarev, of course, had a vested career interest in this conclusion because he had been assigned to track me as far back as my 1958 appointment as Chief Scientist of Special Projects. As my career in the Navy had advanced, so had Pisarev's career in the KGB. Likewise, a decline in my Navy career would be matched by Pisarev's decline in the KGB. But if I were now under cover in the guise of an academic, there would be opportunities for Pisarev to don the Soviet version of sheep's clothing and surface in academia. Such an opportunity would arise sooner than Pisarev could have possibly imagined.

Seymour Hersh would soon be publishing news about American submarine surveillance operations in Soviet waters, a project, he would report, having the code name Holystone. At this late date, it may appear as an absurdity for me to neither confirm nor deny that there was or is a project named Holystone. But the discipline of tight security is such that until you are specifically released from its constraints you must follow the letter of the law to the grave. Many if not most of us who have been cleared for these now public-domain names violate this restriction since there no longer appears to be a rational basis for maintaining secrecy. But by permanently locking all of the code words to which I am privy into a cellar of my brain, I need never have a moment's confusion wondering whether this or that code name has already been leaked to the public. Thus, when a reporter calls and says, "I am calling about Project Whatever," it will elicit the automatic reply, "Project what?"

Inevitably, however, a moment crept in when it dawned on me that there could no longer be any doubt that some segment of the informed public believed that there was an espionage submarine called *Halibut*, that it had carried out a successful mission to locate a sunken Soviet ballistic missile submarine, that I was the project manager, that the CIA tried spectacularly to recover that submarine, and failed. That secret was bared. But the secret residing in the secret— the motivations of that Soviet captain and his crew—had remained intact and that, ironically, is the secret that ought to be revealed.

Although I would discover that Vladimir Pisarev been tracking me for nearly decades, I had no idea who he was when we first came face-to-face in 1976. I was the director of the Law of the Sea Institute and he was plying his tradecraft as a political scientist attached to Arbatov's Institute for the Study of the U.S.A. and Canada.

It was my first year as the institute's director. I had just made a run for Congress. I was backed by the 442nd Regimental Combat Team's veterans of Japanese-American ancestry against a well-heeled, free-spending opponent, and though my campaign was far more cost effective than his in terms of dollars per vote, I lost. When I returned to the University of Hawaii, I discovered that in my absence the Law of the Sea Institute had been transferred there from the University of Rhode Island and that I had been offered the directorship. My first reaction was that there would be no reduction in my other responsibilities and I would be worked to the bone. My second reaction was that I had once more been handed a position of vast international influence on a silver platter, and I could not refuse it.

The institute had been established at Rhode Island because of proximity to the United Nations in New York and the need for a politically unaligned, nongovernmental organization as a forum for diplomats and practitioners to test their ideas and proposals in advance of formal treaty negotiations. John Knauss, an oceanographer from Rhode Island, was its first director and he had set the institute's policy from the very beginning. It was to be open to the presentation of all views on law of the sea issues from any quarter of the globe, First World to Third World.

The success of the institute was the cause of its relocation. Rhode Island had no law school or school of international studies but it had many oceanographers and resource economists, and when LSI's executive board sought invitations from other universities, a couple of entrepreneurial ocean scientists from Hawaii's East-West Center volunteered the University of Hawaii. With a staff borrowed from Hawaii's new law school, LSI structured an ambitious first conference and a distinguished array of ocean law diplomats was invited. Considering the lure of Hawaii and the free transportation, attendance at this first meeting was all that could be asked for.

The Soviet Union sent three representatives. One was Anatoly Kolodkin, the president of the Soviet Maritime Academy. A survivor of Hitler's siege of Leningrad, he was quite well known, the very model of the shrewd, dogmatic, and tenacious Soviet diplomat. Another man, Boris Imerikov, had no certain affiliation, but his role would quickly emerge, and the third was my Pisarev, using his Arbatov institute credential.

I had never heard of him. With a crew cut and academic tweed he could have been easily mistaken for a junior professor at Stanford or Harvard were it not for a slight accent that betrayed his origins. He seemed like a graduate of a Soviet charm school. I engaged him in casual conversation at a coffee break and presuming that he regarded me as a local state official, I told him of a paper I had published on conference topic. He looked at me very carefully and uttered these words that stuck in my memory and rang the full set of alarm bells: "Dr. Craven, I have read every paper you have ever written." It was a very proper thing for him to say. Intelligence operatives on all sides know, or like to think they know, which institutions advertising themselves as nongovernmental or non-defense-oriented are in fact the home of individuals whose primary mission is intelligence. Although many more years would go by before I would find out that Pisarev had been following my footsteps from the time that I was first appointed as Chief Scientist of Polaris, now that I had become LSI director, whatever decline his career had undergone since I had left my positions with the Defense Department had been restored. The KGB could not believe that I was no longer intimately involved in intelligence missions. Such a change in career pattern could not occur in the Soviet Union. The assumption was that my move to Hawaii had been a cover for better proximity to Pacific operations. Now Pisarev could meet with me to his pleasure in the vain hope that he could find out what I was "really" doing.

After our introduction, I invited him and his other two comrades to accompany me for a snorkel tour of the famed tropical fish reef at Hanauma Bay. Pisarev, to be sure, was already trained in snorkel and scuba. Kolodkin could swim well but had never snorkeled and was willing to learn. Imerikov would accompany us to the bay, but he declined the snorkeling. At the bay, I gave Kolodkin a short course and he was a quick learner. All three of us spent about fifteen minutes exploring the shallow-water reef. But there was a veritable snorkler's paradise that lay farther out, accessible only through a small channel in the reef. I would not ordinarily take inexperienced snorkelers beyond the reef, but Pisarev was obviously qualified and Kolodkin was a strong swimmer. We started out and immediately heard a shout from shore. It was Imerikov calling us back.

"I have decided that I will learn to snorkel!"

His position was now clear to me. He was the party functiona-

whose role was to monitor Kolodkin and Pisarev to make sure that they would not defect. Wonderful, I thought, every man must do his duty. So I began to teach Imerikov. He struggled mightily but would not give up. After about an hour he had mastered the art sufficiently and all four of us went beyond the reef and enjoyed its magical underwater beauty.

I had taken the measure of my three Soviets and they had taken the measure of me. For the next thirteen years in annual encounters at LSI conferences in Kiel, The Hague, Rhode Island, Halifax, Seoul, Mexico City, Honolulu, San Francisco, Miami, Tokyo, Wales, and Genoa I would learn from them and they from me the futility of continuing the Cold War. The intelligence game is fearful and wonderful. Both sides will never believe anything that they have not confirmed through intelligence. Therefore, if you wish to give a message of, say, deterrence, you have to allow access to the adversary so that he can see for himself that the deterrent is credible. More subtle, but of greater significance, is the importance to each leader of being in full command and control of his armed forces and in particular his nuclear forces. If one side or the other discovers that command and control is being lost and that the fanatics in his country may try to take over or precipitate a war, the leadership in jeopardy will want to communicate that knowledge to the other side. The medium of the dire emergency hot line lies at one extreme. At the other are the interpersonal exchanges that take place at the international conferences of nongovernmental organizations. In between are actions, debated at the annual conferences, testing the ability of one nation or another to live up to its commitments to international law.

During the Cold War there were a number of significant tests of these commitments, and the Soviets in their later years were increasingly failing. A major issue for both sides was freedom of navigation, the right of commerce and the military to have full access to the ocean. Both the Soviet Union and the United States had declared three-mile territorial seas that allowed both sides to get within that distance of each other's coast with ships and submarines and research vessels. The penalty of being observed was more than outweighed by the opportunity to observe. But other nations of the world were determined to extend the territorial sea to twelve miles, a policy generally driven by domestic fishing interests. One drawback with that distance was that many straits are less than twenty-four miles wide and foreign transit through them would be problematical. Another new regime was that of permitting a right of transit passage in archipelagic waters but declaring the right to specify lanes of travel through these waters. The test of these limitations would not take place in the halls of diplomacy but on the high seas.

Under the Reagan administration the United States Navy challenged the Soviet Black Sea fleet by "innocent passage" through Black Sea territorial waters. In violation of recently enacted protocols, the Black Sea fleet shouldered the United States Navy out of the three-mile limit. Diplomatic protest to Moscow yielded the desired result. The Kremlin ruefully acknowledged that its instructions had not reached the Black Sea fleet. The law of the sea meetings also offered evidence to the Soviet leadership that it was in danger of losing control of its strategic and tactical sea-based forces in a manner that could precipitate nuclear war. No rational, patriotic leader would want to see his nation engaged in all-out war as the result of the actions of chauvinistic zealots. These naval actions played a major role in President Gorbachev's decision to fold his cards in the Cold War and attempt to restructure the Soviet Union through his policy of perestroika.

The restructuring was in evidence in the late 1980s. In November 1988 Kolodkin, in his new role as a member of the board of directors of the Law of the Sea Institute, convened the Moscow Symposium on the Law of the Sea. In his opening remarks, citing Gorbachev's recent speeches, he said, "Today we cannot speak about regulating navigation, marine scientific research, and fishing without thinking at the same time about the safeguarding of peace and security on the high seas and oceans."

The 1988 symposium extended an olive branch. Soviet attendees were carefully selected. Pisarev, Arbatov's Institute for the Study of the U.S.A. and Canada, and the Shirshov Institute were not represented. Cold warriors were not welcome at this love feast.

Pisarev had focused on me, my career, and my influence as one measure of the nature and intensity of U.S. oceanic activity. By 1990, however, this measure was no longer current. I had been replaced as dean of marine programs at the university, I had been retired as director of the Law of the Sea Institute and as Hawaii's marine affairs coordinator. My professional survival—and Pisarev's—appeared to hang on the tenuous thread of my lifetime appointment as an emeritus professor at the university. But Pisarev, always the meticulous observer, had noticed that I had recently founded a for-profit enterprise called the Common Heritage Corporation that had started small but had a powerful board of directors. Its purpose was to manage innovation for the benefit of the common heritage, the resources of the sea. Pisarev targeted the Common Heritage Corporation as his ace in the hole in the coming perestroika reorganization showdown.

In January of 1991 he suddenly showed up at my office in Hawaii. It was certainly a sign of the times that he made a full confession. He was not really a political scientist he told me, and outlined his background as a nuclear scientist and submarine technologist. His current mission, he said, was to establish a perestroika project under the auspices of a newly formed Soviet corporation. It was seeking a joint venture with an American firm engaged in oceanic development projects on one or more Pacific island nations. The primary project that the Russians had in mind would be a sea-farming program employing deep ocean water as the growth medium. The proposal called for the design, construction, and deployment of deep ocean pipes for pumping the deep ocean water to the surface. This part would be a purely Soviet operation. The American technologists would utilize the Soviet-delivered deep ocean water for various aquaculture and agriculture projects designed and developed by the Common Heritage Corporation. The island nation would operate the farm and collect revenue for the joint venturers in proportion to their participation.

His proposal struck me as a fine first step in easing the fundamental conflict between the Soviet Union and the United States but it seemed to have little chance of success. One of many reasons, apart from obvious cultural barriers, was Soviet ignorance of standard business practice. In a rare and surprising gesture meant to pave the way, the Soviets volunteered to pay my way to visit Moscow for an exploratory conference.

I checked with my lawyers and potential business partners, and although there was no legal requirement to do so, I had a few informal meetings with those federal agencies that might have some concerns. They all encouraged me to go with the expectation that the meeting would be educational but that nothing could possibly develop from it. On the other hand, members of my former staff at the Law of the Sea Institute were perplexed. Officially unaware, but privately suspicious, of my prior experience in matters of intelligence and national security, they feared I was being led down a garden path. Someone had the idea of giving me a copy of John Le Carré's novel *The Little Drummer Girl*, about a naive young actress who becomes a pawn in a game of deadly intrigue, with the caveat to read it as though it were historically accurate. Someone else who had already read the book warned me, perhaps in jest, to steer clear of alluring unknown women. My family was simply apprehensive.

I left Hawaii on the Palm Sunday weekend of 1991. After an uneventful crossing and a change of planes in Paris, on the Moscow leg of the journey I found myself in an aisle seat beside a passenger at the window who was bundled in a blanket. When the meal was served, the blanket stirred and unbundled, revealing a beautiful young woman with dark hair and deep blue eyes. She spoke with a soft Oxford accent and though she surely was an alluring unknown woman, I felt safe enough, imagining that she was a British student on her way to visit Moscow. A few minutes of conversation, however, disclosed that she was Russian. I will call her Tatiana. She had studied English at the University of Moscow and was returning home after a refresher course in London. It suddenly occurred to me that she might be available as a translator for my meetings with the Pisarev group. She was. On arrival, a negotiation with her mother and my hosts and verification by a colleague at the Soviet Academy of Sciences that Tatiana was not part of the party apparatus cinched the deal, giving me a voice at all our meetings.

Aided by Tatiana's interpretation and her remarkably perceptive powers, I soon discovered the extent to which the domestic political pot was boiling. The Soviet team was not monolithic as I would have expected. It was as highly politicized as it was polarized. On one side was the corporation, an energy company called Alten (for "alternate energy") composed of outspoken supporters of Boris Yeltsin, and on the other was my old friend Sagalevitch and his Shirshov Institute, taking orders as usual from Gorbachev and the Kremlin. Pisarev and a gray eminence from Arbatov's organization were the discussion leaders. It was clear that this was one of a number of proposed perestroika projects under the management and control of Arbatov. It was also clear that the Yeltsin side was gearing up for a post-Soviet world. By week's end we had hammered out an agreement that would lead to their visiting Hawaii to meet with the American team and newly co-opted members of the Cook Islands government, where the project would take place.

The pot began to boil over on Thursday evening, March 28.

Having left the Alten office, just outside the Kremlin wall, we stepped into falling snow and streets that were lit by the flashing red lights of police and soldiers. The Yeltsin forces were demonstrating at the Kremlin and Gorbachev had given orders to keep it peaceful. I was thrilled to be an observer of this historic moment in Russian history and yet I was uncomfortable because of my presence in the very center of this most intimate family affair. Our meetings concluded, Tatiana invited me and several members of the project to Palm Sunday service at one of Moscow's Russian Orthodox churches, their religious calendar being a week behind that of the Western Christian world. Only one of the communist brethren had the courage to attend. I was amazed at the opulence and grandeur of the church. The service perhaps was a sign of the times. I headed home the next day to prepare the follow-up meetings in Hawaii. In the interim our most irksome problem was communication. My hosts' telephone and fax were both virtually inoperable, and the obsolescent Telex was prohibitively expensive. Tatiana solved the problem by enlisting a communications student at Moscow State University who had access to e-mail. The rapid-fire exchanges that followed made it seem more likely that the project would become a reality.

The significance to me of this one small project was personally overwhelming. I felt that I had been given a crystal ball look into the coming world. Perestroika, glasnost, and life after the crumbled Berlin wall was the pokerlike body language of someone, Gorbachev, about to fold his hand. His "four kings and razor," the gangster's winning hand, was no match for our four aces, and he knew it. The Cold War was over. On August 19, 1991, what Gorbachev most feared, a right-wing coup, materialized. Yeltsin stood definitely on a tank and Gorbachev appeared to be saved, but Yeltsin's action was really a countercoup on behalf of the Republic of Russia. The days of Gorbachev, the Communist Party, and the Soviet Union were numbered.

I e-mailed Alten, saying that I assumed that the project, which seemed more appropriate than ever to the new times, would go forward. I received an immediate reply that "thanks to the glorious revolution" all was well, but the head of the company had somehow found it convenient to depart for the People's Republic of China for "a few months." I never again heard from Pisarev.

But it was not too long before an e-mail arrived from the student communicator. He and Tatiana had made their way to the United States, he to the University of Wisconsin and she to visit with an American church group for whom she had once been a translator. Tatiana, I knew, would be in a difficult position until the political situation in her homeland had stabilized. She would also have firsthand knowledge of the two factions on the Soviet side of our project so my investment partners and I invited her to Hawaii to assess the situation. My Law of the Sea Institute associates were opposed, imagining their warnings about *The Little Drummer Girl* as having come true. My wife was concerned that a young woman, who could not possibly have the beauty, brains, and political perspicacity that I had attributed to her, had taken me in. Nevertheless, Tatiana was invited for a visit of a few days. My wife picked her up at the airport in the morning and by the time I came home later in the day she had decided that Tatiana could stay as long as she had to. Indeed, my staff, my partners, and my family and I took her under our collective wing. The joint venture with the Soviets crumbled like Lenin's statue, but Tatiana stayed on, entering graduate school at an American university and acquiring advanced degrees in international relations. Tatiana is now a senior staff member of a prominent nongovernmental organization not unlike the Law of the Sea Institute.

As for Sagalevitch, he took to selling the services of the Shirshov Institute's Mir mini-subs. He persuaded the makers of the film *Titanic* to use his Mirs in that epic production. The *Keldysch* or the *Mendeleev* will probably not return to Hawaii for a long time, however, and I content myself with mind's-eye images of Sagelevitch in his cabin, bottle of vodka and Spanish guitar in hand, singing the mournful words of the "Two Guitar Duet."

Spring may bloom, but two guitars
we once played down beside the garden wall
are stilled forever, and our songs in ashes lie.

The public has breathed a sigh of relief. The evil empire is no more. But those of us who are concerned about command and control of nuclear weapons worry because they still exist, they are not fully accounted for, command and control has been fractionized and dispersed, and ownership is passing from the hands of recognized governments into private or irresponsible government hands. It is a brand-new game and the preservation of peace has taken on new dimensions. The recent events in North Korea and the Balkans demonstrate that new forms of policing are required. We must guard the undersea and the littorals of the world in the new era of global instability. The coastal zone, the home of our burgeoning population, is also affected by a widening gap between the rich and the poor. The intrepid band that formed the Special Projects Office to deter nuclear war, that formed the Deep Submergence Systems Project to win the Cold War, has given us the technology to occupy ocean space for better or for worse. Those public servants have completed their tasks and have crossed the bar, but they taught us that eternal vigilance is not enough. They taught us that society must organize for the deterrence of nuclear war and the preservation of world peace. These are still missions of the people of the world's free democracies, and we must again organize a band of individuals whose lives are dedicated to these missions.

They taught us that warriors and peacemakers enmeshed in endless conflict, hot or cold, lose the concept of time. There are only new and previously unanticipated missions; needs for instant development and acquisition of innovative hardware to carry out the new missions; and the necessity for instant recruitment and training of personnel for the immediate conduct of the mission. In the turbulent midst of endless conflict all of these processes are telescoped into a multiplexed existential continuum without beginning and without end. Everything is of highest priority and utmost urgency and when called upon to execute the mission, they go. They go as soon as they are called. They go with what they have got. They go and they execute with competence, skill, and dispatch—or they die.

They also taught us to walk softly and display strength; to be wise as serpents and harmless as doves; to prepare a world for future generations that cannot yet speak for themselves; to know that actions speak louder than words and, acting as children of the ocean, in the silence of the ocean deeps, to create a silence that is heard around the world.

Index

291